Reclaiming America

Restoring Nature to Culture

RICHARD CARTWRIGHT AUSTIN

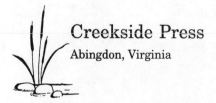

Creekside Press

Abingdon, Virginia

Acknowledgements will be found on page 233-234

Abbreviations

ILL	Inclusive Language Lectionary
JB	Jerusalem Bible
KJV	King James Version
NEB	New English Bible
NJB	New Jerusalem Bible
RSV	Revised Standard Version

Library of Congress Cataloging-in-Publication Data
(Revised for book 4)

Austin, Richard Cartwright, 1934—
    Environmental theology.

    Includes bibliographies and indexes.
    Contents: bk 1. Baptized into wilderness — bk. 2. Beauty of the Lord — bk. 3. Hope for the land — bk. 4. Reclaiming America.
    1. Nature—Religious aspects—Christianity. 2. Muir, John, 1838—1914. 3. Edwards, Jonathan, 1703—1758. I. Title.
BT695.5.A97 1987   231.7   90-080298
ISBN 0–8042–0869–7 (pbk. : v. 1)
ISBN 0–8042–0859–X (pbk. : v. 2)
ISBN 0-8042–0861–1 (pbk. : v. 3)
ISBN 0-9625831-0-3

10 9 8 7 6 5 4 3 2 1
Printed in the United States of America
Creekside Press
P. O. Box 331
Abingdon, Virginia 24210

Printed by McFarlane Graphics, Bristol, Virginia

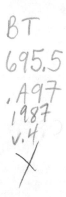
Dedication

To Samuel, John, and Paul

Each is at work reclaiming America

I had fainted, unless I had believed to see
the goodness of the LORD in the land of the living.

Psalm 27:13, KJV.

Contents

Introduction:

On Chestnut Ridge

The current period of history is challenging and dangerous. Humanity and the other species of earthly life are at risk from industrial society's pollution of the biosphere. Radical changes in social policies and personal behavior will be required to stem environmental degradation, for otherwise the earth's ability to sustain life will be damaged beyond repair. Perhaps we will fail to change in time. Perhaps we will intensify both our exploitation of the earth and our oppression of one another until environmental life-support systems collapse beneath human abuse. This dark shadow stalks our path.

Yet the innovative skills that distinguish human culture and that have covered the earth with many constructive artifacts of human civilization are the very skills which can assure good and satisfying lives for most people if we resolve to fashion life-sustaining relationships with the other creatures and natural forces that share this planet with us. Life in communion with God, in harmony with nature, and in fellowship with one another is still possible upon the earth.

This book brings the series *Environmental Theology* to the point of acting on that possibility. Here strategies are formulated to embrace nature within American culture, to protect our distinctive landscapes, to curb America's huge appetite for earth's resources, and to reduce our impact upon the biosphere. This volume also proposes reforms within Christian churches so that our worship and witness may become relevant to the environmental crisis that threatens all God's creation. The ethics and policies proposed here respond to the prophetic challenge that John Muir, America's pioneering environmentalist, addressed to American culture a century ago (see Book 1, *Baptized into Wilderness*). The call for personal awakening to the natural world in Book 2, *Beauty of the Lord,* leads toward the social regeneration proposed in this book. The policies that Book 4 proposes in the language of the American political tradition have roots in the "biblical ecology" proposed in Book 3, *Hope for the Land*. There we saw that the moral quality of human relationships with nature is a central concern of biblical faith. From slavery in Egypt the Lord rescued the Hebrews, who in turn helped liberate both the Canaanite farmers from oppression and their landscape from exploitation, in order to fashion a covenant community. This was a holy people joined to a holy land, sustaining each other in just regard for the needs of both landscape and inhabitants. God sent Jesus to revive this community of redemption and to extend its embrace to all the earth, all peoples, and all creatures.

Now this concluding book proposes strategies for environmental liberation that are both faithful to the biblical tradition and appropriate to modern circumstances.

* * *

The biblical God is an engaging personality who helps us to embrace justice and compassion in our own lives. Christian dialogue about faith and ethics is personal, shaped by the circumstances of each of us and relevant to them. In each of these books I have shared personal experience so that the reader may imagine the circumstances from which I write and may join a human conversation about God's will for us.

This book is written from Chestnut Ridge Farm in the mountains of southwestern Virginia, where the harvest over the past fifteen years has included maple syrup, strawberries, and grass-fattened beef, along with insights that have led me to write. Before the time on this farm, most of my years as a pastor were spent in the coalfields of Appalachia, where I eventually became so alarmed by the ravages of strip mining that I led an unsuccessful campaign to end strip mining in West Virginia and then helped organize a nationwide effort to obtain Federal regulation of this destructive practice. By the time I stood with colleagues in the Rose Garden to watch President Carter sign the Surface Mining Control and Reclamation Act of 1977, I was convinced of a calling to develop the links between Christian faith and the needs of the natural environment. Exhausted by the struggle over strip mining, however, I turned to farming in the hope that building a healthy landscape might restore my spirits.

In the newly rented house on Chestnut Ridge, I was lonely and vulnerable to my surroundings. Briars and cedar trees had taken root in the old hillside pastures, while the few acres which could be plowed looked gray and lifeless from too many applications of fertilizer and herbicide and too many harvests of corn. The farm pond brimmed with life, however, many varieties of birds sang along the lane, the deep woods were stately, and beyond the high ridge ranges of green mountains faded away toward the Kentucky border. I was fearful that a neophyte farmer would not be able to control the complex ecology of southern Appalachian fields, where everything—particularly weeds and briars—grows in such profusion. It would take me several years to learn that a farmer need not subdue the environment but can, instead, interract with it.

Taking title to Chestnut Ridge Farm was like entering a marriage—a sensuous, emotional, engaging relationship. Like a marriage partner, a farm has its own kinship network that includes people who were raised on the place long before. Ownership opened access to a neighborhood culture. Several neighbors, patient with my city-bred ignorance and eager to display skills that had too often been regarded as commonplace, taught me to farm. I am grateful to John "Junior" Peters, Frank Taylor, Morgan Compton, Earl Wolfe, Jean Collins, and Vincent Collins. My neighbor Carl Price is a skillful trainer of mules and workhorses. When I purchased a pair of Belgian mare colts, Carl broke me to the reins behind his experienced mules, then trained my mares, and finally supervised my first plowing behind my own team.

I am an odd farmer, however, since my motives are unusual.

The farm is a secure haven where I need not go hungry, yet I do not depend upon it for my livelihood. This gives me freedom to experiment. Farming is part of my theological exploration, so harvests of inspiration are just as pleasing as healthy produce.

Tending this farm helped me develop the theology of beauty presented in Book 2 of this series, *Beauty of the Lord*. The philosophy that sensitivity to beauty is a useful guide to practical action drew me away from the routines of my neighbors. I was attracted, for example, by the sugar maple trees that grow in unusual profusion on the cool, north-facing ridge crossing the farm. Although our southern climate is marginal for these trees and none of my neighbors tap them, I decided to try to make maple syrup. Communion with these trees each February and March has been satisfying, and so has mastery of the craft of "sugaring." Eight years in ten there has been good production.

The workhorses proved indispensable for hauling the maple sap across muddy slopes to the sugar house. Other work with horses is slow, but there are few acres to till here, and the stately rhythm of the team gives the farmer time to relate to the land. Their "fuel" grows on the farm, while they return nourishment to the soil through their manure. They are beautiful companions. To accommodate the horses, my helpers and I cut straight poplar trees, hauled the logs to a local sawmill, worked with old "Pawdaddy" Corder to saw framing timbers and lumber, and built a new barn.

Farmers in this neighborhood keep beef herds whose weaned calves are sold at auction, trucked away to confinement feedlots, and fattened on corn until they are slaughtered for their meat. Since I disapprove of crowded feedlots and extensive grain feeding, I decided to raise my calves here on the farm so that they might enjoy wholesome surroundings during their short lives. Although these calves don't get as heavy as feedlot calves, customers find the meat lean, tender, and unusually tasty. Pasture management has required much trial and error: after several years of trying to clear brush from the hillsides without using poisons, I realized that so much soil was eroding away that these hillsides needed brush to hold them together until trees could be reestablished. Now I let the hillsides return to forest while I maintain grass in the areas level enough to mow.

From the first, people came eagerly from nearby towns to buy maple syrup. Sometimes they would return for other specialty crops, particularly if enjoying the beauty of the farm remained part of their experience. Beginning with pick-your-own strawberries, I have added red raspberries and apples for picking along with cider making as farm specialties.

I am not a good farmer, technically, because I lack the keen eye and retentive memory for physical detail that a farmer must have to monitor the crops and interact creatively with the surrounding environment. I also lack the decades of hands-on experience that bring wisdom to a good farmer. My calling is theology. However, the once-tired soil of Chestnut Ridge Farm now looks dark and rich, and worms can be found in the earth. The grass stands taller at haying time, and more trees wave from the hillsides. Cattle enjoy their lives in open pastures. Our produce is wholesome and tasty, and the people who eat it are my friends. Chestnut Ridge Farm has become more beautiful.

* * *

When people of faith are ready to join together in efforts to rescue the earth from ecological disaster, we will need—in the spirit of Pentecost—to speak the common idioms of social and political discourse. This book, therefore, translates biblical insights into images appropriate to American social dialogue. Many other languages and cultures are also important to the fate of the earth, but here I specifically address the culture and institutions of the United States in order to present ideas clearly and to suggest specific applications. Christian environmentalists in other countries need equally to devise policies relevant to the political traditions and cultural images that are valued within their societies.

The first part of the book identifies political images from America's history that resonate with the sensuous theology and the biblical ecology discussed throughout the series. "The pursuit of happiness," Thomas Jefferson's inspired substitute for the "right to property," may inspire human relationships with nature that are engaging rather than simply manipulative. Furthermore, Jefferson's hope that independent farmers might form the backbone of a free society is similar to the biblical vision of a liberated people tending a landscape that is also freed from oppression. Building upon such principles, I suggest emotional and moral requirements for satisfying human work. I believe that unsatisfying work may tempt people to compensatory activities that are environmentally destructive, and that inefficient efforts to meet human needs inevitably waste resources.

Part II focuses upon agriculture in order to suggest how society's values and technologies must change in order to meet human needs while protecting environmental vitality. Agriculture disturbs more land than any other human enterprise. Indeed, some environmentalists have called human evolution from hunting-gathering to agriculture a "fall" of our species into techniques of exploitation that inevitably degrade both people and the landscape. The Bible, however, is not pessimistic about agriculture, even though biblical salvation history begins with liberation from agricultural oppression. Within God's covenant agriculture became a moral relationship between humanity and nature which might add to the beauty of the earth. In that spirit I suggest a moral vision of agriculture, one suitable to the needs of the modern world.

Part III proposes political and Constitutional changes to protect the vitality of nature despite the pervasive presence of human culture. Human rights of access to nature are affirmed, in order to correct the constriction of human experience within urban culture. A comprehensive strategy for land reform in the United States is suggested. And an amendment is proposed to extend Constitutional protection to the species of life, to singular natural features, and to the environmental systems that support life.

Finally, Part IV proposes a broader understanding of Christian identity so churches may join their efforts to redeem the earth from destruction. In faithfulness to the Lord who alone is God, churches can help their members achieve communion with the full range of created life. Jesus suffers alongside abused landscapes and endangered species just as surely as he suffers with the oppressed and forlorn within the human family. Congregations may broaden their understanding of *parish* to embrace the needs of the living ecosystem within the sphere of their daily experience, and they may expand worship to enfold the praise and petitions of all creatures. Just as Christians once pioneered communities that expressed visions of social justice and compassion, now churches need to establish communities where people learn to honor the earth, to tend it, and to keep it with integrity. We will experience salvation as we extend it to all that lives.

Part 1.

America the Beautiful

Throughout our history, we Americans have found our country to be a hospitable landscape which meets our physical needs and also fills our senses with beauty:

> O beautiful for spacious skies,
>   For amber waves of grain,
> For purple mountain majesties
>   Above the fruited plain!
> America! America!
>   God shed His grace on thee,
> And crown thy good with brotherhood
>   From sea to shining sea![1]

This beloved hymn expresses our desire to build a human society which is as benevolent as the American countryside. If we celebrate this landscape in poetry, however, we often take it for granted in our policy. Even while we exploit the earth carelessly, we assume it will continue to respond abundantly and shine majestically. Now, however, purple mountains recede behind city smog, once fruitful plains lie poisoned and eroded, and waters shimmer with the scum of sewage and industrial wastes. We must draw this landscape into spheres of moral regard and political responsibility if we wish to protect the beauty that remains and restore vitality to damaged ecosystems. We need to extend our affectionate embrace to all species and systems of life that make America beautiful.

Among the founders of the American republic, Thomas Jefferson had a unique vision of free people joined to the landscape. His values were comparable to biblical jubilee ethics. He believed the land and its people might protect each other from oppression, while farmers might combine productivity with beauty in order to achieve happiness. Today, as agribusiness strips the landscape of both human residents and natural life, this is a poignant vision. If we Americans still wish to pursue happiness, we must reappraise modern culture with a critical eye. Much of our production and consumption not only overburdens the earth but deflects our desires from the more humane, natural, and immediate paths to satisfaction.

This "industrial revolution" has indeed transformed the character of all our work. Although the pay may be better, industrial processes and bureaucratic structures alienate workers from meaningful relationships with the materials of production and the purposes of labor. Work has lost many of its sensual, satisfying qualities. People alienated from the joys of work demand other, compensatory satisfactions, and these growing desires for material consumption burden the natural systems which sustain life. To resolve these dilemmas, we need to develop patterns of work that are both personally satisfying and environmentally responsible. We need industries that are truly efficient in that they meet genuine human needs without waste of effort or dissipation of energy. We can cultivate new tastes that help us achieve personal satisfactions and cultural creativity even as we reduce the burdens that human society places upon the earth.

1. *Jefferson's Vision*

Thomas Jefferson influenced America's revolutionary struggle, our Constitution, and our early federal experience. His views were popular but always controversial. He drafted the Declaration of Independence, contributed to our understanding of human rights, and fashioned America's imaginative Constitutional protection of "religious freedom," which has diffused tensions between churches and civil government. He was a pioneering scientific naturalist and agriculturalist, a brilliant architect, and an innovative champion of public education and higher learning. While serving as president between 1801 and 1809, he made the Louisiana Purchase, which secured the vast lands of the Mississippi and Missouri basins for the westward expansion of the new nation. Wary of the pretentions of power, however, he did not want his presidency memorialized on his tombstone. He insisted it bear "the following inscription, & not a word more":

> Here was buried
> Thomas Jefferson
> Author of the Declaration of American Independence
> of the Statute of Virginia for religious freedom
> & Father of the University of Virginia.[1]

Jefferson's vision of sharing land to support human freedom will begin our moral reconstruction of the place of nature in modern American culture.

Jefferson understood that to become free, people must overcome both political and economic oppression. To remain free, we must avoid both political and economic dependency. Each household, he believed, required a measure of economic independence along with opportunities to participate in democratic decision-making, in order to learn behavior appropriate for a free people, to grow from slavishness toward human dignity, and to discover their stake in the maintenance of a free society. Jefferson enthusiastically fanned the flames of rebellion that led to the Declaration of Independence and the revolution against English dominion. He was less enthusiastic, however, about the proposed Federal Constitution, because it did not define civil rights and because it provided for representative government rather than popular democracy. Jefferson insisted upon the addition of a Bill of Rights as a condition for states' ratification. He also strove to keep representative government limited, and to build beneath it institutions of direct, participatory democracy. Freedom would be secure, he believed, only when all people had the opportunity to gather frequently in local assemblies to debate and vote upon the public questions that affected their lives. He thought that the New England townships, where every citizen had a voice and vote in local decisions, had "proved themselves the wisest invention ever devised by the wit of man for the perfect exercise of self-government and for its preservation."[2] He tried to persuade his home state, Virginia, to adopt this pattern, and he made sure the same opportunity was extended to the Northwest Territories beyond the Ohio River.

Throughout his political career, Jefferson affirmed a human right of access to small landholdings and worked to implement the right in practice. For the majority of people, he believed, subsistence agriculture would be the key to economic independence and a means toward a life of dignity and beauty. Within the Virginia legislature, prior to the Revolution, Jefferson led the effort to repeal English laws of *entail,* which allowed a landowner to restrict land passed to heirs in order to prevent the division of his estate, and *primogeniture,* which gave the eldest son the whole estate of one who had died without having made a will. Each of the states came to adopt similar reforms. Jefferson also tried to amend the Virginia constitution to assure fifty acres of land to any man of twenty-one years of age who did not already own as much, and to extend the voting right to anyone who owned a quarter acre in town or twenty-five acres in the country.

These provisions would have guaranteed both political rights and means for subsistence to any white male willing to receive them.[3] Jefferson would have happily extended these rights to black males as well, but his efforts to end slavery in Virginia, and to prevent its continuance in the new United States, were not successful.[4] Jefferson also alluded to the "natural equality" of women, but he gave no serious thought to political or property rights for women outside the traditional household.[5] Furthermore, he had difficulty recognizing that protection of Native American culture would require patterns of landholding that differed from those valued in white society.

After the American Revolution, Jefferson was dispatched by the Continental Congress to serve as ambassador to France, where he had opportunity to observe huge landholdings farmed by poor tenants while the desperate unemployed looked on. He wrote to his friend James Madison, "This enormous inequality producing so much misery to the bulk of mankind, legislators cannot invent too many devices for subdividing property." Jefferson advocated progressive property taxes with higher rates on larger holdings to encourage the break up of estates. He affirmed that when some hold land idle while others are poor and unemployed,

> the laws of property have been so far extended as to violate natural right. The earth is given as a common stock for man to labor and live on. If for the encourgement of industry we allow it to be appropriated, we must take care that other employment be provided to those excluded from the appropriation. If we do not, the fundamental right to labor the earth returns to the unemployed.

America, he urged Madison, must "provide by every possible means that as few as possible shall be without a little portion of land. The small landholders are the most precious part of a state."[6]

Jefferson came to see the right of access to land as a foundation upon which economic independence, and therefore political democracy, could be constructed. Before the American Revolution, the English king and his colonial administrators had often deeded huge tracts of frontier lands to investors and land speculators. By

acts of 1785, 1796, and 1800, however, Congress opened the rich
farmlands across the Ohio River to small-farm settlement at modest
fees, nearly fulfilling Jefferson's vision. Popular access to subsistence agriculture placed a dignified foundation beneath all economic
endeavors. Here in America, Jefferson would boast,

> every one may have land to labor for himself if he chooses; or
> preferring the exercise of any other industry, may exact for it such
> compensation as not only to afford a comfortable subsistence, but
> wherewith to provide for a cessation from labor in old age. Every one,
> by his property, or by his satisfactory situation, is interested in the
> support of law and order. And such men may safely and advanta-
> geously reserve to themselves a wholsome controul over their public
> affairs . . .[7]

Jefferson saw farming as a means to break the dominion of
economic want over human life. Since farmers can, with the help of
God and nature, provide for the basic needs of their families, they are
spared the moral corruption of dependence upon commerce within
which, to make a living, one person must cheat a neighbor while
another must lick the boots of a benefactor.

> Corruption of morals in the mass of cultivators is a phænomenon of
> which no age nor nation has furnished an example. It is the mark set
> on those, who not looking up to heaven, to their own soil and
> industry, as does the husbandman, for their subsistence, depend for
> it on the casualties and caprice of customers. Dependence begits
> subservience and venality, suffocates the germ of virtue, and per-
> pares fit tools for the designs of ambition.[8]

Jefferson believed that the development of human virtue required a
haven from the pressures of the marketplace. Trade had social
benefits, but dependence upon it was corrupting. Agriculture, however, could enoble the farmer.

Not all farming, to be sure, was uplifting. Jefferson railed
against the practice of growing tobacco in Virginia—"a culture
productive of infinite wretchedness"—because the tobacco market
enticed farmers into slavish dependence upon one cash crop and
tempted them to exploit their families, their stock, and their land:

> Those employed in it are in a continual state of exertion beyond the powers of nature to support. Little food of any kind is raised by them; so that men and animals on these farms are badly fed, and the earth is rapidly impoverished.[9]

Diversified farming on a small scale, however, provided a family with sustenance, engaged all members in creative and productive activities proportional to their age, strength, and wit, and—by surrounding families with the beauty of natural life as well as the companionship and example of dignified and diligent neighbors—stimulated aesthetic reflection, intellectual development, and moral growth. Small freeholds, Jefferson believed, benefited the land itself because the farmer had a long-term interest in its productivity. In Europe he had observed that English tenant farmers with long leases protected the fertility of their soils by using both animal and vegetable manures, whereas French tenants on short leases neglected the soil.[10] The land would benefit even more, he felt, from fully democratic patterns of ownership.

Jefferson undertook farming and gardening projects at his Monticello estate that made it, during his lifetime, America's leading site for agricultural experimentation and research. He corresponded with horticulturalists throughout the world, exchanging seeds and plant material, discussing machinery design and crop rotations, and sharing the results of experiments. No occupation gave him more physical pleasure or provided greater intellectual challenge. When he retired from the presidency, he wrote the following mediation:

> I have often thought that if heaven had given me choice of my position and calling, it should have been on a rich spot of earth, well watered, and near a good market for the productions of the garden. No occupation is so delightful to me as the culture of the earth, and no culture comparable to that of the garden. Such a variety of subjects, some one always coming to perfection, the failure of one thing repaired by the success of another, and instead of one harvest a continued one through the year. Under a total want of demand except for our family table, I am still devoted to the garden. But though an old man, I am but a young gardener.[11]

Because of his concern for personal rights and human dignity, Jefferson is often portrayed as a radical individualist. He was, however, profoundly conscious of how susceptible people are to the quality of their society and the character of their physical surroundings. He believed, as well, that private virtues could not survive without social outlets for their expression. Drawing his psychology from John Locke, Jefferson understood people to be inherently good but vulnerable to the influence of their environment. Universal education was therefore essential to shape people for freedom. "The diffusion of knowledge among the people," he believed, is the only sure foundation "for the preservation of freedom and happiness."[12]

Beyond education, however, people required both a political and a natural environment suitable to wholesome life. Despite the cultural opportunities they offered, European and American cities in Jefferson's day were physically unhealthy. Many of their citizens suffered from economic vulnerability, which undermined human dignity, while those with means and skills were too easily tempted by commercial speculations or unhealthy entertainments. "I am not a friend to placing growing men in populous cities, because they acquire there habits & partialities which do not contribute to the happiness of their after life."[13] On the other hand, the rich American wilderness offered the opportunity to construct a wholesome society where freehold farms would give families security, stimulate their industry, and inspire their aesthetic, intellectual, and moral reflection, while new political institutions would open to them opportunities for dignified, personal participation in shaping their social order. Here a new culture of free people could flourish, unlike anything the world had seen before. His political vision of what farmers might become, as well as personal experience with some of his more industrious and upright neighbors, led Jefferson to write fervently, "Those who labor the earth are the chosen people of God, if ever he had a chosen people, whose breasts he has made his peculiar deposit for substantial and genuine virtue,"[14] and to say again:

> Cultivators of the earth are the most valuable citizens. They are the most vigorous, the most independent, the most virtuous, & they are tied to their country & wedded to its liberty & interests by the most lasting bonds.[15]

* * *

When Thomas Jefferson chose to summarize fundamental human rights in his draft for the Declaration of Independence, he changed the phrase "life, liberty, and property," which the Continental Congress had adopted two years before, to "life, liberty, and the pursuit of happiness."[16] The right to "property" had come to mean different things to different people. To conservatives it meant the right to hold vast estates, whether they were productive or idle, and even to dictate to one's heirs how such lands could be used. This was a view Jefferson deplored. To the farmers and tradespeople who were now ready to sever allegiance to the English king, the right to property meant freedom from any taxation imposed without their political representation. This was the predominant view within the Continental Congress. To the most progressive group, however, the right to property had a radically democratic meaning. The Virginia Bill of Rights, which was drafted by Jefferson's friend George Mason and adopted by the Virginia legislature while Jefferson was in Philadelphia working on the Declaration, interpreted the right to property as a right of access to land and to the means of subsistence, a right that one generation could not withhold from the next:

> . . . all men are by nature equally free and independent, and have certain inherent rights, of which, when they enter into a state of society, they cannot by any compact deprive or divest their posterity; namely, the enjoyment of life and liberty, with the means of acquiring and possessing property, and pursuing and obtaining happiness and safety.[17]

Jefferson supported this fully democratic interpretation of property rights, but he realized that the Continental Congress, as a whole, would not do so. He simplified Mason's text to achieve his now immortal statement:

> We hold these truths to be self-evident, that all men are created equal, that they are endowed by their Creator with certain unalienable Rights, that among these are Life, Liberty and the pursuit of Happiness.[18]

Jefferson may have hoped that in this more subtle version the idea of a universal right to pursue happiness might yet outflank the conservative defense of intrenched property rights. The holdings of a few must not be allowed to block the pursuit of livelihood by the many. Jefferson believed that every human had a "fundamental right to labor the earth," for the "earth is given as a common stock for man to labor and live on." If the laws of a country shielded uncultivated lands from the unemployed poor, those laws violated natural right. Jefferson even affirmed squatters' rights when conditions were desperate: "Every man who cannot find employment, but who can find uncultivated land, shall be at liberty to cultivate it, paying a moderate rent."[19] By 1841 the U.S. Congress itself recognized sqatters' rights within the public domain, and this recognition in turn led to the passage of the Homestead Act of 1862, which allowed settlers to claim tracts of 160 acres of public land and to acquire title after five years' cultivation.[20] Because the United States held such vast public lands—thanks in part to Jefferson's Louisiana Purchase—large private holdings did not prevent public access to land until near the close of the nineteenth century when homesteads were exhausted. (A century later, however, the majority of Americans have been effectively excluded from land ownership. We must now reconsider the right of access to land in a democratic society, a concern to which I will return in later chapters.)

In retirement, Jefferson prepared a careful statement of his conviction that a moral society must allow each person the means to satisfy natural wants, and that laws which block access to the means of subsistence are a social crime:

> I believe with you that morality, compassion, generosity, are innate elements of the human constitution; that there exists a right independent of force; that a right to property is founded in our natural wants, in the means with which we are endowed to satisfy these wants, and the right to what we acquire by those means without violating the similar rights of other sensible beings; that no one has a right to obstruct another, exercising his faculties innocently for the relief of sensibilities made a part of his nature; that justice is the fundamental law of society; that the majority, oppressing an individual, is guilty of a crime, abuses its strength, and by acting on the law of the strongest breaks up the foundations of society . . . [21]

When people need land for livelihood, Jefferson here affirmed, it is not squatters who damage the fabric of society, but the owners and the police who try to remove them from the land.

Of course, these principles made it easier to justify the encroachment of white settlers upon Indian lands that were not being cultivated. Jefferson admired the dignity and freedom of Native Americans, treated tribal leaders with respect, and honored treaties; but he could not detach himself from his own culture or appreciate the value of protecting uncultivated regions large enough to permit Native Americans to pursue their hunting traditions. Instead, when president, he congratulated the chiefs of the Cherokee Nation on their progress in adopting scientific farming, believing this would benefit Cherokees in precisely the same way it benefited white settlers.[22]

Jefferson believed that *"the earth belongs . . . to the living,"*[23] so that one generation cannot bind or inhibit another. This conviction, which undergirded his principles of landholding, led Jefferson to oppose long-term debt, whether public or private, as well. He considered debt a device by which salesmen lured free farmers into dependency. Only during the Revolution, when no credit was available, had the farmer been safe:

> I know no condition happier than that of a Virginia farmer might be, conducting himself as he did during the war. His estate supplies a good table, clothes itself and his family with their ordinary apparel, furnishes a small surplus to buy salt, sugar, coffee, and a little finery for his wife and daughter, enables him to receive and to visit his friends, and furnishes him pleasing and healthy occupation. To secure all this he needs but one act of self denial, to put off buying anything till he has money to pay for it.[24]

To cure the greed of lenders, Jefferson proposed that all debts expire after a generation, which he calculated to be nineteen years. Public debts, which he believed were most often accumulated to subsidize the business schemes of the rich at the expense of the people, should be treated in a similar manner.

I am not among those who fear the people. They, and not the rich, are our dependence for continued freedom. And to preserve their independence, we must not let our rulers load us with perpetual debt. We must make our election between *economy and liberty,* or *profusion and servitude.*[25]

* * *

Jefferson's vision was influential and, to a degree, prophetic. Education proved to be as important to the development of a free people as he had argued, though public education would not release moral qualities within human nature to the extent he had hoped. The availability of land for the family farmer, at first very cheap and eventually free, undergirded American economy, culture, and political institutions for more than a hundred years following the Revolution. Most farmers, however, did not remain content with the rewards of self-sufficient, diversified agriculture. Instead, they imitated the tobacco farmers whom Jefferson deplored and specialized in a cash crop whenever they could, often going deeply into debt to do so. .

Access to the political process has also expanded steadily in this country, although the quality of political life at the neighborhood level—where, Jefferson believed, people should exercise their citizenship and experience their freedom—has rarely approached his expectations. Americans have more frequently accepted representative politics than they have insisted upon participatory politics.

Jefferson was a loving, painstaking student of the teachings of Jesus. Although he did not draw moral insights from the rest of the Bible, his personal and political vision was surprisingly close to what I have called the "biblical ecology." Like the ancient Hebrews, he believed that both the natural landscape and human society could benefit from responsible, family-scale agriculture. The Hebrews had gone further and developed a sense of the moral rights of nonhuman species within the agricultural domain, which Jefferson did not share. Although he loved nature, Jefferson was a child of the scientific enlightenment, which persuaded him that human subjugation of nature was fully appropriate. Like the Hebrews, however, he believed that human ownership of land should be restricted by ethics and limited by time. The powerful must not block access by the weak. Debts, while tolerated, should periodically be forgiven. Where the Hebrews affirmed the jubilee redistribution of land to the landless every fifty years, Jefferson believed in fresh access for each generation.

So long as the American frontier was available to family farmers for settlement, this abundance of land held the more painful question of land reform and redistribution in abeyance. Jefferson, more than any other American leader, inspired this policy of open settlement, which allowed America to grow as the land of the free.

2. *The Pursuit of Happiness*

Modern society overloads the biosphere, and the burden is growing. To reverse the present patterns of environmental degradation, we need to review not only our deliberate treatment of nature, but also the ways we choose, within our culture, to satisfy human desires and aspirations. When we fail to meet our own needs directly and efficiently, our compensatory activities tax the surrounding environment. Nevertheless, I draw hope for the future of the planet from the conviction that the deepest human desires are in harmony with the beauty of the earth.

"I am come that they might have life," Jesus said, "and that they might have it more abundantly. I am the good shepherd" (John 10:10–11, KJV). Even though we have reason to despair for the fate of human society and the natural world, Jesus helps us to revive our engagement with life, open our senses, awaken our feelings, and attend to the vitality about us as well as the life within. Jesus' intervention is critical because, in order to live expressively in a broken world that is painful and threatening, we must trust God. "I had fainted," David cried, "unless I had believed to see the goodness of the LORD in the land of the living" (Psalm 27:13, KJV). God promises a renewed creation if we trust and take courage. Personal desires, social good, and environmental health can support one another within a moral ecology. We can lighten the human burden upon the earth if we learn to meet our needs and desires more directly by cultivating satisfying relationships within human community, and also with natural life.

This is not to suggest that every urge one feels can be pursued without harm to others or damage to the environment. Conscious feelings may themselves be distorted, bent by sin and frustration. We may need to be reborn in order to recover the purity of heart that Jesus recommended—the capacity to know and express desires in a straightforward yet appropriate manner. Neither does this suggest that humanity, which now overpopulates the earth and relies heavily upon destructive technologies, can easily accommodate itself to the needs of the natural environment. Mistakes that have been compounded for generations will be difficult to correct. Yet the finest in human culture can be realized in creative, nonoppressive relationships with our living environment. Human culture has been, at times, a magnificent addition to the life of the earth, and we may again contribute beauty to the earth and enrich the natural ecosystem.

The quality of human culture is important to individuals because the characteristics that make us human are propagated as much by culture as by genes. Thinking depends upon the rich language that culture offers the individual; personal feelings are shaped by the images that one's culture celebrates; personal expression is facilitated by the tools that culture furnishes and is guided by the vocations that it recognizes. Only within a culture can there be artists and poets, teachers and inventors, farmers and traders, healers and preachers. Each of these may contribute to culture and even change it; before one contributes, however, one receives. Personal creativity is rooted in the soil of human culture.

A century of industrialization and swift urbanization have altered the fabric of culture and changed the way each of us fits in. It is true that many rural people had lived difficult lives and moved to the factory towns eagerly, and that some of these and more of their children have benefited from the change. Nevertheless, family relationships were disrupted, contacts with nature were lost, and rapid change led to inner disorientation. People employed for wages and salaries learned to meet more of their needs with commercial products; this stimulated trade and manufacturing and led to further expansion of the wage economy. Spreading industrialization and the accompanying urbanization put strains upon the natural environment as more resources were mined and harvested while toxic wastes were spewed into the air, poured into the waters, and deposited across the landscape. Within the wage economy, people sought satisfaction as consumers, but many of the products and services upon which they became dependent failed to meet their needs as well as expected, and some turned out to be hazardous to their well-being. Today it is becoming clear that the frustrations of modern life are overtaking the rewards. It is time to reevaluate technological society. Although many useful items have been manufactured and some good systems have been developed during the past century, there are alternative ways to meet human needs that are more direct, less costly, and leave less residue of pollution in their wake.

Our lives are so deeply imbedded within modern industrial culture that it is difficult to imagine alternatives that would be satisfying and protect nature as well. Even the most self-defeating cultural patterns can come to be accepted as immutable. Sometimes we submit to conditions that we should protest. Sometimes we are drawn to things that hurt us. Sometimes we limit our thinking to the stereotyped images that are offered through the mass media. Even with the best intentions, we may need help to open ourselves to a fresh perspective.

The Lord offers such help to us. Prophetic moral visions in the Bible, for example, emerged through the ages at times of crisis when people felt the tension between their faith in a loving God and their experience of suffering, oppression, and pollution. At such times God has called people to recreate society and has inspired fresh visions of justice, reconciliation, and peace.

* * *

When, in his revolutionary declaration, Thomas Jefferson said that God gave all people the right to pursue happiness, he was claiming for American colonists the right to remove arbitrary barriers to that pursuit. He argued that, at the very least, governments must not impede the search. The overt issue was British rule, which had become oppressive to the energetic colonists who were eager to build their own lives without interference from overseas and to fashion a freer, more just society. Jefferson knew as well that there were other forms of oppression to which this principle should be applied, such as the laws that deprived some people of access to land for livelihood and, indeed, the laws that kept some people enslaved. The times to remove these barriers would come.

The pursuit of happiness can be viewed as a moral principle referring to the whole cluster of energies, drives, and aspirations that make humans a creative, expressive species. The principle is refreshing because it reverses the usual direction of moral proclamation: rather than a dictate by an authority to control popular behavior, it is an assertion by people in rebellion against restraints that do not serve their needs. It is not a standard for judging personal behavior, but a standard to evaluate the customs and institutions that would constrain behavior. The principle affirms that legitimate political and cultural institutions must facilitate the human pursuit of happiness, not frustrate it. With the success of America's revolution, this principle became one of the values taught by the leaders themselves, extending legitimacy to those who question whether society serves their needs and aspirations. America's government has lasted because its institutions are frequently questioned and sometimes reformed.

When people are denied the freedom to pursue happiness, or when we lose our appreciation of how to do so, the surrounding natural environment shares the burden of our frustrations. Those who would block human aspirations must often resort to violent and destructive measures that not only hurt their human targets but also damage the landscape. The defoliation of Vietnam is one sad example, and nuclear war would be the ultimate illustration of this truth. Ineffective or wrongheaded pursuit of needs and desires also takes its toll upon the surrounding environment.

I once purchased a sleek Jaguar automobile because—I now realize—I was sexually frustrated; many people do similar foolish things. Since the car did not satisfy my real need, I wasted the metals, fabrics and fine leathers, as well as the skills of its builders, and I continued to waste fuel until I found a human relationship that satisfied my real need and made an opulent, inefficient vehicle unnecessary. Judging from the sexual and emotional content of advertising intended to attract us to products and services, a great deal of what we consume in our affluence—straining the earth's resources—may result from our inability to satisfy desires in a straightforward fashion.

At the other extreme live the poorest and most desperate people, who are deprived of relevant technologies. On the African plains people cut scarce trees for firewood and thereby hasten the desertification of the land they depend upon for crops and livestock grazing, because simple stoves that save fuel, although manufactured, have not been made available to them. The poorest in Latin America clear the rain forest to graze their cattle briefly before the weak soil is exhausted, because Japanese will buy the timber and Americans the beef, and because the regional governments are too unstable and impoverished to devise sustainable economic alternatives. The world's richest and the world's poorest—the beneficiaries and victims of injustice—do the greatest environmental damage. Within the affluent culture people choose to abuse nature; within the culture of poverty people are forced to do so.

To protect the earth's ecosystem, governments will need to curb many corporate enterprises and redirect many human activities. Coercion by itself, however, will not be effective, since people will not observe restrictions that simply frustrate their efforts to meet their needs. Coercion exaggerates the gulf between the weak and the powerful and tempts those in authority to abuse their power and profit from corruption. On the other hand, social policies that improve justice, protect freedom, and support the pursuit of happiness are more likely to find popular acceptance. People need to taste the benefits that a society more attuned to nature can provide. When we are encouraged to meet our own needs efficiently and effectively, we are more likely to include the needs of other living things within our family of concern.

* * *

God's new covenant, the kingdom that Jesus announced, embraces the life of this world—animal and vegetable as well as human. As Christians come to appreciate this we will be able to join the earthly pursuit of happiness with less hesitation. At times we have felt we must turn away, not only from the culture of injustice that the apostle Paul calls "the world," but also from the life and landscapes that surround us, in order to invest our affections in a place detached from this earth. Indeed, some faithful people have been so bruised by life that such an otherworldly hope is their only consolation; we may respect their hope and trust that God will meet their needs. When God revives our lives, however, and helps us to stand erect, then yearnings that lead us away from our fellow creatures, and from the earth itself, become less appropriate. Other-worldly desires overlook too many whom God loves as well as the ecosystem of great beauty in which God delights.

Christians are called, rather, to form a community that embraces God's creation and maintains fellowship with our living companions of all species. This calling requires that we open our hearts to the earth and expand our sensory contact—seeing, hearing, tasting, smelling, and feeling—so we may come to know the lives that share our communion with the Lord. Many people will find sensuous involvement with natural life to be a new experience—exciting, but perhaps also frightening and disorienting. Many Christians may find it challenging to integrate this experience with their more familiar religious emotions and convictions. The earlier volume *Beauty of the Lord* addressed these concerns in order to help Christians respond to fresh experiences of God's beauty and the beauty of the earth with moral integrity. When we cultivate our taste for beauty in its sensual and moral dimensions, and when we enjoy God, our companions, and the natural world more fully, these experiences will help us to become both livelier and more responsible. With God's help we may engage all of life with confidence.

When we open ourselves to the needs of the natural world we will also feel more pain, for nature has been wounded. Already many Christians who serve the afflicted or stand with the oppressed expose themselves to suffering that they might have avoided had they remained detached. Additional suffering is likely when we sympathize with nature and feel within ourselves the distress of a polluted world. However, the joy of being alive to the beauty of nature will outweigh the suffering. Indeed, in order to feel pleasure we must accept vulnerability to pain. The psychotherapist Wilhelm Reich observed that "the ability to endure . . . pain without becoming embittered . . . goes hand in hand with the ability to receive happiness and to give love."[1] As we come to empathize with the natural life around us, our experiences help make nature's interests our own.

Just as I feel sorrow when a good friend dies, so I also grieve when an old sugar maple I have tapped puts forth no more leaves. I empathize with a load of steers even as we drive to the slaughter-house. The pain is acute when destruction exceeds the need: when a stand of trees is entirely clear-cut rather than thinned for the best timber, or when hills are destroyed for the seam of coal within them. Sometimes grief and anger inspire a fight for change. Even when no reform seems possible, it is better to have loved the trees and hills that are beyond rescue. They need those who see their beauty, for to die unloved is the hardest death of all.

Some Christians have been tempted to cultivate suffering, but this is a mistake. Suffering is an inevitable by-product of our compassion for other lives, but it is not the purpose of these relation-ships. We live for joy, to receive it and to give it. "The chief end of man," in the words of the old Westminster Catechism, "is to glorify God and enjoy him forever." To endure suffering may be a sign of love and strength, but to cultivate suffering is a sign of sickness, and those who recommend suffering to others may soon become their oppressors. Christians must be intolerant of the suffering that results from exploitation. Our gospel is a call for liberation directed to all people and to the earth. If we recognize that suffering is evil, even when we choose to share it, we are more likely to take pity on the weak of the earth and to accommodate their needs.

Ethics for sexual expression that are relevant to environ-mental crisis pose a particular challenge. Among life's pleasures, most people need to enjoy their sexuality if they are to live happily while not overburdening the earth with displaced desires. Human vitality—with all its joys and sorrows—is rooted in sexual energies. Yet sexual anxieties have become ingrained within the biblical and Christian traditions, making it difficult for some churches to ac-knowledge the contribution that sexual expression makes to human happiness, and even more difficult for them to offer a moral guidance that supports human expression while cautioning against population growth that overburdens the earth.

Since the God revealed in the Bible is not a sexual being, biblical faith at its best has humanized sex and separated it from worship. The authors of the Bible proposed a moral vision of human sexuality that fused desire, love, and justice so man and woman might help to fulfill each other while contributing creatively to the society that sustains them. However, centuries of competition with pagan cults, which employed fornication in the worship of sexual deities, left a residue of anxiety about sexuality in the Bible which was augmented within the early Christian church as it struggled to survive the decadent Roman culture. A reactionary conviction formed that celibacy promoted holiness and protected, in particular, the purity of the clergy. Sexual expression became a secondary value justified only by one's desire for children within an approved family setting.

Sexual decadence within our own culture may reenforce sexual anxiety, while the perils of overpopulation may give sexual abstinence new social relevance. Nevertheless, the sexual drive is a vital part of the energetic system that makes humanity a broadly creative species. Expressiveness in humans—unlike most animal species—is supported by a sexual drive that tends to be constant rather than periodic. Most adults need satisfying sexual expression to experience our personhood and fire our creativity, while the blocking of sexual expression may have consequences that are personally disturbing and, at times, socially alarming. "The importance of sexuality . . . can be wrongly estimated," Paul Goodman observed, "when it is free, it is only one among several productive forces; but when it is repressed it is the most important destructive influence that there is."[2] The repression of sexuality feeds the pornography that pollutes our culture. It also undergirds the commercial exploitation of unsatisfied sexual urges to sell products and services. Furthermore, some people are driven by sexual repression to compensatory aggression and violence. When sexual desire is systematically denied gratification, as Wilhelm Reich oberved, "Hate develops as a result of the exclusion of the original goal of love."[3] This frustrated energy can be exploited by totalitarian leaders who manipulate mass rage and direct it at targets to serve the leader's ambition.[4]

When sexual expression is modified by birth control, it can remain satisfying without burdening the earth. From an environmental perspective, therefore, it is essential to speed the trend—which modern birth-control technologies make possible—to separate sexual pleasure from reproduction. A healthy world ecosystem, with living space for other creatures as well as people, cannot be restored until the human population is stabilized or, better still, reduced. When pregnancy is avoided, sexual desire can be satisfied with far less stress upon the natural environment than is required to meet other basic human needs such as food, shelter, and clothing. There may be side effects of separating sexual expression from reproduction that we do not yet understand, and we need to select carefully those birth control techniques that are healthy and socially appropriate. Nevertheless, the need for all people to practice birth control is morally compelling.

Particularly in an age when the moral evaluation of sexuality is in transition, people need safe places to reflect upon their feelings and their behavior. In Western culture, religious institutions have served as the primary interpreters of human sexuality. Today, as the needs of life change, churches have special opportunities to help people allay their sexual anxieties and fashion moral contexts for the expression of their desires. It is appropriate for churches to offer moral guidance, but it is not appropriate for churches to encourage sexual repression. Anxious religious training, particularly the indoctrination of children, has often led to a repression that pushed desire below the level of awareness so that its impact upon one's behavior was unrecognized. Jesus, in contrast, preached straightforward expression from the core of one's personality, and he offered new life to those who needed to untangle their desires and needs. When we experience our sexual desires, acknowledge them, and praise God for them, we can fashion appropriate ways to express them and learn to avoid those expressions that might hurt ourselves and others. When we are not conscious of our desires, or when we cannot accept them, they are more likely to rule us in devious ways. Loving Christian couples should be able to sing of faith and passion together, as did the sixteenth-century poet Edmund Spenser:

> This joyous day, dear Lord, with joy begin,
>   and grant that we for whom thou didest die
>   being with thy dear blood clean washed from sin,
>   may live for ever in felicity.
> And that thy love we weighing worthily,
>   may likewise love thee for the same again:
>   and for thy sake that all 'like dear didst buy,
>   with love may one another entertain.
> So let us love, dear love, like as we ought,
>   love is the lesson which the Lord us taught.[5]

* * *

The pursuit of happiness requires education. Thomas Jefferson believed that popular education was the foundation for a democracy where people could shape society to suit their needs: "I think by far the most important bill in our whole code is that for the diffusion of knowledge among the people."[6] Jefferson drafted Virginia's statute providing for comprehensive public education; he developed the curriculum and designed the buildings for the University of Virginia; and he made sure that federal lands were allocated for the support of education in frontier communities. Although he usually wanted to limit government so it did not threaten people's liberty, Jefferson wanted all levels of government engaged in providing the education that a free people and their children required.

Since first an ocean and then a revolution came to separate Americans from the corrupting influence of European traditions, Jefferson anticipated a unique opportunity for popular learning:

> If all the sovereigns of Europe were to set themselves to work to emancipate the minds of their subjects from their present ignorance & prejudices . . . a thousand years would not place them on that high ground on which our common people are now setting out.[7]

Although American education might dispense with European prejudices, the frontier would not thrive on ignorance. The common sense of free people by itself, Jefferson observed, was no substitute for sound learning even if some brash Americans thought it were:

> Every folly must run its round; and so, I suppose, must that of self-learning, and self sufficiency; of rejecting the knowlege acquired in past ages, and starting on the new ground of intuition. When sobered by experience I hope our successors will turn their attention to the advantages of education. . . . I hope that necessity will at length be seen of establishing institutions, here as in Europe, where every branch of science, useful at this day, may be taught in its highest degree.[8]

The pursuit of happiness requires education because human personalities are, to a significant extent, cultural constructions. We become persons through our developmental interractions with family, school, church, work, and other cultural institutions that surround us. Culture, in this broad sense, helps humans achieve perceptions, feelings, talents, and aspirations that are beyond the capabilities of other species. We form our identities by making aspects of culture our own, and at times we expand our identity by fashioning new ways to contribute to our culture. Without the language, learning, values, and techniques that culture offers us, however, even the most creative among us would remain unfulfilled.

In modern America, educational institutions are under pressure to mold students narrowly and to equip them for the specific needs of ascendant industries—at the expense of educating people for critical and creative roles in a democratic society. Church-supported schools, as well, are sometimes defensive of doctrine rather than affirmative toward human expression. Organs of news and information—which, in America, remain surprisingly free and critical—are nevertheless financed by commercial advertising, which entices us to remain greedy children dependent upon products supplied by others rather than become resourceful adults.

Many Americans remain ignorant of the most convenient paths to happiness. We are not taught the skills to embark upon independent work. We are not sufficiently familiar with literature and the arts to enjoy them as observers, much less to participate as creators and performers. We are not asked to take responsibility for our health, nor are we encouraged to attain an emotional maturity sufficient to maintain satisfying relationships with others. Ignorance of the paths to happiness leads to greater destruction of the life around us as we grope for and discard compensatory satisfactions, many of which strain our environment. Indeed, modern technologies augment our power to act out our frustrations upon the living landscape.

In order to bring human society into harmony with the natural environment, men and women must now undertake reforms as profound as those Jefferson imagined at the birth of a free people. At every level of society, people will need to develop new understanding and skills to replace familiar attitudes. Such extensive reform of human behavior requires education and cultural support. New perspectives will need to be institutionalized within family life, in schools and churches that teach appropriate values and skills, in new technologies of production and patterns of work, and in government policies.

We now have no ocean to isolate us from the corrupting influences we wish to avoid. We live within the exploitative culture we need to reform. Since we seek to protect the earth from destruction—and not simply to rescue ourselves from a dying earth—we cannot avoid dealing with the institutions that foster destructive activities. Redeeming the earth from destruction is a political task that will intensify our interraction with the broad range of human society. While it may be necessary for some groups to separate themselves temporarily, to develop new techniques and to train their children in new values, perpetual isolation would defeat the intention to change society as a whole for the benefit of the earth.

The pursuit of happiness requires continued access to the finest arts and skills within our cultural tradition. The most satisfying of these are environmentally benign. The environmental revolution, therefore, should be deeply conservative of culture as well as nature, protecting priceless human traditions and skills that have contributed to human happiness through the centuries while we reform destructive techniques. This is a delicate, difficult task.

3. *Good Work*

If we develop our work to be satisfying, socially useful, and environmentally responsible, we may help reunite culture with nature for the benefit of both. Nature would benefit if we modified the modern, myopic view of work as a means to cash income upon which we then rely to purchase our satisfactions. Good work should be a rewarding end in itself as well as a means to other ends. The trend to substitute an economy of rewards for a culture of satisfying work is not a happy one. Too many people are exploited for their labor and left unfulfilled in their leisure, while the consequent processes of production and patterns of consumption burden the natural environment. There is an alternative, however: society may surround its economy with strong values to guard the integrity of human work while protecting the vitality of nature. God proposed such a society to the Hebrews who rebelled against agricultural oppression, and Jesus offered a similar vision to a people frustrated by Roman occupation. Today the Lord calls us to rescue both humanity and nature from abuse by the modern industrial economy.

We need not abandon technology or return to the preindustrial era, though some modern techniques need to be forsaken and many others require modification. The ancient Hebrews who accepted God's covenant did not renounce agriculture but struggled to make it just. The early Christians did not reject government but tried to build loving, participatory communities which were free from exploitation. Modern technology needs to be subdued within a moral framework so that it may be used more skillfully to support human welfare and sustain the life of the earth.

Karl Marx described work as the appropriation of nature for human requirements, producing "use-values"—things of benefit to humanity—from the substance of the earth. Such work is "the everlasting Nature-imposed condition of human existence . . . the necessary condition for effecting exchange of matter between man and Nature." He observed that while capitalism organizes people into increasingly sophisticated productive units, it requires that labor produce "surplus-values," which are retained by the enterprise as wealth. These are benefits that the worker does not enjoy and for which he or she is not compensated.

> The English languge has two different expressions for these two different aspects of labor; in the Simple Labor-process, the process of producing Use-Values, it is *Work;* in the process of creation of Value, it is *Labor,* taking the term in its strictly economical sense.[1]

Marx did not wish to change the techniques of industrial production, which he admired, but rather to redress the exploitation of labor by placing ownership of these enterprises in the hands of the people as a whole. This remedy as applied by socialist and communist states has not, however, given workers a quality of life superior to that enjoyed by workers in capitalist countries. Industrial society— whether it is socialist or capitalist—has problems even more fundamental than the structure of ownership.

The social critic Lewis Mumford probed the unsettling character of modern technology in four studies, beginning with *Technics and Civilization* in 1934 and concluding in 1970 with *The Pentagon of Power*—a particularly valuable analysis of the impact of modern science, bureaucratic organization, and industrial processes upon the human spirit. Mumford saw *anomie,* personal alienation from social structures and values, spreading throughout industrial society in both the East and the West. This alienation he described as endemic to the technologies we now employ.

> We confront a mass society whose typical interests, pursuits, and products do not provide a sufficiently meaningful life even for its most prosperous beneficiaries, still less of course for those who are exploited or, even worse, neglected.
> What is more, the whole apparatus of life has become so complex and the processes of production, distribution, and consumption have become so specialized and subdivided, that the individual person

loses confidence in his own unaided capacities: he is increasingly subject to commands he does not understand, at the mercy of forces over which he exercises no effective control, moving to a destination he has not chosen.... The machine-conditioned individual feels lost and helpless as day by day he metaphorically punches his time-card, takes his place on the assembly line, and at the end draws a pay check that proves worthless for obtaining any of the genuine goods of life.

Machinery and bureaucracy set the style of production until the worker must abandon personal creativity and lose touch with the qualities of natural materials employed, the dynamic of the industrial process, and the usefulness of the product:

This lack of close personal involvement in the daily routine brings a general loss of contact with reality: instead of continuous interplay between the inner and the outer world, with constant feedback or readjustment and with stimulus to fresh creativity, only the outer world—and mainly the collectively organized outer world of the power system—exercises authority: even private dreams must be channeled through television, film, and disc, in order to become acceptable.[2]

It would be excessive to claim that we have declined from an age which was more humane. Preindustrial society had important virtues, yet many people endured grinding labor with limited opportunities. They were more vulnerable to natural calamities and the perils of disease than we would find tolerable today. The challenge is to reform technological society so that work may become more satisfying, while preserving the modern techniques that are truly valuable.

* * *

During the religious reformation of the sixteenth century, Martin Luther reaffirmed the moral value of "work" while he attacked "works." He deprecated the endless duties, payments, rituals, and observances—the "good works"—administered by medieval ecclesiastics using an arcane calculus of merit. These were supposed to secure peace with God, but instead they conditioned the believer to perpetual anxiety. Luther announced that such "works" could be discarded in favor of reliance upon faith and baptism as sufficient signs of God's favor. To replace all this medieval religious trivia Luther recommended *work,* arguing that conscientious labor in any useful craft or trade could be a vocation as pleasing to God as the holy orders of priests and nuns. As the Protestant Reformation spread, Luther's antidote to religious anxiety and his encouragement of practical endeavors helped to stimulate the expansive release of human energies that made the early modern period so creative.

Now, at the end of the twentieth century, we must reform work again in order to liberate humanity from the alienated labor and the compulsive consumption to which the managerial priesthood of modern society would hold us captive. People need release from labor that has no inherent dignity or beauty, from the sterile monotony of work that has no sensual rewards within it, from fashioning products without social value, and from providing services that fail to achieve humane or natural ends. People also need release from the constant lash of advertising to consume huge quantities of these same products and services. As Isaiah cried, "Why do you spend your money for that which is not bread, and your labor for that which does not satisfy?" (55:2, RSV). Though we may in fact be anxious and unsatisfied, the priests of the modern economy urge us to continue our numbing, perpetual works for a pay that can provide only part of what we desire. We walk a treadmill as tiresome as the one against which Luther led his rebellion.

Let us reject the false god of an economy that is sheltered from cultural supervision—an economy that is not held accountable to humane values, to the needs of the earth, or to justice as set forth plainly by God. While recognizing the usefulness of free markets when they are set within a strong framework of social values, let us reject the idolatry of market that would exempt it from social scrutiny. Let us rebuild a humane understanding of work from its Hebraic and Jeffersonian roots and learn to respect the productivity of the natural ecosystem. Society, in order to prosper, does not need to depend upon alienated labor, oppressed workers, foolish products, or rapacious exploitation of nature. Through sensitive work we can draw adequate sustenance from the earth while we return beauty to the world.

The industrial revolution adapted workers to the needs of machines. Men, women, and children were trained to behave like gears in a well-oiled device which, under the control of an engineer, discharged a stream of uniform products. Research centers and bureaucracies, often far removed from the factory floor, developed the knowledge required to make the industrial system productive. Researchers and managers might be innovative and yet remain isolated from the social consequences of the technologies they perfected. The "knowledge explosions" of science propel powerful splinters of technology that sometimes tear the fabric of society. As Lewis Mumford observed,

> Because of our concentration on speed and productivity, we have ignored the need for evaluation, correction, integration, and social assimilation. In practice this results in an inability to use more than a small fragment of the existing corpus of knowledge—namely that which is fashionable or immediately available, because it can be commercially or militarily exploited.[3]

We are not well aware of the knowledge we have lost through the destruction of traditional cultures, the breakup of small communities, and the displacement of crafts by manufactures. Through the many centuries of development prior to the industrial revolution, humanity has accumulated a vast array of information, useful skills, and wisdom relevant to particular cultures and environments. Mumford compares these to the "gene pool" of diversity that helps natural life adapt to change and evolve creatively:

> Similarly, one may talk of a technological pool: an accumulation of tools, machines, materials, processes, interacting with soils, climates, plants, animals, human populations, institutions, cultures. The capacity of this technological reservoir, until the third quarter of the nineteenth century, was immensely greater than ever before: what is more, it was more diversified . . . than that which exists today. Not the least important part of this technological pool were

the skilled craftsmen and work teams that transmitted the colossal accumulation of knowledge and skill. When they were eliminated from the system of production, this vast cultural resource was wiped out. . . .

The result is that a monotechnics, based upon scientific intelligence and quantitative reproduction, directed mainly toward economic expansion, material repletion, and military superiority, has taken the place of a polytechnics, based primarily, as in agriculture, on the needs, aptitudes, interests of living organisms: above all on man himself.[4]

On Chestnut Ridge, for instance, I have restored a small farmhouse, built in the 1920s, which features a unique curved porch contrived by a carpenter of that period; it remains a work of art. When I added a deck with a matching curve, the best available carpenters admired the original, but they were not inspired to replicate its carefully warped wood and fitted timbers. The modern work is comparatively crude. Somewhere the older skill may survive, but it is no longer generally available.

* * *

New crafts that are developed with aesthetic, social, and environmental sensitivity can help reverse these trends toward the impoverishment of human work. The spread of dignified work throughout society will require new values and new laws and policies; it will depend upon changes in technologies, industrial organization, and financial management. Nevertheless, many of these changes will begin with individual ingenuity, group and neighborhood efforts, and small-business innovation. Small-scale initiatives, however inconsequential in appearance, are particularly appropriate if the goal is to restore the ability of individuals, communities, and small organizations to express their distinctive creativity, to sustain themselves more efficiently, and to build a more complex, diverse, and humane culture than now exists.

Even people who feel trapped within jobs they dare not leave can begin to improve the quality of their work. I do not mean necessarily by tightening one's bolt on the assembly line with greater precision and enthusiasm. Rather, I am speaking of behavior that requires emotional risks: becoming aware of one's feelings on the job, including those which are painful or unpleasant; opening one's senses to the work environment; and learning the needs of one's co-workers. Transforming a meaningless job into a purposeful vocation may require study—on one's own time and at one's own expense— to learn more about the productive process, the health and safety risks within it, and the economy that surrounds it. It may require communication skills, including the receptive gifts of listening and empathy. Even within a job from which all creativity has been scientifically removed by efficiency experts, opportunities will appear to express oneself and to contribute to the welfare of others. One person may help organize a union, another may blow the whistle on a safety violation. One may give management ideas to improve the product, another may inspire a quality circle to reshape the productive process. Still others may resign in order to build a better product in their own shop. Of course, some will be ridiculed by co-workers, and some will be fired by management. Creativity is always risky, but it is rarely dull. Creativity leads to life, even when insecurity and anxiety accompany it.

A person's feeling for beauty can help to make work more creative. Perceiving beauty in people, in materials, or in environments draws us into deeper relationships with them while it also excites our imagination and stimulates our creativity. When we become more sensitive to beauty we also experience ugliness more keenly, but the pain we feel may motivate efforts to heal what is broken or correct what is deformed. A sense for ugliness, which helps us detect poor design and shoddy workmanship, makes an essential contribution to fine work.

The true opposite of beauty is not ugliness but *insensibility*— the inability to feel either pain or pleasure, either ugliness or beauty. Insensibility is the disease of the modern workplace. Tastes of beauty, along with twinges of pain, begin the cure. Of course, if our working environment is so desperate as to arouse little more than pain and disgust, then we need compensatory experiences in order to tolerate our work while we look for ways to initiate change. Indeed, all good work requires periodic "sabbath" rests, such as happy weekends with good food, a bottle of wine, making love, a long hike in the woods, and heartfelt worship.

When work is performed expressively and beauty is perceived within it, then work and leisure begin to intertwine. No matter how much we enjoy our craft, work is never the same as leisure; we will always need rest from even the most engaging labor. Yet leisure can be a time when we celebrate our work, rather than escape from it, and so complete the creative process. In his stimulating study of the subject, Sebastian de Grazia defines leisure as "a state of being in which activity is performed for its own sake or as its own end."[5] Good work partakes of this quality: besides having social value and providing the worker with pay or other instrumental benefits, good work provides sensual and emotional satisfactions that stimulate and nourish the worker. After rest, we want to return to such work; we grieve if illness or age keep us from work. Reflecting on the preindustrial economy, Lewis Mumford paints a suggestive picture of how leisure may mingle with labor:

> Had this craft economy, prior to mechanization, actually been ground down by poverty, its workers might have spent the time given over to communal celebrations and church-building on multiplying the yards of textiles woven or the pairs of shoes cobbled. Certainly an economy that enjoyed a long series of holidays, free from work, only fifty-two of which were Sundays, cannot be called impoverished. The worst one can say about it is that in its concentration on its spiritual interests and social satisfactions, it might fail to guard its members sufficiently against a poor winter diet and occasional bouts of starvation. But such an economy had something that we now have almost forgotten the meaning of, leisure: not freedom from work, which is how our present culture interprets leisure, but freedom *within* work; and along with that, time to converse, to ruminate, to contemplate the meaning of life.[6]

Good work benefits the worker in pay or sustenance, and also in sensual satisfaction, intellectual stimulation, and community respect. If work does not appeal on such terms, it should not be considered acceptable. When "the good of the community" or "the requirements of industry" are used to justify labor that is perpetually onerous and unsatisfying, then work has become servitude.

On the other hand, work that is inherently fulfilling should release the worker from an unhealthy preoccupation with money: "For the love of money is the root of all evil: which while some coveted after, they have erred from the faith, and pierced themselves through with many sorrows" (1 Timothy 6:10, KJV). Money is a flexible instrument, one which helps us exchange labor for goods and services that may meet some of our needs. Money's value is entirely instrumental, however; it does not meet any needs until we exchange it wisely for something more substantial. Therefore money is not, properly, an object of desire. Because money is so versatile in trade we are tempted to desire it for itself and, even more commonly, to worry that we do not have enough of it. Anxiety about money can so preoccupy the mind, in fact, that one loses feeling for the underlying needs that money may, or may not, help to meet. This anxiety may become so intense as to obscure from view any obvious opportunities to meet needs directly. Preoccupation with money binds us, emotionally, to the cash economy.

Although I know better, I am sometimes consumed with worry about money—a depressing and usually unproductive experience. It is striking how this anxiety can affect rich and poor alike, since anyone can imagine circumstances that might overwhelm one's resources, and since we all have desires that are not presently satisfied. To overcome this anxiety, I try to discover the particular needs underlying my concern: am I worried about food, shelter, retirement, or health? Do I need resources for a creative project? Sometimes, when needs are identified, they may be met in ways that do not require greater income. Sometimes one becomes aware of a need—such as desire for affection—which no amount of money could allay; yet, when unrecognized, it may feed one's sense of financial insecurity.

Modern Americans are conditioned by advertising to attempt to meet every need with a cash purchase. Breaking this conditioning is an essential step on the road to personal health, and it is also necessary if we are to protect the natural environment. I used to repress everyday anxiety with the help of tobacco, but when I stopped smoking I gained strength for work on the farm and also improved my health insurance, in effect, at no cost. Human needs and desires extend far beyond the cash economy, and many needs may be met most efficiently outside the world of trade.

When money becomes a substitute gratification—an idol distracting us from real needs—it fails to satisfy. Those who rely upon it, whatever their level of income, are impoverished. One antidote to an anxious idolatry of money is to become acquainted, again, with one's real needs. Another is to pursue good work within which there are the sensual, intellectual, and communal rewards. Another is to trust the Lord.

* * *

In order to develop new crafts appropriate to our age, some people return to old crafts. One friend of mine has found her vocation as a storyteller, visiting schools to share myths and tales from the children's Appalachian heritage. Another is a gifted musician who moved to the mountains to tap the rich musical heritage within this culture. If I could begin my vocation again, I would reverse its course and start out by farming with the aid of a team of horses, for no work I have tried is more satisfying; then I would add theology and—from this settled posture—develop my ministry. Wendell Berry, an insightful critic of modern culture, stays with his farm and his team in order to ground his prose and inspire his poetry.

Others with similar values develop new crafts. When a lawyer I know became appalled at the expense of conventional household plumbing, its consumption of scarce water, and its waste of useful nutrients, he diversified his practice by selling composting toilets. Some who train for conventional professions search for new ways to apply their vocation to the healing of our age. A recent graduate in forestry refused jobs with timber companies that harvest trees in ways that destroy the forests; he and his family held out for an anxious year until he found work protecting the forests whose beauty inspired him to his profession.

Developing new crafts is not an individualistic endeavor. Just as business must study the market, so a craftsperson must come to know the human community and the natural environment within which he or she wishes to work. Good crafts draw carefully from nature in order to serve the real needs of a human community. This gives good work a moral quality. Crafts achieve efficiency by respecting the character of the community within which they are useful. "A sound and viable technology, firmly related to human needs, cannot be one that has maximum productivity as its supreme goal," argues Lewis Mumford; "it must, rather, seek as in an organic system, to provide the right quantity of the right quality at the right place in the right order for the right purpose."[7]

Modern crafts can adhere to such values while making use of machinery, technology, and modern information systems. New crafts can inspire technological improvements to make productive processes more efficient, useful, and benign. Good work will harness technology to serve personal, social, and environmental values. Good work, by using tools well, will honor the Lord.

4. *Elegant Frugality*

This title phrase was coined by an innovative physicist, Amory Lovins, to convey the ethical and aesthetic implications of energy conservation. "Personal values . . . that could sustain life-styles of elegant frugality are not new," he said; "they are such values as thrift, simplicity, diversity, neighborliness, humility and craftsmanship."[1] Lovins' famous essay ("Energy Strategy: The Road Not Taken?") surprised even those alert to the energy crisis in the wake of the 1973 Arab oil embargo. In the pages of *Foreign Affairs Quarterly,* Lovins demonstrated that America wasted most of the energy it drew from the ground or purchased abroad and that, furthermore, multibillion-dollar schemes to build more nuclear power stations and to employ more exotic technologies such as coal gasification and oil shale extraction would compound the problem. Lovins proposed a "soft energy path" to meet forseeable energy needs, less expensively, through improving the efficiency of energy use. He claimed that conservation—supplemented by diversified, small-scale power generation—would hold down costs, bring production and consumption into balance, and increase employment.

Lovins' analysis transformed the energy debate. Although his specific proposals have met institutional resistance from governments, electric utilities, and energy conglomerates, his principles have held up under technical criticism and now influence energy planning. Philosophically, Lovins considers efficiency to be elegant—that is, beautiful. Ethically, Lovins believes that frugality can satisfy human needs more directly than our current habits of indulgence, while it also slows the depletion of natural resources.

Earlier studies of energy efficiency focused upon individual machines and discrete productive systems: measuring, for example, the friction in a motor that diverts energy to waste heat, or comparing the cost of fuel to the value of the product. Lovins broadened the perspective to evaluate the entire culture of energy extraction, conversion, and application, as well as the usefulness of the final product or service:

> How much primary energy we use—the fuel we take out of the ground—does not tell us how much energy is delivered at the point of end use (the device that does the kind of work we desire), for that depends on how efficient our energy supply system is. End-use energy in turn says nothing about how much function we perform with the energy, for that depends on our end-use efficiency. And how much function we perform says nothing about social welfare, which depends on whether the thing we did was worth doing.[2]

In the 1970s many experts who were concerned about America's growing dependence upon foreign oil suggested expanding the electric utility system to provide energy that could replace the fuel oil used to heat homes and commercial buildings, as well as some of the oil used by industry. Large nuclear and coal-burning power plants could be located far away from cities to reduce pollution and safety risks, and could be connected to urban areas by a network of high-voltage transmission lines. Power plants that use coal or nuclear fuel nonetheless waste about 60 percent of the energy in the fuel they consume when they heat water to steam in order to drive electric generators; the wasted energy dissipates it into nearby air and water as surplus heat. But very little waste results when fuel is burned directly in a building's furnace. Lovins argued that employing a nuclear power plant—the most complex, sophisticated, and dangerous technology we know—in order to provide energy for simple space heat would be as cumbersome as using a chain saw to cut butter. A more efficient strategy to reduce oil consumption, argued Lovins, would be the careful design of new buildings so they might draw heat from the sun in winter, yet shade their own interiors in summer. This could nearly eliminate space-heating requirements while also reducing air-conditioning demand. He also proposed that small electric power stations using fluidized bed combustion, a new technology that burns coal more cleanly, be located right in urban neighborhoods.[3] Then the surplus steam, once a polluting waste product, could be piped directly to nearby office buildings for space heating or to factories for process energy. Carefully designed, such elegant *cogeneration* of electricity and useful steam energy could double the efficiency of an electric generating station and therefore reduce by half the need for new power plants.

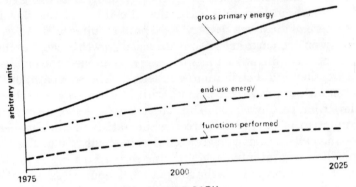

(a) A HARD PATH

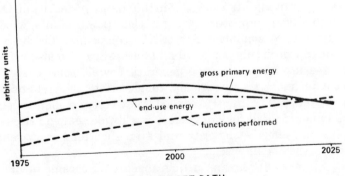

(b) A SOFT PATH

Lovins characterized as a *hard path* the conventional planning for energy sufficiency: building complex facilities to meet the ever-growing demand without modifying the character of that demand. The hard path will continue to deplete the earth's resources at an ever-increasing rate. He called his own approach a *soft path:* it is an array of measures to increase efficiency and promote conservation, combined with solar design, and the use of dispersed wind generators along with other small-scale power options. This more diverse system would mobilize technology in order to bring needs and resources in line with each other. Lovins used the sketches shown here to illustrate that the hard path requires vast increases in energy extraction to keep pace with social growth because as more exotic and more distant sources of energy are tapped, the efficiency of conversion and distribution will decline. The soft path, on the other hand, improves the efficiency with which energy is applied to achieve what people require. This path offers hope of reducing gross consumption of energy resources while satisfying human needs more adequately than conventional development would. The hard path will be capital-intensive, draining resources away from other parts of the economy, while the soft path will require less capital but more labor, increasing employment and spreading investment through society in a more equitable manner. The hard path will require vastly increased use of both coal and nuclear power to compensate for decreasing availability of oil and natural gas and to overcome declining efficiency within the energy system itself. On the soft path, Lovins proposed closing nuclear power plants, which he considered unreasonably dangerous. To compensate for these closings and for declining use of oil and natural gas, he also proposed increased use of coal for one generation while solar design and efficient technologies are spread through society; then reliance upon coal, as well, can be greatly reduced. More recent evidence that the combustion of fossil fuels increases worldwide temperatures—the "greenhouse effect"—suggests that even such temporary reliance upon coal may be unwise.

Shortly after Lovins' article appeared, I became involved in similar energy planning. In 1977, American Electric Power Company (AEP), the nation's largest investor-owned utility, began to study mountains and valleys in my area as potential sites for a $2 billion, three-million-kilowatt "pumped-storage" power plant, proposed to be the largest facility of this type in the world. This project threatened a forest so beautiful it was being evaluated for inclusion in the National Wilderness System; it also threatened a municipal reservoir, some state hunting lands, and the farms and homes of a hundred families. AEP proposed to construct large reservoirs in two valleys, one at the base of a mountain and one at the top, and to bury a huge generating station inside the mountain between them. High voltage transmission lines would connect this facility with a dozen other power plants in the AEP system. These plants, often idle at night and on weekends when demand for electricity was low, could continue to operate at those times in order to generate electricity, which would be wired to the electric turbines buried here in the mountain. They, in turn, would consume the energy in order to pump water from the lower reservoir to the higher. At times of day when demand for electricity might exceed the capacity of other plants, the water here would be allowed to flood back through these turbines to generate supplemental electricity for the system. This pumped storage facility would act like a giant "storage battery"; however, it would waste about 40 percent of the electric energy it received, compounding the 60 percent waste of primary fuel energy among the generating plants that supplied it. The cost of that waste, plus the cost of amortizing the $2 billion required to build the pumped-storage facility, would have raised electric rates alarmingly for consumers in a seven–state region.

Residents of the areas immediately affected by the proposed facility decided to oppose the plant and to argue their case on on the grounds of economic waste and energy inefficiency. We organized a coalition of ratepayer and environmental groups embracing all seven states served by AEP and drew together people affected by other AEP expansion plans as well. We contested the pumped storage in court and before several federal and state regulatory authorities. We also took our concerns directly to the company's stockholders. As part of our appeal, we commissioned an independent study of development possibilities for the American Electric Power system, which turned out to be more sophisticated than any planning done by the utility itself. Our consultants modeled alternatives to pumped-storage construction, including new rate structures to discourage waste and give conservation incentives to customers, utility investment in home insulation, laws to improve appliance efficiency standards, time-phasing controls on air conditioners and hot water heaters to reduce peak demand, and cogeneration. The study showed that a package of such reforms could meet the same needs as the pumped-storage proposal but at far less cost to the utility and its customers. After a five-year struggle, AEP reluctantly abandoned the pumped-storage proposal, though it has refused to implement most of the alternative reforms we suggested. Such a stalemate, which does not make sound provision for the future, is common because most regulatory authorities do not insist that public utilities undertake imaginative conservation planning.[4]

The soft path, nevertheless, presents difficulties of its own because it requires us to change our living habits as well as our machinery. Large and complex systems such as dependence upon automobiles for urban transportation, as well as familiar small systems like household heating-and-cooling units, will have to change. One change will increase household self-sufficiency, but another may limit our personal mobility. The soft path does not abandon all large, integrated systems in favor of small, dispersed systems, but it does propose to change the social mix of these systems. To Lovins, the issue is not size, but appropriateness.

> The concept of matching scale to end use . . . is the essence of the soft approach—not the predetermined predominance of a particular scale, small or large. That is why conservationists are consistent in desiring both generally smaller energy systems and more urban mass transit, and why their adversaries, with equal consistency, tend to desire both gigantic energy systems and the universal primacy of private cars.[5]

Both hard and soft paths require sophisticated planning, both depend upon technological innovation, and both need political direction. Although the soft path is relatively more flexible, diversified, and participatory, it is vulnerable to indecisive political leadership because critical conservation policies and efficiency standards must be defined and applied by governmental agencies. The soft path facilitates democratic participation in the energy system, but it requires farsighted political leadership.

Some soft-path techniques also depend upon personal supervision. For example, although a passive solar home saves the owner money throughout the year, residents must participate by adjusting blinds and ventilation more than is required in a home with automatic electric heating and cooling. People who prefer to remain passive consumers, and who can afford the additional expense of such convenience, may not favor some conservation strategies. On the other hand, those who resent the control of their lives by institutions they cannot influence are likely to welcome many of the soft-path technologies. Those who care about the natural environment will also favor them. Lovins acknowledged that the choice is political as well as economic:

> The giant energy facilities essential to the hard path are arcane, remote, unfamiliar, and so overwhelmingly impressive as to be threatening. Huge sums are at stake, experts argue over esoteric technologies and unimaginable risks, national interest steamrollers local doubts. It is not surprising, then, that these facilities breed public distrust and alienation... by denying public participation not only in the procedural but in the psychological sense. . . .
>
> Soft technologies, on the other hand, use familiar, equitably distributed natural energies to meet perceived human needs directly and comprehensibly, and are thus . . . "convivial" to choose, build, and use.[6]

Even so, the soft path may make some people anxious. To walk along it we must awaken from the false comfort—indeed, the idolatrous fantasy—that distant experts will invent a solution to every problem. We must become involved with the energy systems that undergird our lives and shape our communities.

If, as Lovins forcasts, nuclear power can be abandoned, fossil fuel consumption can be stabilized and—in time—reduced, and society meets human needs more efficiently and effectively, the benefits to the natural environment from reduced mining, radiation, and thermal pollution, as well as reduced acid and toxic pollution, will be enormous. Nature will benefit additionally if wood, metals, and other natural materials are conserved with the help of comparable strategies to meet human needs more gracefully through better design, more careful manufacture, improved durability, and the recycling of discarded materials.[7]

* * *

If we follow the soft path, we will also need to mobilize our ethical and aesthetic sensibilities. Amory Lovins suggested that the values of "thrift, simplicity, diversity, neighborliness, humility and craftsmanship" can help us to achieve "elegant frugality." We might add to this list the values of expressiveness, attention to one's environment, and delight in things that work well, look good, or bring pleasure. For instance, my sensibilities have changed through attention to the natural world. In the mid-1960s I built a home complete with electric heat and air conditioning. Ten years later, remodeling another home, I chose a wood stove and passive solar design for heat, and for cooling I decided to trust an old porch, a hillside site, and fresh breezes. The second house is more enjoyable. Fueling the wood stove requires communion with the woods, selecting the trees to be removed without damage to the health of the forest. Trees are cut one winter in advance, before the sap rises, while the wood is dry. Splitting wood is pleasant exercise, and if it becomes tedious I prefer hiring a neighbor to help rather than hiring the power company.

"Simplicity" is a concept that is often misunderstood. When, for example, we admire the grace of Shaker chairs, we suspect that this quality of design may relate to the faith and simple life-style of those who crafted them. Indeed, having gathered in settlements to express heaven on earth, Shakers communicated their sense of perfection through their crafts. Shaker communities, however lacking in luxuries, were nevertheless complex economic organizations. Jobs were rotated to prevent boredom and to provide members the full range of experiences that the settlement afforded. To remain in a Shaker community, the typical convert had to master many more skills and trades than one person was required to learn in ordinary society. Shaker society was the result of careful efforts to protect purity, to practice humility, and to sustain community sufficiency. To realize the simplicity so admired by outsiders, this ingenious sect invented many devices, from flat brooms to sophisticated roof trusses, so their buildings might be more useful and their daily labor more efficient. The quality of "simplicity" that we admire is not a lack of social complexity but a lack of confusion. It is "elegance," as Lovins uses the term. It is a quality manifest by those who are clear about their desires and choose direct means to achieve them. Shakers achieved simplicity by holding the techniques of their day to the scrutiny of religious convictions, improving upon the methods they chose to employ, and inventing new technologies where the existing ones were not adequate.[8]

Individuals and families who attempt "elegant frugality" will encounter frustrations. There are so many changes we might like to make that cannot be achieved without the support of a neighborhood or a community, and many others that require political action at the state or even the national level. Personal efforts to conserve the earth's resources will soon convince us how dependent we are upon our society and how deeply we participate in many of its environmental abuses—no matter how much we wish otherwise. Christians may call this cultural bondage "original sin," our heritage from a society that has forsaken wholesome relationships. This understanding may help us cope more gracefully. Trusting God's forgiveness when we fail, we can stay alert to the earth's needs, modify our personal habits, and look for opportunities to join with others to achieve comprehensive social reforms. We will serve the biosphere by making a few changes skillfully, rather than attempting many things that turn out poorly. A sense of vocation, calling us to particular efforts, may be more helpful than the gnawing sense of duty that pulls us us in all directions until we are tired and defeated.

A commitment to "elegant frugality" can give scope to our aesthetic sensibilities. When my wife Anne and I added a dining room to our house, we asked a local woodworker to build the table, in preference to a manufactured one. We desired heavy walnut, soft and warm to the touch. We wanted a table so well suited to the room that it would be cared for as long as the house stood, so the beautiful lumber would not be wasted. Such a table could not be found in a showroom, but required design responsive to the room itself. We achieved all of this with the help of a skilled craftsperson who enjoyed the challenge and charged no more than we might have spent at the store.

If we express our social and moral convictions with aesthetic sensitivity, people are more likely to respond. Some of those who enjoy our dining room may be inspired to use solar design and local crafts themselves. The terms, *trend setting* and *style setting* sound tawdry because the rich and the slick have so abused these roles, but they represent important social functions. Those with resources and imagination can promote environmental responsibility by doing some things so beautifully that others are induced to follow. We need many good examples to help us learn lifes-tyles that can ease the human burden upon the earth.

Part II.

Agriculture

Early one recent August morning I drove down the back roads in western Ohio. The gently rolling landscape was silent, and no creatures could be seen. The planted fields were growing either corn or soybeans. Although many fields remained fallow, there was no livestock grazing them. Some of the farmhouses were well maintained, but there were few vegetable gardens. I looked for human activity, but in my two-hour drive I did not see any men, women, or children in the gardens, around the barns, or in the fields—even though this was the cool of the day. Life had left the landscape. Agriculture was dying.

A few mornings later, one hundred miles to the northwest, I drove down other back roads near Shipshewana, Indiana. Most of these farms belong to Amish families. The landscape was alive. Horses and dairy cattle could be seen on every farm, and on many there were pigs or sheep, chickens or geese. The roadsides hummed from insects, rabbits darted into the brush, birds sang on fenceposts, and the fresh air bore various aromas—most of them pleasant. Beside every farmhouse was a large vegetable garden with a beautiful flowered border. Children were outdoors weeding the gardens. Men were adjusting equipment in the barnyards. Nearly half the farms displayed signs advertising some service performed on the premises: "Harness Shop," "Small Engine Repair," "Quilts for Sale," "Miller's Greenhouse," "Firewood, Landscape Timbers, Fence Supplies," even "Yoder's Book Store." Along the gravel roads a steady traffic of horses and buggies carried men and women upon various errands. The landscape was alive, agriculture was thriving, and the scene was beautiful.

Agriculture affects our natural environment more broadly than any other human activity. It is the most essential vocation for human survival. Christians concerned about the environmental crisis may want to think first about the ethics of agriculture. Our religious sense of justice toward nature has its roots in the agricultural society that was God's "holy land," so biblical ethics may be more applicable to modern problems of landholding and food production than to problems that were less prevalent in biblical times, such as air pollution, water pollution, and toxic wastes. For this reason I have chosen to focus in this part upon the ethics of agriculture, and in the next part on the ethics of landholding, rather than attempt a distinctive Christian contribution to the environmental ethics that may apply to other productive activities such as mining, forestry, petrochemicals, and manufacture.

Modern agriculture is failing because we have turned away from the culture of living systems in order to adopt "businesslike" methods. Since we are accustomed to hearing that the American farmer is the most productive on earth and that our farms feed the world, this announcement of failure may startle some readers. This statement of failure is based on standards that differ from those commonly employed by politicians and agricultural experts. Here, less emphasis is given to high production and low price, while more attention is paid to the quality of human life and the vitality of the landscape.

Despite the problems of modern practice, however, resources for truly productive agriculture—which may support the richness of human life and protect the integrity of nature—are more available today than ever before. If we choose to listen, we can learn from the wisdom of traditional groups such as the Amish, who still farm well. We possess biological knowledge and environmental insights that were not available to previous generations of farmers. Our technological capabilities could support high-quality farming if they were applied with ethical discernment. To farm successfully, we need to bring both land and livestock within the embrace of moral regard. Sensitive, humane agriculture will help the world feed itself more securely than will the pattern of exploitative agribusiness that is today spreading across the world.

I owe a debt to Wendell Berry, Kentucky farmer and poet, who believes that human culture must keep its roots in the soil. I am inspired as well by Wes Jackson, a Kansas geneticist studying the tall-grass prairie, who wishes to lead agriculture to moral and biological integrity. The lanky, shy writer and the rotund, ebullient scientist are fond of each other. Once, Berry reports, they discussed how to motivate farmers to care for the soil:

> Some time ago, in a conversation with Wes Jackson in which we were laboring to define the causes of the modern ruination of farmland, we finally got around to the money economy. I said that an economy based on energy would be more benign because it would be more comprehensive.
>
> Wes would not agree. "An energy economy still wouldn't be comprehensive enough."
>
> "Well," I said, "then what kind of economy would be comprehensive enough?"
>
> He hesitated a moment, and then, grinning, said, "The Kingdom of God."[1]

There is hope for the culture of the earth, but achieving what is possible will require a profound deepening of human values.

5. *Failures*

During the quarter-century following the Civil War, Americans had the opportunity to fulfill Thomas Jefferson's dream for them. Congress, in 1862, had passed the Homestead Act, which opened vast public lands to those willing to invest five years of labor for a 160-acre freehold. The following year President Lincoln issued the Emancipation Proclamation to free slaves in states at war with the Union. When the southern plantation system collapsed following the Civil War, some of the poor white tenants and some of the black freedmen were able to obtain land where they lived, while others joined the tide of settlers moving west to claim homesteads. Many newly independent farmers did not succeed, of course; while others, as soon as they secured title to land, sold it to land speculators. Even so, by 1880 three farms in four were tended by the owner, while only one in four was worked by a tenant.[1] This may have been the high water mark for agricultural independence in the United States.

Nevertheless, most farmers were not animated by Jefferson's vision of self-sufficiency. In particular, they did not share his suspicion of the entanglements of commerce. As early as the 1830s Alexis de Tocqueville observed that Americans "carry over into agriculture the spirit of a trading venture, and their passion for industry is manifest there as elsewhere."[2] When railroads knit the east together and then reached across the great prairies, many farmers seized the opportunity to supplement their return from subsistence farming and local trade, and eagerly grew whichever cash crops railroads were offering to purchase and transport to markets. With the prospect of cash income, many of these borrowed money for new equipment or additional land. This burden of debt forced them to grow cash crops whether the market price was high or low, and so they became captive to the boom-and-bust cycles characteristic of capitalist agriculture. On the frontier, many were like Daniel Muir, John Muir's father, who hurriedly burned useful timber from his virgin land to plow the ground for cash crops and then less than a decade later, after the soil had been exhausted by thoughtless tilling, moved to another homestead.

There were also many who farmed wisely and well. Sociological studies suggest, for example, that farmers of German heritage—typically more conservative than those of Yankee background—retained their farms for successive generations because they valued family self-sufficiency along with strong community relationships. They diversified production to use family labor wisely, and they were cautious about cash crops, expansion, and debt.[3] In addition to the freehold farms that spread across the land during the nineteenth century, there were many rural experiments inspired by religious, socialist, and perfectionist visions: the Shaker settlements that scattered from New England to Kentucky, the Amana community in Iowa, the Mormons who trekked as a church body to Utah, and countless others. Most of these fellowships built distinctive cultures of worship, education, and manufacture upon an agricultural base. Crops and livestock were raised primarily for the needs of the community rather than for trade, while the techniques of farming were shaped by moral vision and improved by cumulative group experience upon a particular landscape. Hard work and plain living could be onerous, as one Shaker brother cheerfully lamented:

> All full of bus'ness night and day;
> With scarce a moment's time to play;
> I've work enough that's now on hand
> For 15 years for any man.
> I'm overrun with work and chores
> Upon the farm or within doors. . . .
> How can I bear with such a plan?
> No time to be a gentleman!

Another Shaker, however, saw communal support and good order as the realization of God's kingdom on earth:

I've not a word to say, nor dare I breathe complaint,
I live in God Almighty's day and call'd to be a saint,
I've plenty that is good, to eat & drink & wear;
I've decent clothes and wholesome food, enough & some to spare.
My bed is soft & sweet, my room is nice & clean,
No court on earth is kept more neat, for any King or Queen
My Brethren are my friends, my sisters kind to me,
Whoever plows or knits or spins are all at work for me.
Is this what Jesus meant, an hundredfold to give?
Then I've the whole in present time, yea every day I live.[4]

In 1862, along with the Homestead Act, Congress had passed the Morrill Act, endowing each state with large tracts of public land. Proceeds from the sale of these lands were to be used to establish colleges of "liberal and practical education" in "agriculture and the mechanic arts."[5] These pioneering educational ventures stimulated innovation in farming and the other trades essential to rural life, but land-grant colleges, and the extension services that reached out from them to assist farmers, exhibited serious deficiencies as well. These schools have been practical but rarely liberal: they train farmers to apply the techniques of agriculture with competency, but they do not teach them how to evaluate these techniques. They do not educate farmers for independent observation and critical reflection upon farming practices, economic arrangements, and social conditions. The Jeffersonian vision is not present. Extension agents, the field representatives of agricultural universities, patronize their constituency, encouraging farmers to depend uncritically upon expert direction rather than developing their own abilities to experiment and evaluate. Although land-grant institutions have become the research centers for modern agriculture, they fail to evaluate critically the fads in farming technology that sweep across the country. Indeed, agricultural extension has pandered for business interests, promoting standardized technologies that require farmers to increase their capital investment and to specialize in the crops most vulnerable to economic cycles.[6] The most careful farmers, and the most inventive, are now turning elsewhere for counsel.

Rural Americans have typically turned to churches to interpret life, to guide personal behavior, and to inspire moral values.

Book 2 of this series explored the American beginnings of a style of evangelical piety that came to predominate in the countryside, in order to explain how a faith so voluntary, expressive, and participatory could yet discourage men and women from integrating their daily experience of the natural world into their religious faith. Certainly the biblical ecology portrayed in Book 3 of this series, with its rituals and disciplines of moral reflection upon livestock, land, and wildlife, has rarely been replicated in the rituals and teachings of American Christian churches. In response to the rigors of daily life, churches have usually devoted more attention to providing immediate comfort, along with hope for redress beyond the grave, than they have to fashioning temporal moral strategies that might make life better and bring God's kingdom closer. When religious imagination is thus deflected from daily life to another realm, it is easier for churches to give tacit support to the social prejudices of their members and to condone their environmental abuses. When the most fundamental relationships of rural life, such as human work with land and livestock, are not undergirded by religious celebration and ethical reflection in the country church, then it is hard for the farm family to develop moral vision and to sustain it.

Ironically, the vast territory that Jefferson purchased to provide all Americans with the opportunity for self-sufficiency became an occasion to avoid moral reflection upon social justice and care for the earth. Justin Morrill, author of the land-grant college act, understood that

> the very cheapness of our public lands, and the facility of purchase and transfer, tended to a system of bad-farming or strip and waste of the soil, by encouraging short occupancy and a speedy search for new homes, entailing upon the first and older settlements a rapid deterioration of the soil, which would not be likely to be arrested except by more thorough and scientific knowledge of agriculture and by a higher education of those who were devoted to its pursuit.[7]

As long as the free land lasted, problems of social injustice and environmental degradation could be deferred with slogans such as "Go west, young man!"

When the supply of homestead land suitable for farming was depleted late in the nineteenth century, when racial segregation was reimposed across the south, and when single-crop farming depleted soils in many regions, farm tenancy began to rise again at the expense of freehold ownership. Most farmers never learned how to control their vulnerability to the wide variations in price for the crops they sold on the free market. Although, in principle, freehold farm families should by this time have been the most secure members of society, since they could provide their food—and often shelter and clothing as well—through labor upon their own land and barter with their neighbors, in fact they had become the most vulnerable class. Eager for cash income that would enable them to purchase manufactured products, many farmers mortgaged their land to buy mechanical equipment and to expand their holdings for efficient cropping on a larger scale. Once in debt, the farmer was vulnerable to fluctuations in commodity prices—more so than the traders, transporters, and shopkeepers who also earned their livelihood in the chain of food distribution, since prices that farmers paid for goods and services might rise even while the price offered for crops fell. Just so, in the early 1920's the farm economy was devastated when agricultural commodity prices collapsed while other prices remained high, sustained by urban prosperity. By 1930, when the whole nation had been plunged into depression, 42 percent of America's farms were operated by tenants.[8]

Shocked by the spread of tenancy and the abject poverty of most tenant families, President Franklin D. Roosevelt proposed a program of land reform—the first in America's history to treat farmland as a scarce resource subject to the claims of distributive justice. In 1937, Congress established the Farm Security Administration with authority to grant mortgage loans to tenants who wished to purchase the land they farmed, and also to guarantee similar loans offered by commercial banks. The agency was required to establish standards in every region to assure that these farms were an appropriate size for family operation: not so small as to be economically unworkable, nor so large as to constitute government assistance to those who might not need it. When loans proved insufficient, the government added grants, along with health assistance, relocation assistance, and a variety of other services. The program reached over two thousand rural counties, and eight hundred thousand farm families were helped in some way. Because the program did not bow to traditional restrictions imposed by racial segregation in the South and disturbed accepted patterns of land ownership everywhere as well, it came under heavy attack as "Communist" and "un-American." In 1946, Congress replaced this agency with the more conservative Farmers' Home Administration, which would pursue land reform of quite a different character.[9]

* * *

If rural society had been healthy in the decades before World War II, farmers after the war might have been more cautious about new technologies. However, farming had been in economic distress since 1920 due to overdependence upon major cash crops, the resurgence of racial bigotry, and the closing of the social escape valve that homestead land had once provided. A whole generation of rural Americans had grown up knowing little but poverty and hard, unrewarding toil. The quality of social life in small towns and rural communities was declining as the fabric of rural culture weakened: schools were generally poor, churches often dispirited, politics corrupted, the arts and literature largely unknown. During the war, many young men and women had gained new experiences in military service or in defense plants and, following the war, many were determined to leave the countryside or to change it.

Changes came indeed: rapid mechanization; new fertilizers, herbicides, and pesticides; consolidation of farms and rural depopulation. Farm tractors were improved to operate an amazing variety of equipment designed to speed plowing, planting, cultivating, and harvesting. The horses and mules that had performed this labor on most farms were retired, for tractors could cover many more acres in a day. Farm fields were enlarged so the machines could work more efficiently. Where a farm family using horses or mules might have tended forty acres, they could manage two hundred acres with their tractor; indeed, they needed cash crops on additional acreage to retire the loans for their new equipment. They were familiar with the

Tenth Commandment, God's first rule for agriculture —

> . . . neither shalt thou covet thy neighbor's house, his field, or his manservant, or his maidservant, his ox, or his ass, or any thing that is thy neighbor's. (Deuteronomy 5: 21, KJV)

— yet new technology appeared to change the rules. Progressive farmers could not utilize modern equipment efficiently unless they added their neighbor's fields to their own. The neighbor's draft animals were of no further use, and his farm labor would need to be discharged, but his cropland was coveted.

Distributors of farm machinery, bankers with money to lend, and experts from land-grant colleges agreed: farms must consolidate to be productive, competitive, and profitable. It was time to transform *agriculture* into *agribusiness*. The most promising farmers were urged to expand. The Farmers' Home Administration (FHA), as successor to the Farm Security Administration, which had once tried to succor tenants and marginal farmers, now enforced consolidation as government policy. Having determined that larger farms were more likely to succeed, the FHA offered Federal loans and guarantees to those who were willing to expand their holdings to a size appropriate to modern machinery. During the 1950s landlords across America evicted their tenants, while banks and the FHA encouraged consolidation by witholding credit from small-farm owners. These policies were popular in the southern states because they offered a resolution of longstanding racial tensions: blacks were evicted from the land they farmed and forced to leave the region. During the 1950s and 1960s, millions of poor Americans without adequate education or employable skills streamed from these farmlands to the slums that swelled within northern cities.

Today, many of the larger farms created at the expense of the poor are themselves collapsing; although others who farm more modestly, with imagination and community support, survive and even thrive. Children and grandchildren of those uprooted from tenant farms continue to live listless, hopeless lives in urban slums. Although they may have forgotten their rural heritage, these people have a moral claim to land, as do other Americans as well.

Just as new machinery supported the illusion of curing rural poverty by removing poor people from the landscape, so fertilizers, pesticides and herbicides seemed to overcome the exhaustion of soils that accompanies one-crop farming. Phosphates and potash are strip-mined and shipped to farming regions where they are combined with nitrogen fertilizers manufactured from natural gas. When enough of these nutrients are spread upon fields, then wheat, corn, and other major crops will grow despite the inherent character of the soil. Scientists also learned to reassemble petroleum molecules to form an array of deadly poisons that support the dominance of desired crops by killing competing life and predatory organisms. The first pesticides—such as DDT—lingered in the food chain to kill insects and birds and threatened humans as well. The herbicides and pesticides developed more recently are designed to focus their destruction upon more limited targets and to decompose more swiftly; however, they are being applied in such vast quantites that they poison farm workers, pollute groundwater, and sometimes contaminate food. Their continued use across huge regions will have broad environmental consequences.

Good soil is a complex ecosystem filled with organisms and bacteria that digest decaying life and transform it into nutrients for new growth. This organic aspect of soil—called *humus*—retains water, holds particles of earth together, interracts with sunlight, and feeds the roots of plants. It can often be observed in soil as dark color and resilience to the touch. Strong applications of fertilizer bypass the humus and inject specific nutrients directly into the roots of crops. This disrupts the biological processes within soil and leads to gradual decline in humus content. Soils that survive continual application of fertilizers often have a grayish appearance: they hold less water and erode more rapidly. Herbicides kill life in the soil directly and accelerate this process.

Soils erode more quickly on modern farms than on the best traditional farms—a degeneration process that is further assisted by the removal of fence rows, contour strips, and other unplowed barriers to erosion, in order to accommodate large machinery. It may now cost four bushels of Iowa topsoil, lost by erosion, for each bushel of corn harvested there.[10] To control soil depletion, the U.S. Depart-

ment of Agriculture and university extension agents are now urging
farmers to adopt "no-till" techniques: rather than turning the sod
under with a moldboard plow, no-till farmers drill corn or wheat
seeds directly into the stubble-covered ground left from the previous
year's harvest, so surface structure is retained and erosion is reduced. However, this method usually requires even larger applications of herbicides to inhibit weed growth. As rain soaks the earth
and carries herbicides deep within, ground water is contaminated.
Thousands of midwestern farmers have had to stop drinking the
water from their wells, and many rural towns are also discovering
that their water supplies contain unsafe levels of cancer-inducing
herbicide residues.

The most important ingredient of modern agriculture is
petroleum, which serves as feedstock for fertilizers and chemicals as
well as fuel for trucks, tractors, and machinery. The world's reserves
are being depleted so rapidly that petroleum will be scarce and
expensive in a generation. Like the opportunity for frontier settlement a century before, the temporary availability of petroleum has
been a means to defer ethical demands and practical decisions. The
massive application of petroleum to agriculture has created new
problems of environmental degredation and it has facilitated the
social injustice of farm consolidation. When the resource is depleted
and price of oil soars, petroleum derivatives will be too costly to
spread across our fields. We need to begin the reformation of food
production now, before this crisis is reached.

In traditional agriculture, healthy soil and the sun's radiant
energy fed the plants that became grasses for livestock, grains and
other foods for humans. Indirectly, the sun provided the horsepower
needed for cultivation, since draft animals lived from the land along
with the farm family. A farm was an ecosystem modified by the
farmer's ingenuity to convert solar energy into food and fiber to meet
human needs. Now the modern farm consumes more energy in
tractor fuel alone than than is converted from sunlight by the crops,
while the energy required to make farm equipment and, in particular, the energy in fertilizer, multiply this input many times. Once a
net producer of energy for human culture, agriculture is now a net
consumer. By contrast, one organic farm that grew crops without

relying upon petroleum-based fertilizers and pesticides, used—in a controlled experiment—one-third the energy of a conventional farm.[11]

Since 1940 the number of Americans in farm families has declined by 80 percent, while total employment in farming has declined by two-thirds. However, employment has increased in other areas to bring resources to the farms and produce to the table: factory workers who assemble farm machinery, truckers, food processors and packagers, wholesalers and retailers, restaurant and fast-food employees. The number of these jobs, and their quality, must be considered in evaluating modern agriculture. America grows more food today, yet the variety of produce grown near major cities is declining as agriculture becomes more specialized and production is concentrated in particular areas. Outside California and Florida, most regions are less self-sufficient in food today than they were during World War II. After forty years of modernization, American agriculture remains an unstable system that continues to exhaust our soil while it consumes scarce resources and pollutes the natural environment. From his Kentucky farm, Wendell Berry writes dolefully:

> That one American farmer can now feed himself and fifty-six other people may be, within the narrow view of the specialist, a triumph of economics and technology; by no stretch of reason can it be considered a triumph of agriculture or of culture. It has been made possible by the substitution of energy for knowledge, of methodology for care, of technology for morality. This "accomplishment" is not primarily the work of farmers—who have been, by and large, its victims—but of a collaboration of corporations, university specialists, and government agencies. It is therefore an agricultural development not motivated by agricultural aims or disciplines, but by the ambitions of merchants, industrialists, bureaucrats, and academic careerists. We should not be surprised to find that its effect on both the farmland and the farm people has been ruinous.[12]

* * *

In 1920 nearly 32 million Americans lived in farm families, and the majority of these families owned their own land. By 1979 the farm population had dwindled to 7.5 million, and it has continued to decline since then. Only one million farm operators (whether individuals or family groups) now live on farmland they own, while another half-million live nearby. A slightly larger group (1.4 million people, sixteen years and older) work on farms regularly, while 3 million additional people do seasonal farm-work, many of these as migrant laborers. Although the number of those who work on farms has remained relatively constant since 1950, the number of owners has declined by half.[13] A growing proportion of those who work the land occupy marginal, unstable jobs; those with the security of ownership are a dwindling group. As agriculture becomes industrialized, the Jeffersonian vision fades.

Most agricultural commodities are now produced on very large farms. In 1982, the 5 percent of farms with sales over $200,000 a year accounted for half of all farm income; within this group, the 1 percent with sales over $500,000 a year accounted for a third of all farm income. More than half of America's farms sold less than $20,000 each: these farms together accounted for less than six percent of total farm income. Of the major agricultural commodities, only tobacco is still grown primarily on smaller farms: farmers' opportunity to raise tobacco is still protected by a Federal allotment system dating from the Great Depression. Indeed, most farm famlies do not earn the majority of their income from the land. Even in 1978, during the most recent farm boom, the average farm-owning family earned only 43 percent of their cash income from the farm, though many raised food for the family in addition. It is common for one or more persons to work away from the farm and, since many farm families are now elderly, Social Security and other transfer payments provide a significant share of income. Being a "farmer" or "farm family" is as much a question of self-understanding as the source of one's income. Many who love their farm choose to work elsewhere to subsidize its operation.[14]

American farms comprise about one million acres, slightly less than half the total land area of the United States (including Alaska and Hawaii). Farm ownership is being concentrated in fewer and fewer hands. The U.S. Department of Agriculture reports that

in 1978, less than 3 percent of the total population owned all of the farmland. About 0.14 of one percent of the total U.S. population—or five percent of the farmland owners—owned 48 percent of those farm and ranch acres.[15]

Small farmers used to obtain cash income by selling some of their produce to neighbors. They also bartered, taking produce to the general store to exchange it for other goods. Now the general store has been replaced by a supermarket that only buys large quantities of standardized and packaged produce, which are likely to be shipped from distant states or foreign countries. Sales to neighbors of certain farm commodities are now considered illegal. Berry observes that

> nowhere now is there a market for minor produce: a bucket of cream, a hen, a few dozen eggs. One cannot sell milk from a few cows anymore; the law-required equipment is too expensive. Those markets were done away with in the name of sanitation—but, of course, to the enrichment of the large producers. . . . The germs that used to be in our food have been replaced by poisons.[16]

Even for larger farms, the free market is shrinking rapidly. Few dare to specialize in milk, broilers, turkeys, fruits, or vegetables without a contract from a corporate buyer who sets the price, prescribes details of operation, and may also require the farmer to buy feed and equipment from the company. Cattle fattening and hog raising are coming under the control of such companies as well. By 1979, about one-quarter of agricultural production was governed by these vertical management arrangements; the proportion has been growing steadily ever since.[17]

During the 1960s and 1970s, when grain prices were rising, the federal government urged farmers to plant every available acre to feed a hungry world and improve America's balance of foreign trade. Farm exports, which had drawn 10 percent of farm production, rose to 30 percent by 1979. A later chapter will consider why these exports were ineffective in combating hunger abroad. They did, however, create a boom in land values at home. When it appeared that a hungry world required more and more American grain, many farmers again looked covetously at their neighbor's land, and many others traded equipment for larger and more

elaborate machines. Since land values were rising, banks were eager
to write mortgages to finance these transactions. Farmers both here
and abroad devoted every available acre to crops moving in international trade, and they eventually grew more food than the world
could purchase. Inevitably, early in the 1980s, commodity prices
weakened and then collapsed. Farming areas were plunged into depression. When land prices also tumbled, bankers foreclosed mortgages to protect their investments, and many farmers had to surrender their farms. Larger farms, more leveraged with debt, have
generally been more vulnerable to foreclosure than smaller farms.

In August 1986 the *New York Times* reported that "Imported
food is flooding the market at prices that American farmers can't
possibly match," and, for the first time in American history, food
imports exceeded farm exports.[18] In July 1987 the *Times* reported
that when Tex-Cal Land Management Company—a 7,300 acre
grape- and almond-growing conglomerate—went bankrupt, it de-
faulted on loans from the Farmers' Home Administration totaling
$68 million dollars.[19] Mortgages, loans, and subsidies to agribusi-
ness have proved to be just as insecure as the aid offered poor tenant
farmers fifty years ago. The solution requires more than economic
analysis. It is time to reconsider the character of agriculture itself.

6. *Roots*

Agriculture is a form of cultural interraction with the natural environment, a meeting of social values and technology on the one hand, with the vitality of the earth's ecosystem on the other. Although agriculture is not the only human practice in which culture and nature respond to each other, here each of the two systems is unusually susceptible to the other's influence. Indeed, the genius of good farming is to increase this mutual vulnerability. The best farmers, alert to their environment, adapt to the particular characteristics of the lands they tend; to the climate of sun and rain, heat and cold; and to the living community of animals, plants, and organisms with which they work. Their farms yield a harvest for human consumption that is gathered without diminishing the vitality of the system of life, because these farmers not only modify natural systems to meet human needs but also return to the living community a quality of care that helps it to flower more abundantly. The landscape of a good farm has been changed from the wild, yet many grasses, trees, birds, insects, and microorganisms that were present in the wild state remain, and the farm continues to sustain a complex ecosystem of diverse and abundant life. Though no longer wild, a good farm landscape is again beautiful.

Those who farm well are themselves changed as they till the land. To meet their own needs they have formed a relationship with a place that becomes precious to them. A good farm, like other living companions with whom one shares intimacies, becomes a beloved friend respected for its own character as well as for its usefulness. The qualities of the land we know affect our work and our recreation, as well as our emotions and mental images, our memories and hopes.

Families that remain on the land for several generations deepen their attachment because the farm, unlike human companions, need not die. The homestead links the living with those who have gone before and those yet to come. The farm contributes to the family's identity. Thus, while people shape the land, the land supports and shapes human culture as well.

Agriculture has a purpose—at once practical and moral—that can be stated in terms of three interdependent values: *sustenance, conservation,* and *production.* Since each of these values modifies the others, all three must be joined to form sound agricultural ethics that may inspire farming techniques and guide public policy. When society elevates production to the exclusion of conservation and sustenance—and this is the modern practice—then the *culture* within agriculture erodes, and the degradation of lands and their inhabitants is sure to follow.

Sustenance, as I use the term here, refers to the immediate nurturance received by the farmer and the farm family, the benefits that flow directly to their community of face-to-face acquaintances, and the support of creatures who share the farm landscape as well. Sustenance embraces the food, fuel, and fiber from the farm of which all of these partake; it also includes the joy of work, the quality of relationships, and the sensuous rewards of beauty. Sustenance is the first objective of agriculture and its absence is the first warning of malpractice. Masanobu Fukuoka, the Japanese philosopher of farming, writes that "the ultimate goal of farming is not the growing of crops, but the cultivation and perfection of human beings." He also states, "I do not particularly like the word 'work.' . . . Other animals make their living by living."[1] If there is no joy in farming, if the practice does not nurture the farmer, then the work is not good.

Many farmers have given up this quest for personal satisfaction and the disciplines of subsistence agriculture as they imerse themselves in the frantic practices of industrial food production. They work exhausting hours at repetitive tasks; they plow under those patches of beauty remaining on their land; they drive themselves to ever greater production; they eat meat, bread, and vegetables from the supermarket instead of from their farms; then they look for something else to buy to make them happy. They start each day tense and anxious. The joys of the land are wasted on them.

The pursuit of sustenance may appear to compromise commercial productivity, but some of the competition among these values can be resolved upon reflection. One farm family may withdraw some land from cash crops in order to provide for a garden, an orchard, and a woodlot, as well as grazing lots for "4–H" livestock tended by the children. The vegetables, meats, fruits, and firewood that these lots produce may not be cheaper than those avilable at the market, but since they provide education, recreation, relaxation, and a sense of well-being for the family, other expenses—for amusements and even medical care—may be reduced. Another farmer who loves horses may employ them instead of a tractor even though this restricts the land he or she may plow and limits the crops which can be grown for sale. However, the contented farmer may also have less need for goods manufactured elsewhere. Furthermore, horses are more energy-efficient than a tractor and recycle natural resources rather than exhaust them. Even though the horse-powered farm may have a smaller exchange with the off-farm economy, it may make a greater net contribution to society. There is an additional social contribution when a farmer tends less land and thereby makes room for more farm families in the neighborhood. This can be an important benefit to a crowded world.

Sustenance, as defined here, includes the benefits to the farm family and also to the face-to-face community near the farm. The produce shipped beyond this circle should be considered production. This is an important distinction, because personal exchanges that build community add value to what is otherwise only produce. Eggs direct from the farmer may or may not be superior to those at the supermarket, but a word with the farmer once a week, along with a personal appreciation of where food comes from, creates a relationship that nourishes the human community while the eggs feed the body. As a part-time farmer I barter with my neighbors. Sometimes the exchanges are formal: a quarter of beef with a specified value is traded for chickens and turkeys, or perhaps for some plumbing and carpentry work. Often the exchange is an informal neighborliness: I let my neighbor hang his tobacco in my barn to dry; later, when he sells his timber, he doesn't allow the stand which I view from my porch to be cut. These exchanges are pleasant in themselves and build a satisfying community. The physical beauty of the neighborhood and the pleasures found in walking, hunting, or fishing are also part of human sustenance within a rural community.

Sustenance includes the vitality of the landscape and the subjective experience of the creatures who inhabit it, even though much of this experience may remain beyond human comprehension. Wildlife retains rights in an agricultural setting, and on healthy farms it is usually abundant. Domestic animals, well fed and thoughtfully used, also enrich the landscape. Native species are often restricted for the sake of production, but none needs to be eliminated altogether. If a farmer is able to enjoy the surrounding environment then the costs of maintaining a healthy ecosystem are repaid; it is a delightful place for a family.

Sustenance leads to satisfaction. Satisfaction in a beautiful farm is a feeling one wishes to share with friends. The prophet Zechariah spoke about such farmers: "On that day, says the Lord of Hosts, you shall all of you invite one another to come and sit each under his [and her] vine and his [and her] fig-tree" (Zechariah 3:10, NEB, alt.).

Conservation is the most expansive of the agricultural values, and as the environmental crisis deepens it becomes urgent. Conservation requires the farmer to attend to the whole biotic community, to understand the landscape's past and to safeguard its future. As a conserver the farmer enters deeply into the human vocation "to cultivate and take care of" the garden of God's creation (Genesis 2:15, JB). When we do this well, men and women exhibit the image of God to nature.

Much of modern agriculture is fundamentally incompatible with conservation. Conservation expresses the ethical conviction that living systems have value; it also responds to the knowledge that resources are finite. Many modern farming technologies are based upon the assumption that living systems can be simplified or even replaced without adverse consequences, and that limitless resources are available to sustain an artifice created by human ingenuity. Conservation requires the farmer to be sensitive to the natural environment so the diverse potentials of living systems are protected for future use. Modern agriculture, in contrast, attempts to reduce the farm ecosystem to fewer components so that the farmer may control these more rigorously. Petrochemical fertilizers are designed to bypass the soil's biotic community, while herbicides and pesticides are designed to kill the species which might prey upon or compete with a crop. Sad to say, modern agriculture kills a great deal.

Conservation ethics require us to protect the systems where life and death interract creatively—the very systems herbicides and pesticides would destroy. Microorganisms, plants, and animals feed upon one another, while decay replenishes the soil. However, the ecological awareness of the interdependence of life and death also poses a problem for the traditional Christian viewpoint. We may no longer regard death as the enemy of life. It was the apostle Paul, interpreting God's intention to bring the cosmos into fellowship with Christ, who said that "the last of the enemies to be done away with is death" (1 Corinthians 15: 26, NJB). However, when life within this world is healthy, death need not be an enemy. Abusive and untimely death threaten the quality of human life, just as as herbicides and pesticides threaten natural life; but death in its proper place leads to new life. Just as the moral integrity of Jesus' death gave life to the world, so all appropriate deaths nourish creation. Wendell Berry extols this moral reality:

> The soil is the great connector of lives, the source and destination of all. It is the healer and restorer and resurrector, by which disease passes into health, age into youth, death into life. Without proper care for it we can have no community, because without proper care for it we can have no life.
> It is alive itself. It is a grave, too, of course. Or a healthy soil is. It is full of dead animals and plants, bodies that have passed through other bodies. For except for some humans—with their sealed coffins and vaults, their pathological fear of the earth—the only way into the soil is through other bodies. But no matter how finely the dead are broken down, or how many times they are eaten, they yet give into other life. If a healthy soil is full of death it is also full of life: worms, fungi, microorganisms of all kinds, for which, as for us humans, the dead bodies of the once living are a feast. Eventually this dead matter becomes soluble, available as food for plants, and

life begins to rise up again, out of the soil into the light. Given only the health of the soil, nothing that dies is dead for very long. Within this powerful economy, it seems that death occurs only for the good of life.[2]

Conservation requires protecting the character of the soil while we use it, and rebuilding soil to health if we find it depleted. Conservation also requires protecting the range of life possible on a particular landscape. Forests may be opened for farms, but some woods should be retained or restored on every farm where trees will grow. Native prairies may have been plowed to plant wheat, but the traces of prairie remaining can be protected and encouraged to expand—even within farms. Habitat for birds and wildlife should be considered. A farm where fields are not too large makes one of its finest contributions when birds and small animals thrive in the many fencerows and brushy boundaries. Lakes, streams, and marshes need to be protected, and livestock should be fenced away from some stretches so their banks may grow wild. Where water is scarce, constructed farm ponds serve wildlife along with the domestic economy. The farmer who thoughtfully hosts the life of the region is blessed with bees for polination, birds and toads to consume insects, worms and bacteria to maintain soil, all within a balanced ecosystem that is less likely to succumb to diseases. Such a farm will be beautiful.

The trend to replace people with larger machinery has not served the interests of conservation. Caring for a diverse, healthy landscape requires closer attention and more specialized labor than the maintenance of vast, standardized fields. It is true that many of the farmers displaced were indifferent to conservation. Yet a well-populated landscape is likely to have more room for natural life than one given over to large equipment. People have a variety of needs and interests; compared with the uniform requirements of machines, people are more compatible with nature. When the people who live on the land also love it, their presence can be a defense against the schemes of remote planners to usurp the life of the earth for some technical endeavor.

Society's interest in conservation should be supported with

economic incentives to influence farmers' behavior. Farmers care for nearly half America's land area—the half that produces our food as well as many other benefits. Erosion of this agricultural capacity threatens the health of the nation. Another 40 percent of America's land area—forests, grasslands, parks, and other territories—is owned by state and federal governments. In return for the timber, grazing, recreation, and other benefits that public lands contribute, society invests in the maintenance of public lands through the tax-supported agencies that administer them. It is equally appropriate for the public to invest in the conservation of farmland, and for farmers—if they manage their lands in the public interest—to receive some payment for these efforts in addition to conventional income from the sale of crops. When society pays only for production we, in effect, bribe the farmer to neglect conservation and to overwork the land for quick returns.

Production is most beneficial when it is secured along with sustenance and conservation. Produce is likely to be of higher quality, and the supply more reliable, when both land and farmer are healthy. Most Americans will continue to live away from rural communities and will depend upon farmers for their food. Those farmers who specialize in cash crops to the exclusion of subsistence farming renounce the most secure rewards of their craft and place themselves in unnecessary economic jeopardy, yet all farmers need some production for sale. Even those who farm in neighborhoods with a diverse economy, such as the Amish, need items that are not made locally, and for these they require cash income. The market for agricultural commodities can guide farmers to raise what society really needs; indeed, a free market is the most effective planning mechanism. In addition, the knowledge that one helps to feed others is one of the principal satisfactions from farming.

When people are forced from the land in order to make way for larger machinery to achieve higher production, some of this production must be devoted to feeding those who can no longer eat from their own gardens. If more people lived in rural communities, less food would need to be shipped to the cities. More people could engage personally in gardening and farming; more needs could be served through face-to-face exchanges; and a healthy balance among production, conservation, and sustenance would be more likely to prevail. Today's farming is not an adequate agriculture.

* * *

Among Americans who farm well, the Amish have earned particular respect. Shunning many modern technologies, this frugal people cultivate lands that have retained their vitality for generations. Although they refuse government aid whenever possible and even decline Social Security payments, the Amish draw a wholesome living from the land and care for one another so well that poverty is virtually unknown among them. Despite the group's frequent refusals to accommodate to modern ways, most Amish children embrace the faith as adults, though some do choose to depart. The sect has grown to ninety thousand people who live in a hundred rural settlements scattered among twenty states. They demonstrate that it is possible to select farming techniques on the basis of moral principles, and to thrive in consequence. They also illustrate the deep personal dedication and strong group discipline that ethical farming may require.

A Christian people, the Amish are a conservative branch of the Mennonite tradition, which took hold soon after the Protestant Reformation among peasants near the common borders of France, Switzerland, and Germany. The Amish were such resourceful farmers that landowners sought them for tenants; however, since they were considered heretics they were usually not permitted to own land themselves. In 1738 some Amish migrated to Pennsylvania, where they were welcomed and allowed to purchase land. Immigration by small groups continued for more than a century until most Amish believers found homes in North America.[3]

The Amish sharply distinguish good from evil. Nature is good, as represented by the garden of Eden, which God created for humans to tend, and so farming and the other trades which remain close to the land are also blessed. In their view, however, prevailing human culture has fallen into evil ways and Christians must separate themselves from it. The Amish pursue the apostle Paul's positive injunction "Do not be conformed to this world but be transformed"

(Romans 12: 2, RSV), and they also heed his negative warning "Do not unite yourselves with unbelievers" (2 Corinthians 6: 14, NEB). They are a separated community, determined to depend upon God and one another. Their plain dress and habits, as well as their distinctive horse-drawn buggies, are signs of bonding with each other and parting from the predominant culture. They exemplify the counsel given in the sixteenth century by Menno Simons, founder of the Mennonites: "Rent a farm, milk cows, learn a trade if possible, do manual labor as did Paul, and all that which you then fall short of will doubtless be given and provided you by pious brethren."[4]

David Kline farms in Ohio with his wife Elsie and five children, as part of a large Amish community. He works six heavy horses in the fields and keeps three light horses for road transportation, while he employs a diesel engine to drive a conveyor belt to a silo and another to run a milking machine. A portable fence to contain livestock is the farm's only electrical appliance; shunning the electric company, Kline energizes the fence with solar-powered photovoltaic cells. In the evenings the family home is brightened with kerosene lamps. Kline sells milk from twenty-four cows to a plant that makes Swiss cheese. He also sells occasional calves and pigs, and some wheat. He rarely uses fertilizer or herbicides, but relies instead upon a good crop rotation to maintain healthy soil and sustain good yields.

> Many of our practices are so traditional that the reasons are almost forgotten. The rotations of our field crops work so well that they are seldom questioned. This is a four or five year rotation, which means a field will be in corn every fourth or fifth year. The corn is followed with oats, and in the fall after the oats are harvested, the stubble is plowed and then sowed in wheat and a grass seed, usually timothy. The growing wheat is top-seeded the following March or April with legume seeds. After the wheat is cut and threshed in July, the stubble are mowed and almost miraculously the wheat field converts to a hay field. The next summer several cuttings of hay are taken and then the field is pastured in the fall. In a five year rotation the field remains in hay for two years. Then during the next winter, the old sod is liberally covered with straw and manure. In late winter or early spring the sod is plowed, and in May it is planted again to corn. The rotation is completed.[5]

Kline believes the community's adherence to horses protects the moral quality of Amish life: "Staying with horses has restricted expansion." Not only do horses limit farm size, "they are ideally suited to family life." While the team rests the family eats together, and work is suspended at dusk since "God didn't create the horse with headlights." Whereas heavy tractors compact soil in the fields, horse-powered cultivation helps the earth remain light and aerated, while ample applications of manure sustain the humus. Kline cites research by Oberlin College suggesting that, in a heavy downpour, tilled cornfields on Amish farms absorb six times the water that nearby no-till cornfields can hold before run-off begins to carry erosion.

Kline's description of his farming seasons is lyrical:

> The field work begins in March with the plowing of sod. This is leisurely work, giving the horses plenty of time to become conditioned. This is what the Quakers call quiet time, a time to listen to God and his creatures, as we are not just observers but a part of the unfolding of spring. The creaking harness and the popping of alfalfa roots, the tinkling sound of the hornet lark, the lisping of the water pip—it's a wonderful time. April is for plowing corn stalks and sowing oats—and for spring beauties and lovely hepaticus. In May, glorious May, we plant the corn. Then we turn the cows and horses out to pasture and revel in warblers and morel mushrooms. Haymaking in June, and strawberry shortcakes, pies, and jams. The bird migration is over and summer settles in. Work on the farm peaks in July: threshing, second cutting hay, transparent apples, new honey, blackberries, and the first katydid. August already hints of autumn and silo filling—the whine of silo fillers is heard throughout the land. We fill our silo with the help of four neighbors. Sowing wheat and McIntosh apples means September. October is corn harvest, cider making, and loving the color and serenity only October can offer. As the month draws to a close, so does the field work.
>
> A lot of what you may consider recreation, we get on our farm. Year to year is a never-ending adventure. This year we had four firsts: our first Kentucky warbler, our first luna moth and imperial moth, and after waiting for over thirty years I saw my first giant swallowtail butterfly. Very exciting!
>
> I like to look at our farm as an artist would behold his or her painting—a variation of colors and designs. Never a bare spot of

canvas should be left exposed. The bare spots on our farm, such as cow paths along the hill, are covered in November with straw or horse manure to prevent erosion. In wintertime we cut wood, which is a real pleasure, and then we rest. But we have a lot of barn chores that take several hours in the morning and several hours at night, and then there's feed grinding. We haul 300 or 350 loads of manure a year. Once a week we clean out the horse stables: that's usually Saturday mornings, so if we get company on Sunday the barn is clean.

Kline's serenity and his sensitivity to the farm environment are supported by a rigorous cultural discipline. The church district, which forms the essential context for Amish life, is sufficiently compact so families with horse-drawn buggies can assemble conveniently. Worship is held every second Sunday at one district farm or another, and members of the district meet frequently for work and companionship. While Amish church districts are self-governing, they remain very traditionalist. The several ministers who lead worship and oversee the life of the district are chosen by lot from among the most respected farmers. The patterns of daily life follow well-worn customs, and any proposed innovation may be pondered by the ministers—in consultation with ministers from other districts—for years. By refusing electricity, telephones, and automobiles, the Amish limit their economic ties to the larger society and control its intrusion upon the family and the community. "We don't think the telephone or the automobile or the tractor is sinful," Kline explains. "We think their influence to the family can do harm." The Amish develop many personal and economic relationships with the larger society within which they live, but they consider the nature of these contacts with care. It is their strong self-definition, even more than their isolation, that makes their society work.

Within the Amish community there is a sense of social security. Many parents save money to help their sons begin farming on their own land. Most Americans have seen pictures of large groups of bearded Amish men gathered on such a new farm to erect a barn in a day. When the elderly turn their farm over to their children, they continue living with dignity in a smaller house beside the main house. Most important, when sickness or disability strikes, the community responds, as Kline remembers fondly:

> Eight years ago I had an accident which required surgery and a hospital stay. My wife now tells me that the first words I told her in recovery were, "Get me out of here! We've got to cut the wheat!" Of course she couldn't, and I need not have worried because I have neighbors. While my Dad bindered the wheat, the neighbors shocked just as fast, and when our team tired my brother brought his four-horse team. By supper time the twelve acres were cut and shocked.
>
> This year we could help a neighbor who had come to help me. Since his bout with pneumonia in July he hasn't been able to work much, so last Thursday six teams and mowers cut eleven acres of his alfalfa hay. Then last Saturday afternoon, with four teams and four wagons and two hay loaders—and fifteen men and about as many boys—we had the hay in his barn in less than two hours, while he sat in the shade. As a matter of fact, we spent almost as much time afterwards sitting in a circle under the maple tree with cold drinks and fresh cookies.

* * *

The Amish experience illustrates that good farming requires a supportive culture. When neighbors share common values and take a similar approach to their tasks, they can encourage, assist, and correct one another. When, in addition, neighbors truly care for one another and support each other in need, then farmers can afford to take the risks required to practice good agriculture on a scale appropriate to human sustenance and the conservation of nature. True agriculture is a moral system joined to productive techniques. Providing for humanity while protecting nature requires a culture that can integrate technology with sound values.

The Amish also demonstrate that the practice of good agriculture need not await economic recovery or changes in government policy. If a group of people can pool a variety of known skills and contribute dedication to their task and commitment to one another, they can farm well. Although it is never easy, human communities can still flourish on the land. The resources they choose to provide for one another in the neighborhood are more important than distant political and economic powers.

Reclaiming American agriculture will require many new experiments to supplement the wisdom preserved by traditional groups. The Amish have designed their communities to shield them from the dominant culture; they do not see their calling to be agents of social reform. Their traditionalism has protected them from many mistakes common to modern agriculture, but it also isolates them from some useful new knowledge. Along with such groups that preserve proven traditions, society needs other groups that work on the advancing edge of discovery, yet apply moral and ecological sensitivity within their practice. Those who labor to reform deeply intrenched social abuses are as valuable as those who have held themselves apart from those abuses. Many approaches to reform are needed, for a healthy culture becomes nearly as complex as a healthy ecosystem.

Farming is one of the most complicated professions that humans pursue. It requires an intimate knowledge of soils, plant life, animal husbandry, climate, technology, and markets, as well as wisdom and moral sensitivity in the application of this knowledge. Since individuals are unlikely to master so much information and to develop relevant skills and sensitivities without assistance, good farmers need a culture that provides them with education and training, assists them with practical and moral evaluation, and helps them screen the stream of new information. The higher our standards for farming, the more important such cultural support becomes.

The prevalent myth that farming is an appropriate occupation for backward or simple-minded people reflects the cultural poverty of many farming areas during the 1920s and 1930s. Rural communities often failed to work as problem-solving networks and as systems providing social support. Indeed, despite Thomas Jefferson's vision of vital agrarian democracy, many American small towns and rural communities have functioned poorly in these respects. Our characteristic inventiveness, our voluntarism, and our sense of fairness have frequently been overwhelmed by our individualism, ambition, and greed. The widespread failure of churches to deal with social and environmental ethics, and the common intellectual inadequacy of the public education system—these two pillars of

American rural society—have contributed to the weakness of agriculture just as much as the periodic collapses of commodity prices.

This cultural weakness opened the way for the application of industrial methods. Farmers needed help. Machines that gave them power, and techniques that simplified the farm environment, were immediately appealing. After World War II, many farmers submitted to direction from agricultural bureaucrats who were linked to regional centers of expertise. Although the new system surrounded farmers with complex charts and technical jargon, in fact they needed to know relatively little to make it work. Each farmer grew greater quantities of fewer crops, guided by distant experts and assisted by powerful chemicals that subdued competing life. Agribusiness moved into the void left by the collapse of a workable culture of farming on the local level. Farms became factories, and the land was rendered nearly as sterile as a factory floor.

In order to reclaim the half of America's landscape devoted to farming, we need to reestablish rural communities where those who wish to develop a culture of farming can support and guide one another. If farmers are to be more than field hands within a bureaucratic system of food production, then they must form networks of support on a face-to-face level with others who are also committed to a healthy biosphere and who can contribute a diversity of skills—so the earth may be tended, knowledge improved, and practice perfected. People within these communities will need dedication not only to the earth but also to one another, for good farming must include mutual assistance to survive losses and setbacks without succumbing to abusive practices. Rural communities must make group decisions about the agricultural standards and techniques, so that a culture may develop that is both moral and coherent. If we wish to liberate land and people from bureaucratic mismanagement, then farmers and other local contributors to agriculture must be willing to submit to reasonable discipline from one another. This is difficult for Americans, but it is the beating heart of an agrarian democracy.

7. *New Growth*

The agricultural depression of the 1980s forced many farmers to reexamine their practices because they could no longer afford the high cost of fertilizers and chemicals. Fortunately, in nearly every state some farmers had been experimenting for a decade or more with agricultural techniques requiring little chemical assistance. These "organic farming" pioneers were once considered a peculiar cult; indeed, many of them rejected artificial chemicals as much from religious conviction as scientific understanding, while many employed exotic "natural" compounds to stimulate plant growth and control predators. When some of these organic techniques proved effective, and the problems with industrial agriculture became more apparent, organic practices began to enter the mainstream of American agriculture. Some people prefer to label these practices "regenerative," "biological," "natural," "sustainable," or even "low-imput" agriculture, in order to avoid appearing extreme.

Many who are now organic practitioners were traditional farmers resistant to modern ways. Some were people with professional backgrounds and environmental concerns who entered farming in mid-life or upon retirement in order to find meaning through working with the soil: I myself am one of these. At the core of the organic movement, however, are farmers who adopted chemical farming with enthusiasm but later became disillusioned. Dick and Sharon Thompson, whose three-hundred-acre Iowa farm has won national attention, are representative of this group. Dick Thompson tells how they began farming in 1957:

We grew nothing but corn, using a lot of fertilizers and pesticides. But a nagging voice inside was saying there had to be something better. Things weren't working. The cattle were sick. The hogs were sick. We were hungry for change.

During that time, a minister told us that God was going to teach us how to farm. Here I had two degrees in agriculture, and I had lived on a farm all my life, and a minister was telling me it's going to be different! Well, within a couple of weeks, a friend came along and took us to a meeting on natural farming. The speaker said we were going down a blind alley. It was like he hit me over the head with a two-by-four. So we quit using chemicals cold turkey.

Twenty years later, their farm has become a showcase for natural farming techniques—visited annually by hundreds of people, both farmers and agronomists. The Thompsons grow corn and hay in rotation, use the corn to raise thirteen hundred hogs a year, raise cattle on the hay, and recycle manure, along with nutrient-bearing sludge from a nearby water treatment plant, to the soil. They began organic farming on faith, trial, and error; they now add careful scientific evaluation of their practices. "I can govern my life by faith and hunches," Dick explains, "but that doesn't mean anything to other people. I need to understand what's going on, so I can explain it to somebody else."[1] He consults with state and federal agronomists, and he conducts research supported by the Robert Rodale Regenerative Agriculture Association in Emmaus, Pennsylvania. He heads the Practical Farmers of Iowa, a hundred farmers who disseminate information about biologically responsible practices. He is particularly delighted that birds and small game are returning to his land.

Another popular approach to organic farming is to manage, on a small acreage, a dense ecosystem of plants, trees, and animals for human use. High-quality fruits and vegetables can sometimes be sold to nearby restaurants at premium prices. Even better, customers who want wholesome produce free of chemical contamination will come to the farm to pick their own fruits and vetegables. To make a living from a small farm, it is often best to bypass conventional food distribution systems, which pay low prices to the farmer and require rigidly standardized produce. Selling directly to the consumer is more profitable. People from nearby cities and towns enjoy visiting a beautiful farm with a rich variety of trees, plants, and animals, and they will pay well for good produce. Booker T. Whatley tells farmers:

> Stay small, but get smart. . . . start thinking less about big tractors and more about marketing. . . .
>
> Think of your farm as a vacation spot or a retreat for your customers. Many come there to enjoy the country atmosphere and get away from the hustle and bustle of the city, as much as they do to pick fresh fruits and vegetables.[2]

A vigorous black agronomist at work for half a century, Whatley is an evangelist for intensive farming. As part of an experiment at the headquarters for Domino's Pizza near Ann Arbor, Michigan, Whatley has developed an unusually complex one-hundred-acre farm ecosystem that is expected to draw thousands of visitors and to yield 2.5 million dollars worth of produce each year. The farm raises a wide range of fruits, vegetables, and herbs; lamb, venison, quail, pheasant, duck, and catch-your-own fish; mushrooms, honey, and Christmas trees.

Several grocery chains in California feature pesticide-free fruits and vegetables certified by an independent testing laboratory that monitors the farms where the produce is grown. At the minimal grade, this produce must show no detectable pesticide residues, whether "natural" or chemical; for intermediate grade produce, any chemicals used must have decomposed completely so the farmer's soil and water also test pesticide-free; and to raise the highest grade of produce the farmer must refrain from applying pesticides of any kind. Farmers receive a premium of as much as $2.50 for a carton of top-grade peaches and $5.00 more for a carton of top-grade grapes.[3] In another helpful strategy, several states have begun programs to strengthen the market for regional produce. Massachusetts gives coupons to low-income mothers that may be redeemed at urban farmers' markets for fresh fruits and vegetables. This stimulates enough trade to make it worthwhile for farmers to haul their crops into town, and it also induces mothers to try fresh foods. "Some young mothers had only used canned or frozen vegetables before," reports

Kathleen McCabe, who manages one of the markets. "The farmers enjoyed sharing some of their best recipes and the women learned better than in a formal teaching situation."[4]

* * *

As creative agronomists and biologists reexamine agriculture from an ecological perspective, they see possibilities for new techniques that may sustain the world's human population while protecting the soil and even reclaiming regions that have been abused. One of the most promising of these is "forest farming" for food. A tree sends roots into the soil in a pattern as large and complex as that formed by the branches it raises into the air. This deep network holds the soil together while tapping nutrients that smaller plants cannot reach. Some tree species, such as the locust, are *legumes;* such trees draw nitrogen from the air and fix this critical nutrient in soil just as do other leguminous plants (beans, peas, and clover, for example). These trees can help revive depleted soils. In their book on forest farming, Sholto Douglas and Robert Hart point out that certain trees yield far more food upon an acre of ground than it is possible to raise using grains or livestock:

> Whereas livestock rearing in temperate regions produces an average of about two hundredweight of meat per acre and cereal growing an average of about one and a half tons per acre, apple trees can yield at least seven tons per acre, while leguminous, bean-bearing trees, such as the honey locust, can provide fifteen to twenty tons of cereal-equivalent.... As a 'machine' for supplying the necessary factors for sustaining human and animal life, the tree, with its deep, ever-questing roots, seeking out the riches of the subsoil, and its mass of foliage high in the air, utilizing atmospheric minerals and solar radiation by the scientific process of photosynthesis, is far more efficient than any system devised by man.[5]

A sufficient mass of trees will improve the climate by holding rainfall and expiring water vapor. Reforestation can combat the spreading aridity—commonly called "desertification"—that afflicts Africa and is beginning to touch other continents as well. Tree farming may increase food production in some regions where famine is common. Douglas and Hart recommend that plantings of productive trees be interspersed with open grazing strips for livestock; the animals would also consume the tree pods to produce meat, milk, eggs, wool, and other items for human use. However, in many cultures the proper care of trees will require major changes in customs and values.

At the Land Institute in Kansas, Wes Jackson is leading research that might reconstruct agriculture on the world's vast prairies where grasses, not trees, are the natural climax species. In the Mississippi basin, nearly all of America's tall-grass prairies were plowed under a century ago by homesteaders, and much of the short-grass prairie in drier regions further to the west is now gone as well. In their place stand "the amber waves of grain" we celebrate in song, vast fields of wheat or corn spreading toward the horizon. However, the hardy soils that the tall-grass ecosystems formed over millennia are being eroded and depleted through the intensive cultivation of a few species. Jackson compares this fine soil to the membrane in a mother's womb that transfers nourishment from her body to the newly growing life.

> Soil is a placenta or matrix, a living organism which is larger than the life it supports, a tough elastic membrane which has given rise to many life forms and has watched the thousands of species from their first experiments at survival, many of them through . . . successes and even dominion before their decline and demise. But it is itself now dying. It is a death that is utterly senseless, and portends our own.

Jackson explains that "In nature the wounded placenta heals through plant succession; enterprising species cover wounds completely." However agriculture—"the monoculture of annuals, the enslavement of enterprising species"—has interrupted that succession.[6] To grow the grains we favor, farmers have disrupted a natural ecosystem developed through evolutionary trial and error over thousands of years; an ecosystem rich with biological information carried in the genes of the countless plants, animals, and soil organisms that together sustain it; an ecosystem which, driven by energy from the sun, heals its own wounds and rebuilds its own life. "When humans destroy this information," Jackson argues, "they must substitute cultural information, apply more energy, or do both."

> The point is . . . that if the soil and water are to be maintained where till agriculture is practiced, the jobs done by the prairie biota now must be done by humans and their domestic species.[7]

We are manifestly failing to perform these tasks.

Jackson hopes to replace traditional agriculture with a new culture of perennial grain crops which would form "herbaceous perennial seed-producing polycultures."[8] Rather than uniform stands of grain planted every year upon soil that has been plowed, poisoned, or both, Jackson is experimenting with native prairie grasses and the plants that surround them in their natural environment to see if systems might be developed to produce grain for human consumption without annual planting. He hopes that such new ecosystems, adaped from the prairie ecology, will thrive on energy from the sun without fertilizer, resist blight and disease without herbicides, hold the soil, and contribute to its vitality. The Land Institute incorporates a surviving stand of native prairie as well as test plots for the development of grasses and grains adapted to human needs and for experiments that combine species in a variety of environmental configurations. Jackson's goal is not simply to adapt a few native species for grain production. He wishes to evolve a whole ecosystem toward higher yields of palatable seeds while retaining its inherent health and vitality. Progress toward this challenging goal will be slow and results remain uncertain. However complex the developmental process proves to be, Jackson hopes for a result that will make farming simpler, safer, and "resilient to human folly."

> Ecosystem agriculture will be more *complex* than population (crop) agriculture, but the management of agro-ecosystems may not be more *complicated*. Ecosystem agriculturists will take advantage of huge chunks of what works. They will be taking advantage of the natural integrities of ecosystems worked out over the millennia.[9]

Although Jackson argues that "the best agriculture for any region . . . mimics the region's natural ecosystems,"[10] we should not imagine a return to primitive practices. Indeed, "ecosystem agriculture" is more sophisticated, not less, than industrial farming. Like conventional agriculture, it is supported by the ability of scientists to breed plants selectively in order to speed the evolution of desired characteristics. Ecosystem agriculture requires further, however, that these improved species be integrated back into a community similar to the environment from which they emerged, so relationships that nourish particular species and protect them from disease are not lost. While some plants within a community produce food for human use, the system as a whole must sustain within itself the activities for which industrial agriculture employs plows, fertilizers, and herbicides: preparing soil, providing nourishment, and resisting disease. Only recently have scientists acquired biological knowledge sufficient to imagine how we might integrate agriculture within self-sustaining ecosystems, rather than pushing nature aside to make room for farms. This vision might even create a living community that embodied the biblical vision of a just ecology: that is, a network of considerate relationships that permit the domestic and the wild to occupy a landscape together and serve each other's needs.

If agriculture continues to pit humanity against nature, both will lose. On a crowded and vulnerable planet, human knowledge must incorporate the natural wisdom of ecosystems that have learned to thrive without destroying the foundations for future life. We still have a great deal to learn. Modern agriculture overwhelmed nature to construct fragile colonies of productivity that must be heavily subsidized with petrochemicals and constantly managed. We have relied, Jackson argues, upon technologies of conquest and colonization:

> But colonization is based on plunder and is inherently violent and wasteful, a fact we have been slow to acknowledge. The antidote to colonization is discovery. We need to discover how the world works to know better our place in it. In this sense, the true discovery of America is before us.[11]

* * *

In 1970 a blight spread across America's cornfields in the Southern states, attacking plants with a particular genetic construction that had been bred into the hybrid corn varieties by scientists. Unfortunately, 80 percent of the corn planted that year contained these "designer" genes. Although all available supplies of seeds without this genetic configuration were rushed to the infected areas for planting in 1971, 15 percent of the nation's corn succumbed to the blight that year. In 1972 the National Academy of Sciences concluded:

> The corn crop fell victim to the epidemic because of a quirk in the technology that had redesigned the corn plants of America until, in one sense, they had become as alike as identical twins. Whatever made one plant susceptible made them all susceptible.[12]

The characteristic that made corn so vulnerable to blight was not, indeed, a "quirk" in technology but a forseeable consequence of the genetic manipulation and standardization of modern agricultural commodities.

Techniques for seeding, breeding, and cultivating that improve species for human use are nearly as old as agriculture itself, although scientific knowledge and practical manipulations have accelerated dramatically in the modern era. In the Old Testament the patriarch Jacob was revered for his ability to breed sheep and goats selectively to secure the characteristics he desired. Nez Percé Indians were the only Native American tribe to breed horses selectively; in consequence they eluded the U.S. Cavalry longer than any other tribe. Sad to say, when the army overwhelmed them at last, officers took revenge by ordering the slaughter of all of the Nez Percé's swift, surefooted Appaloosa horses. Today virtually every type of animal and plant domesticated within human culture has been deliberately altered to strengthen characteristics that serve human interests.

These "improvements" have side effects. Species altered to respond to cultivation are often more dependent upon human management. Some domesticated species have lost traits that contribute to survival in "natural" environments, and they become vulnerable to predators and diseases that move from uncultivated edges into farm fields. They may also be more susceptible than their wild progenitors to the diseases that evolve within agricultural environments because they have been standardized and carry less diversity into the field. As Jackson explains,

> Successful plant breeding tends to narrow the genetic base of any crop roughly in proportion to its success. The better adapted to the human purpose a population is, the narrower its genetic base and, therefore, the fewer options it has available to meet future threats of insects and pathogens.[13]

Pesticides may be required to protect modern, productive grains from diseases that posed little threat to "less advanced" varieties.

The exchange of plants and animals among different regions also has costs which must be listed alongside the benefits. People throughout the world have a better diet thanks to the discovery of Indian corn, potatoes, and tomatoes in North and South America, although they are also burdened with the tobacco discovered here. However, by 1845, Ireland had become excessively dependent upon one variety of potato, the Lumper, which had no resistance to a blight which raged across that land for three years. Because of this unwise specialization in a species novel to the region, a million people died of starvation and a larger number were forced to emigrate.[14] A bark fungus was accidentally carried from Asia to the United States in 1906, and within thirty years the most useful hardwood species on this continent, the American chestnut, had been entirely destroyed. When organisms that are balanced within one ecosystem are introduced—deliberately or inadvertently—into another, the effects are unpredictable.

The emerging science of genetic engineering will complicate these problems. Until now, deliberate genetic changes have depended upon the controlled propagation of plants and the insemination of animals. The time required for this guided evolution gave scientists—and sometimes farmers—opportunities to observe characteristics in successive generations and to evaluate their ability to survive and thrive in the agricultural environment for which they were designed. Now that scientists may remove genes, alter genes, and insert new genes into particular organisms, species can be changed more quickly. Particular genes may be inserted because there is evidence they will produce a desired effect, but the subsequent interactions among genes within an organism are beyond the ability of scientists to predict, while the interraction of an altered species with its environment is even more uncertain. This is why political decisions concerning the "release" of genetically altered organisms into the environment are so controversial.

Scientific interest in genetic engineering has been fueled by the profit motive since 1980, when the U.S. Supreme Court upheld the granting of a patent on a genetically engineered bacterium. This decision creates the opportunity to "own" life forms by taking a patent on the subspecies developed by genetic manipulation in the laboratory. In the opinion of the court, "the relevant distinction was not between living and inanimate things, but between products of nature, whether living or not, and human-made inventions."[15] This unfortunate decision ignores the continuing partnership between nature and invention, both within the altered life form and also in its interractions with the biosphere. The issue will probably be argued again in terms of the ownership of more complex plant and animal life that is shaped by genetic manipulation. Meanwhile, the potential profits from patents on living organisms are attracting hundreds of millions in investment dollars.

Among those most interested in genetic engineering are the companies that produce herbidices. For example, *triazene* compounds, such as "Roundup" from Monsanto, account for a billion dollars in herbicide sales annually. When applied to fields, triazene blocks photosynthesis in plants, causing them to die. Since field corn contains enzymes that detoxify this chemical, the corn thrives without competition. However soybeans—legumes that return to the soil some of the nitrogen that corn removes—are commonly planted in rotation with corn, and residues of triazene compounds attack this legume as they would a weed. Therefore genetic researchers are working to transfer to soybeans a capacity to produce the enzyme that corn plants employ to overcome the herbicide. If they are successful, chemical companies will sell more herbicides while they retain patents on the only seeds that can grow in the soils they have contaminated. While the earth withers, profits will soar.

America is awash with milk, so much so that the federal government pays dairy farmers to reduce their herds. Nevertheless, several companies are seeking approval to market "somatropin," a bovine growth hormone that, in tests, has increased cows' milk production by 30 percent. Dairy cattle are already a highly stressed, uncomfortable breed. The cattle receiving the growth hormone will have a lower heat tolerance and will experience more medical and reproductive problems. Most dairy farmers are resisting this technology because they realize that increased milk production will overwhelm government support programs and depress the price, driving family farms out of business. If the hormone is approved, however, many farmers will decide to employ it in order to remain competitive. Consumers will drink cheaper milk of uncertain quality, cattle will suffer, and the largest remaining segment of family farming may collapse. Nevertheless, a few companies will prosper.

With prophetic fury, Wes Jackson charges that those who create such agricultural freaks have become monsters themselves, while their baleful influence upsets "whatever is left of the balance of the human."

> Such dehumanized monsters, devotees of human cleverness, have already been created by the biotechnology now available. These are people who see nothing wrong with breeding featherless chickens to cut butchering costs, or who have entertained the notion that the gene for eyelessness should be introduced into hogs in order to provide an economic gain for those raising hogs in close confinement. Blind hogs would be less nervous and would gain weight faster.[16]

The potentials for catastrophe in this field are so surreal that we may need the help of poets and artists to imagine the consequences of human arrogance. The film *Soylent Green* portrayed a future in which rural areas administered by agribusiness have become too polluted for human habitation and even industrial cropping systems are breaking down. Urban life is intolerably crowded and oppressive.

The government looks for techniques to augment the daily ration of soy-lentil powder that gives the film its title. It offers volunteers the alternative of entering crematories where they will be pacified with injections and treated to films of rural landscapes as theese appeared many years before. Once the volunteers die—surrounded by images of natural beauty—their remains are recycled to feed the living.

In America we still have the opportunity to choose between agribusiness and agriculture. Now is the time to act, however, for the freedom to choose may not last long.

8. *Cattle Culture*

The place of animals within agriculture deserves special attention. Indeed, the affliction of animals under modern livestock management must be morally repugnant to Christians who are aware that God, in the Bible, commanded just treatment toward the creatures that share the earth with humanity. Biblical law regulated the use and abuse of animals in much the same way that it limited a farmer's power over human servants. Domestic animals were entitled to rest as surely as people were. Working animals could not be muzzled to keep them from eating as they labored. They were not to be abused as by harnessing together species with different strengths. An animal in distress was to be helped even if it belonged to one's enemy. The careful tending of flocks and herds was so highly respected within Hebrew culture that Ezekiel made it a metaphor for God's care of the chosen people, while Jesus recalled the shepherd's anxious concern for a lost sheep to interpret his own attention to notorious sinners. The Bible's moral ecology gave wild creatures rights within agricultural districts: birds were not to be killed indiscriminantly, while not just the human poor but also wild beasts were to be allowed gleanings from fallow fields and unpruned vines.[1] In short, the Bible commanded that people and animals establish moral relationships with each other, and it distributed rights and responsibilities among the parties.

This series has considered how important for modern science was Descartes' elaborate fiction that animals lack sensibilities and that humans may therefore adopt a technical, unfeeling posture toward them. Although this point of view has prevailed among the Western scientific elite for three hundred years, people who work creatively with animals have always known better. As Vicki Hearne, a gifted animal trainer, explains,

> implicit as well as explicit in the trainers' language is the notion that animals are capable not only of activities requiring "I.Q."—a rather arid concept—but also of a complex and delicate (though not infallible) moral understanding, which is so inextricably a function of their relationships with human beings that it may well be said to constitute those relationships. (By "moral understanding" I mean that, as far as the trainer is concerned, a dog is perfectly capable of understanding that he ought not to pee on the bedpost even though he might want to. Characterizing the dog's own formulation of this understanding is a separate matter. . . .)

A human who works creatively with animals, Hearne continues, must assume moral responsibilities as well.

> So a rider who is a true rider, and no mere keeper of horses, is someone who continuously earns the right to question the horse and the horse's performance, and it is the horse's performance that answers the rider's questioning. . . . The rider is the person who shoulders the burden of knowing—through "the talent of understanding, the skill of commitment"—what the horse means.[2]

John Muir's observed that "God takes care of everything that is wild but he only half takes care of tame things."[3] When we modify ecosystems, society must assume a share of responsibility for the vitality of these processes that were once natural. Likewise, as we adapt species to human needs we take upon ourselves responsibility for their welfare. Beyond our duty to protect living systems in the interest of future generations, we have a moral obligation to maintain the quality of the lives we shepherd. Yet Muir noticed a century ago that while domesticated sheep yield heavy cuttings of wool and grow plump with mutton, these benefits have been achieved by inflicting upon them a distinct loss in personality. In the wild, sheep move with "intelligent independence," whereas the creature bred for human use is so bound to the herd as to be "only a fraction of an animal, a whole flock being required to form an individual." Muir also noted that the domestic sheep, in a general way, is expressionless, like a dull bundle of something only half alive, while the wild is as elegant and graceful as a deer, every movement manifesting admirable strength and character. The tame is timid; the wild is bold. The tame is always more or less ruffled and dirty; while the wild is as smooth and clean as the flowers of his mountain pastures.[4]

Since it is morally repugnant to treat animals simply as objects, we must learn the character of each species and respect the needs of those in our charge.

* * *

Some of the most alarming modern abuses of animals have been facilitated by the development, following World War II, of medical antibiotics that kill a wide range of bacteria including varieties that cause infections. The same antibiotics that are prescribed for humans—penicillin, streptomycin, and others—work well for animals. People do not usually take antibiotics except to cope with an active infection. In the 1950s, however, it was discovered that when livestock and poultry were fed antibiotics as part of their regular diet, they could be penned together in large numbers with little disease. Indeed, the antibiotics appeared to reduce the creatures' stress under crowded conditions and to promote weight gain as well. By 1979 all commercial poultry were being raised on feed that included antibiotics; 90 percent of hogs and 70 percent of beef cattle are now also raised this way. Young beef cattle are taken from farms when they are less than a year old to be fattened in crowded feedlots on a ration of grain and antibiotics until they reach slaughter weight. An increasing proportion of hogs are raised in confinement buildings, while nearly all poultry are raised in small cages, thousands to a building. From hatch to slaughter, chickens may never see the sky or touch the ground. Dr. Thomas Jukes, one of the first to feed antibiotics to chickens and pigs, observed with pride:

It was the discovery of the effectiveness of drugs as feed additives in these conditions that led to the concentration of the meat industry.

For the first time, farmers could confine a large number of animals and still keep them healthy.[5]

In hospitals, meanwhile, the use of antibiotics to prevent infection had alarming side-effects. During the 1960s new bacterial strains appeared that were resistant to these drugs, and some of these spread novel infections to patients. Since antibiotics suppress the majority of bacteria within a human body, those few that are insensitive to the drug have the opportunity to flourish without competition. Bacteria mutate quickly, so new strains can develop rapidly in this artificial environment. By the end of the 1960s epidemics caused by antibiotic-resistant bacteria were being reported around the world. To limit these developments, most physicians became more conservative in their use of antibiotics, saving them for patients with acute need.

In the livestock industry, however, daily antibiotic feeding continued because the whole industry had been reorganized in response to this technological opportunity. Sustained by a constant diet of antibioitics, animals raised in confinement became incubators for mutant strains of bacteria that resist the very antibiotics humans also depend upon.

Orville Schell, in a major study of the problem, explains that there are several ways for antibiotic resistance cultivated in animals to migrate to the bacteria that attack humans:

> Animal bacteria resistant to antibiotics may colonize human beings directly; or they may transfer their capacity for resistance to other species of bacteria within the animal, which may then colonize human beings; or resistant animal bacteria that end up in the intestinal tracts of human beings may transfer their capacity for resistance to indigenous human bacteria. The pathways are numerous and nefarious.[6]

Not only do bacteria, reproducing by simple cell division, multiply very rapidly, but genetic plasmids that resist antibiotics can migrate from one type of bacteria to another.

Public health authorities have traced several epidemics of illness and death to specific shipments of such meat. The people most susceptible to infection are those who eat meat or poultry while they are themselves receiving antibiotics: the drugs that suppress bacteria broadly leave patients vulnerable to invasion by resistant strains. For several years the Food and Drug Administration has been considering whether to prohibit routine feeding of antibiotics to livestock, but the political influence of the meat and poultry industries has been strong. An administration closely associated with business interests is unlikely to issue a ruling that might devastate the confinement feeding industry so recently constructed. Meanwhile, all commercial meat and poultry remains a potential threat to public health, particularly to those who may themselves require antibiotics.

A similar problem arises from the widespread administration of synthetic sex hormones to cattle and poultry in order to stimulate the development of muscle tissue which we consume as meat. In Puerto Rico, from 1979 to 1982, doctors observed an alarming increase in the number of girls under eight years of age with premature sexual development, and a similar increase in infants and small children with ovarian cysts. The evidence pointed to synthetic estrogen, a sex hormone fed to livestock and poultry. Apparently some farmers administered inappropriately large doses of hormones to old dairy cows in an effort to fatten them for sale; others did the the same to hens. When the scandal was publicized the practice diminished.[7]

In 1979 the U.S. Food and Drug Administration banned the most popular form of synthetic estrogen for cattle, diethylstilbestrol (DES), because residues of this carcinogen survived in meat prepared for human consumption. Other synthetic hormones continue to be permitted at levels that the United States government currently considers safe, but the European Economic Community has forbidden the use of synthetic hormones in beef raised for the European market.

Americans should also be concerned about imported meat because many countries do not enforce standards for the safe use of antibiotics and hormones. The drugs, marketed by American companies, are often administered by people with no understanding of the dangers. Carol Tucker Foreman, who directed meat inspection in the

Carter administration, has testified to a congressional committee: "There is a good chance that the American public consumes meat with violative residues of carcinogenic and teratogenic [causing abnormal fetal development] chemical residues with some regularity."[8]

Mutant bacteria that attack humanity are ecological revenge for our abuse of livestock. The ancient Hebrews understood that when a community of life absorbs as much injustice as it can tolerate, the living community may be expected to erupt upon its oppressors. "You shall keep my statutes and my ordinances," God commanded in the Holiness Code, "and do none of these abominations . . . lest the land vomit you out, when you defile it" (Leviticus 18: 26—28, RSV). Although the Hebrews lacked modern knowledge of ecology, they understood nature to be a responsive system, and they appreciated in particular the moral dimension of nature's relations with humanity. We need to acknowledge the immorality of our present practices so that, once we are repentant, we may envision a moral culture that treats livestock with respect.

* * *

My own experience raising beef cattle for fifteen years has led me to ponder this troubling moral relationship. I have formed convictions about cattle culture—the raising of beef—and from these I make more tentative inferences about the raising of livestock and poultry with which I do not have personal experience.

Modern practice afflicts cattle with confinement and with inappropriate diet. It burdens the land with excessive grain production while depriving the soil of animal wastes. It degrades people by substituting exploitative relationships for traditional cattle culture. Also, the food produced is less wholesome.

It is the nature of cattle to range and to eat grass along with other roughage. Their complex stomachs convert grass to flesh efficiently, producing meat that can be lean, tender, tasty, and nutritious. When cattle are confined to feedlots they are violated twice: their instinct to range is frustrated, while the fast-fattening diet of grain without roughage does not suit their stomachs. The cattle are uncomfortable, and their flesh is marbled with fat that tenderizes the meat at the price of loading the consumer with unhealthy cholesterol.

The scientists, businessmen, investors, and farmers who construct concentration camps for thousands of cattle, as well as the luckless laborers who work as attendants amid the filth and penetrating stench, imagine that cattle have no feelings or that the quality of their lives is a matter of moral indifference. Although modern cattle are not prepossessing intellectually, in a suitable habitat they can be both graceful and resourceful. Some bovine sensibilities still exceed the human. Orville Schell points out that "taste and smell play an extraordinary part in the sensory apparatus of animals. A man has about nine thousand taste buds, whereas a cow has around thirty thousand."[9] Such acute senses are violated by feedlot confinement.

Livestock confinement also leads to abuse of the agricultural landscape and depletion of our natural resources. For every pound of meat added to its frame in a feedlot, the average steer consumes fourteen pounds of grain plus two pounds of soy meal. In addition, for one calorie of beef protein available to the consumer, seventy-eight calories of fossil fuel are used to grow and transport this feed and to maintain the feedlot steer. Livestock raised in America consumes ten times the grain that we eat directly, and most of the grain we export also goes to feed livestock, not to feed people immediately. Of the 200 million tons of grain used each year to produce meat, about 145 million tons are fed to cattle. The remainder is consumed by hogs, turkeys, and chickens, all of which require some grain and use it more efficiently than cattle.[10] Compounding the absurdity of confinement feeding, the enormous quantities of manure generated in these small areas are a serious pollutant, whereas the same manure spread upon farmland would provide important nutrients and would protect the tilth of soils that artificial fertilizers now destroy. If confinement feeding were abandoned, half of America's grain crop would no longer be required to sustain this practice. Perhaps a quarter of our grain is raised on land so fragile, dry, or steep it should never have been plowed. Without demand from feedlots, this land could be returned to grass, which would support the raising of cattle on the farm. The productivity of good grain land could then be protected through crop rotations, including some years in pasture to support cattle. Fencerows, windbreaks, and erosion barriers could be reestablished on our farms to guard the soil and to provide shelter for wildlife. The health of our soils could be conserved for the generations to come who will surely need their capacity.

The abuse of livestock in order to obtain high production at low cost leads directly to oppression of people who work in the meat industry. The managers of food conglomerates that sponsor feedlots also force working conditions in slaughterhouses that brutalize workers to an extent not seen since Upton Sinclair wrote *The Jungle* at the dawn of this century. Workers who cut carcasses suspended from fast-moving chains must employ strong, repetitive movements at a rapid pace. They develop "carpal tunnel syndrome" which blocks nerves leading to their hands. Workers must force their hands to close around their knife handles in the morning, and pry them loose at the end of the day. Reporting to *The New York Times* about "Misery on the Meatpacking Line," William Glaberson wrote in the summer of 1987 from from Sioux Falls, South Dakota, where the packing plant is operated by Morrell, a division of the United Brands food conglomerate:

> The workers cut themselves. They cut each other. They wear out their insides doing repetitive-motion jobs. They are sliced and crushed by machines that were not even imagined when Sinclair published his book in 1906. . . .
> A meatpacking house has always been a grisly place to work. But after years of improvements, life in the packing house has been getting worse again. . . . Last year, one out of every two of the 2,500 workers here had serious job-related medical problems. . . . The meatpacking industry has topped the Bureau of Labor Statistics' most-hazardous-industries list for five years in a row. . . .
> Dick Brown, the head of the union's safety committee, said that the beef chain moves 84 percent faster than it did in 1979. In that time, he said, the Injury rate has increased by 76 percent.[11]

As work has been accelerated, real wages in the meatpacking industry have fallen by a third.

This type of "productivity" does not benefit Americans so much as it undermines our freedom. The abuse of animals, land, and people are interdependent problems with similar causes. The correction requires moral imperatives that embrace them all.

Cattle can play an important role in the environmental integrity and social usefulness of agriculture, though they should not be so numerous as they are now. Inefficient as they may be at digesting grain, cattle are splendidly efficient converters of grass into high quality proteins palatable to humans. Whether dairy or beef, cattle make a useful contribution to a diverse farm ecosystem in which some thin soils and sloping terrain are devoted to grasses while cropland is also renewed by periodic rotation to grass. America has extensive prairie grasslands where cattle are appropriate, including a great deal of fragile land that has been plowed unwisely and should be returned to permanent grass cover.

The western prairies can be managed better than is the case when the open range is fenced into sections of private property. Grasslands thrive in response to intense grazing and trampling, which breaks up soil and pounds stems to mulch, followed by long recovery periods for new growth to reach maturity. The prairie ecosystem exhibited this pattern when herds of bison, elk, deer, and other game roamed the plains. If cattle are grazed continually on fenced grasslands, they nibble their favorite grasses so frequently that these species cannot grow well, while other plants thrive because cattle find them less palatable. Grasslands would produce more meat for human consumption if herds were diverse, supplementing cattle with elk, bison, deer, and sheep. Each species favors certain grasses and, where they have room to range, several species make more efficient use of grasslands. In Africa, where there are twenty species of herbivorous mammals, research suggests that a mix of species can yield between two and eight times the flesh for human consumption as cattle alone. In the short-grass regions of the western high plains, meat harvests could increase if fences were removed and herds of cattle, sheep, bison, deer, and elk were allowed to range. "Your nation is at stake," says Allan Savory, who emigrated from Africa to encourage grassland management reform in the American west, "I think we're going to have to go back to the days of cowboy herding."[12]

Livestock have been bred for human use, and so responsible management requires continual human attention. Industrial livestock management has relied upon the segregation of species, confinement, and the poisoning of predators and parasites to increase human control while reducing the costs of labor, but the consequences have been ruinous. Responsible livestock management can reverse these trends and reintegrate livestock into productive agricultural ecosystems where animals and fowl may utilize resources efficiently, thrive with health, and return their wastes to fertilize the land. This will require more human supervision. We will need greater numbers of cowboys, cowgirls, shepherds, pig herders, and those who tend chickens, ducks, turkeys, and geese. If land ownership were shared more widely and the jobs were more satisfying, this increase in labor would be a social benefit outweighing the economic cost, for satisfying work is hard to find. The day-to-day tending of animals can be rewarding "entry-level" work: some of it is useful to train children in responsibility; some appears desirable to young men and women who enjoy the physical activity, beauty, privacy, and adventure that farm and ranch work can provide. Reorganizing the culture of animals and the economy of meat will put the jobs out where the pleasure is. If we had fewer adolescents boxing hamburgers at McDonalds and more of them herding cattle, elk, and bison on the Great Plains, we would raise a happier and more purposeful generation.

Rebuilding cattle culture will require ethical constraints upon the genetic manipulation of livestock species. Three criteria should be respected: the health of the ecosystem, the welfare of the species, and its usefulness to human society—not just the last of these. Regard for the health of the ecosystem requires extreme caution in genetic manipulation, so that forms of life are not released with which the environment cannot cope. The welfare of the species itself is something we know very little about, because Western culture has deliberately suppressed this question for three hundred years, pretending that animal species are objects rather than subjects for moral regard. Concern for animals' genetic welfare can open exciting questions requiring personal observation and scientific investigation. As a preliminary axiom, I suggest that the genetic welfare of domestic animals is enhanced when their sensory capacities and physical abilities are improved rather than diminished; and that wild members of the species, or wild ancestors to the species, may be considered normative to defining improvement. However, one need not feel compelled to develop capabilities in livestock that would frustrate the animals in their domestic setting within a healthy agricultural ecosystem. For example, while I would like cattle to be more alert so they might enjoy life more fully, it would frustrate cattle intended for life within the fences of an eastern farm to be bred as frisky and ranging as cattle upon the open prairie might become.

* * *

Consumers can influence American agriculture and the treatment of livestock. Prudent buyers should reduce their consumption of commercial beef, veal, pork, chicken, and turkey—whether in restaurants and fast-food outlets or from supermarkets—until the government prohibits the routine feeding of antibiotics to livestock and poultry and removes artificial sex hormones from the agricultural system. Those wishing to reduce stress upon the agricultural environment, and those worried about the risk of heart attack, will limit their consumption of commercial beef in particular. Patients receiving antibiotics should refrain from commercial meat and poultry altogether.

Substitutes can be found. Frances Moore Lappé, in her popular book *Diet for a Small Planet,* explains the principles of sound nutrition using little or no meat, and she provides appetizing recipes. Families owning freezers can find farmers in their region who will supply them with quarters of beef, as well as pork and poultry, raised without hormone additives or antibiotics.[13] When my customers buy an interest in a beef "on the hoof," I arrange slaughter, butchering, wrapping, and freezing to their specifications. Some farms deliver meat. Patrons who take the time to visit farms and understand how livestock are raised will feel most secure about their meat. The meat may cost as much as supermarket cuts, or even a little more, but it should have superior qualities. Indeed, when a family makes friends with a farm community, they will receive satisfaction as well as nourishment.

Alternatively, consumers may ask their supermarket to carry meat raised without hormones or antibiotics. If several consumers join together to form a "Clean-Meat Club" and generate publicity about their concern, they are likely to find a store that offers to supply meat to their specifications. When supplies of healthy meat are available, then customers can raise this issue at favorite restaurants. Few should worry, however, about occasional consumption of commercial meat, for overwrought concern can be as crippling as infectious bacteria.

I do not encourage the total renunciation of meat on moral grounds or for reasons of health. Human society does not need to withdraw from other animal species—that would be a moral loss—but we must improve the quality of our relationship. Moderate and responsible consumption of meat, poultry, and fish expresses humanity's place as one of the earth's predatory species within the web of life. If we are to be predators in a moral manner, we need to satisfy our needs without abusing other creatures. We need to build a culture within which all forms of life have an honored, secure place.

In 1988, Sweden enacted a remarkable new animal protection law. As summarized by the Humane Farming Association, this law specifies the following:

All cattle are to be allowed to graze.

All hens are to be let out of cramped battery cages.

Sows are no longer to be tethered. They are to have sufficient room to move. Separate bedding, feeding and voiding places are to be provided. Sows and piglets are to have access to straw and litter in their stalls.

Technology must be adapted to the animals, not the reverse. As a result, it must be possible to test new technology from the animal safety and protection viewpoint before it is put into practice.

All slaughtering must be done as humanely as possible.

The government is empowered to forbid the use of genetic engineering and growth hormones which may mutate domestic animals.

The drugging of animals for competitions and entertainment events is prohibited.

This Swedish statute also includes the fundamental principle that "domestic animals must have the right to a favorable environment in which their natural behavior is safeguarded."[14] When such a moral standard wins respect in other countries, animal rights and human needs may yet be reconciled within a culture of justice and compassion.

9. *Harvesting Justice*

Can environmentally responsible agriculture feed the world? Evidence indicates that the human community will feed itself adequately only when society learns to respect the earth's ecosystems while giving women and men throughout the world the opportunities that justice requires. New technologies can enhance our ability to raise food and to distribute it to one another, but technologies are less important than justice.

Before agriculture was developed, hunting and gathering left natural ecosystems unimpaired, for human populations were sparse and technologies were primitive. We have much to learn from preagricultural peoples whose relationships with nature were sensual, personal, and religious. Nevertheless, people in hunting and gathering cultures did not usually have to make conservation choices other than the decision to move if their presence in one place depleted the resources they depended upon. Although Native Americans in New England seriously damaged maple trees by slashing the sapwood to obtain sap for sugar, their behavior had little consequence because maples were so abundant relative to the human population. Today, however, when Africans gather firewood for cooking as Native Americans once did, the impact of large populations depletes the forests and may even alter the climate.

Agriculture may have developed after human populations in certain regions grew too large to sustain themselves by hunting and gathering alone. Earliest agriculture was often "slash and burn": fires were set to clear ground, and the resultant ashes fertilized the soil. When the soil was depleted following several crops, the tribe moved to clear other plots and allowed grasses and trees to invade the former cropland and reclaim it until the tribe returned many years in the future. Native Americans along the eastern seaboard practiced this type of agriculture when Europeans first encountered them. Indian agriculture changed the ecology of southern New England by clearing land, but because population pressure remained light the natural environment continued to be a healthy ecosystem producing abundant life.[1]

When settled agriculture developed in the ancient world and populations grew, human congestion upon agricultural landscapes stimulated three social phenomena that we may label as *oppression, technological innovation,* and at times *moral protest.* When resources become scarce the strong may overwhelm the weak to protect, and then to enlarge, their share. They may also look for new techniques to produce wealth. If this search is expensive it may be supported by taxes upon the poor, who are thus pushed deeper into poverty in order to finance the schemes of the powerful. In response to these pressures the poor, and others as well, may develop moral sensitivity and may attempt to correct or even to overturn the prevailing systems of oppression.

I presented the thesis in *Hope for the Land* that biblical history began at such a point. Old Testament ethics were addressed, first and foremost, to the crisis of agriculture. Moses and Joshua were revolutionary in that they called for the overthrow of oppressive agricultural systems and the formation of a covenant to redistribute land. Their proclamation was also environmentally innovative in that they proposed to resolve the tension between human needs and the health of the landscape by incorporating lands as full participants in the covenant community. All species upon these "holy" lands within the covenant, whether wildlife or domestic animals, had rights of access to sustenance, while livestock in particular was protected from abuse. To perpetuate justice among people and toward the earth, debts were to be forgiven regularly and the land was to be redistributed periodically so each generation might have access to means of subsistence and the landscape itself might be rescued from impersonal exploitation.

Thus the rudiments of social ethics and the rudiments of environmental ethics emerged at the same point in human history.

The rigorous requirements of these relationships were summarized in the Ten Commandments, injunctions that any person could remember and understand. The covenant that united a holy people with a holy land was liberating because it was not an arbitrary scheme that the powerful might manipulate, but a gift from the Lord who created the earth and its inhabitants. Nevertheless, justice always appears risky and sometimes foolhardy, so the Hebrews needed God's frequent reassurance that a just society could function and even prosper:

> If you listen to these laws and are careful to observe them, then the LORD your God . . . will bless the fruit of your body and the fruit of your land, your corn and new wine and oil, the offspring of your herds, and of your lambing flocks . . . (Deuteronomy 7: 12—14, NEB)

As Hebrew culture developed along the ambiguous paths of human history, it retained a burning hostility to oppression as well as a cautionary appraisal of technology, particularly when new techniques were introduced by the powerful as substitutes for recognized ethics. Although social ethics developed more vigorously than environmental ethics during the period covered by biblical history, Hebrews from Joshua to Jesus retained the conviction that the earth is the Lord's, while they regarded the landscape in all its lively complexity as a full partner within the covenant and as a hopeful beneficiary of God's promises of redemption.

This biblical perspective, now three thousand years old, is the agricultural innovation most relevant to the needs of the modern age. I believe that solutions to the problems of a hungry world lie less in technologies yet to be developed and applied, however helpful some of these may become, than in these principles of justice that are already embedded within our cultural tradition. Throughout the history of agriculture, the health of affected environments has depended upon the quality of human justice. Now that the world is so crowded with people, human injustice corrupts all aspects of the earth's ecosystem and threatens the survival of life itself.

* * *

The much-heralded "Green Revolution" in agriculture during the 1960s and 1970s provides evidence that, in the absence of regard for social justice and environmental integrity, new farming techniques cannot reduce world hunger significantly. At the dawning of this technological revolution, scientists supported by the Rockefeller Foundation developed in Mexico new varieties of wheat, rice, and corn that yielded far more grain upon each stalk and more tons per acre than the traditional varieties of these crops grown in underdeveloped countries. With the enthusiastic support of Western governments and the institutions that channel aid to poor countries, these "miracle seeds" were introduced during the 1960s in Mexico, India, Pakistan, Taiwan, the Philippines, Sri Lanka, and other countries where traditional practices of peasant agriculture remained common. Yields of corn, wheat, and rice increased dramatically.

This was no miracle, however, for cultivating these seeds required costly new farming techniques. Since the new varieties were not adapted to local climates and soil conditions, they required nourishment from artificial fertilizers along with the protection of mechanical cultivation. Most of these varieties needed heavy applications of pesticides to protect them from diseases, while many required more extensive irrigation than the native varieties they displaced. Throughout the world, small farms were consolidated into larger units that might employ the machinery and techniques required for the cultivation of these productive varieties.

The Mexican government, in support of the Green Revolution, directed agricultural investment to those regions where irrigation could be developed. The government encouraged the consolidation and mechanization of farms even though this deepened chronic unemployment. Farmers with small plots, and those in regions not suited to irrigation, were not extended technical assistance or marketing support. In consequence, millions of hapless peasants streamed to Mexico City or waded across the border into the United States. The owners of these consolidated, irrigated farms soon discovered that it was more profitable to grow cotton, coffee, and winter vegetables for export to nearby American markets than to grow grains for consumption in their own country. By 1975, Mexico became a net importer of food for the first time in the nation's history, and the balance of its food trade has deteriorated steadily since then. Meanwhile, 90 percent of those who remain in rural areas suffer malnourishment.[2]

The government of India, which had imported huge amounts of grain during the mid-1960s, implemented the Green Revolution eagerly. Indeed, food production in India rose 250 percent from 1950 to 1984, and the country even began to export rice and other commodities. The benefits have not reached the poorest people, however, particularly India's huge village population. Farm consolidation added to the numbers who cannot grow food for themselves, while mechanization raised rural unemployment. The proportion of India's population consuming less than the 2,250 calories per day required for minimum adult nutrition has remained near 40 percent for decades, not because food is unavailable, but because poor people cannot afford to buy it. The Worldwatch Institute reports that

> India . . . used the expanded production of the late sixties to offset its dependence on costly grain imports rather than to significantly increase food consumption among the poor. A drain on the country's treasury was plugged but there was little progress in raising per capita food consumption.[3]

Indeed, as Jack Doyle reports, the drain upon India's treasury has in fact grown rather than diminished:

> India's bill for fertilizer imports between the late 1960's and 1980 rose by more than 600 percent, an amount greater than what the country spent for food imports in the worst years of famine. And fertilizer wasn't the only Green Revolution ingredient . . . there were also tractors, combines, irrigation pumps, and pesticides.[4]

Indian environmentalists note that the livelihood of rural people has also been degraded by fertilizer and pesticide pollution of waters used for drinking, by the clearing of woods and fencerows that people depended upon for firewood, and by the reduced availability of fish from streams, milk from free-ranging cows, and other traditional foods. Sumanta Banerjee and Smitu Kothari charge that the cycle of development can become a vicious circle. Even though food production is rising faster than population growth,

> . . . malnutrition is increasing among the rural population of our country. The reason is that *food resources such as forest foods, food crops, fish, milk as well as fuel to cook food with, are being systematically diverted from the rural areas, where the bulk of our population lives, to the large urban centers or else exported* so as to earn foreign exchange with which to finance further development which must inevitably lead to the further diversion of food resources from where they are most required.[5]

In neighboring Bangladesh, where 70 percent of the people are chronically anemic, the government has also adopted a policy of exporting rice in order to earn foreign exchange for development schemes and to pay interest in international debts.

Modern agricultural development has been imposed upon some rural societies with unusual brutality. In Brazil, military leaders deposed the elected government in 1964 and embarked upon a program of development that achieved increases in the "gross national product" so great that the Western world hailed them as an economic miracle. All possible means were used to attract huge foreign investments to be repaid with the export of industrial and agricultural commodities. Hundreds of thousands of peasant families were forcibly evicted from their subsistence farms to open the way for new sugar, cocoa, soybean, and coffee plantations to serve the export market. Many people fled to city slums, while others worked on the new plantations for near-starvation wages. The Catholic bishops in northeastern Brazil reported that by 1983 the per capita income of the bottom 45 percent had fallen to

> 2,550 cruzeiros a month, or 25 dollars a year, lower than any per capita income in any country on earth, and below the level of absolute poverty. There are constant reports of laborers dying of starvation and children of six months fed only on sugar and water.[6]

By 1986, when export commodity prices had plunged, the "economic miracle" had collapsed, the generals had resigned, and creditor nations were pressing Brazil to maintain interest payments on its huge foreign debt, the Brazilian economist Marcos Arruda cried out, "The masses die of starvation. There was never a period in Brazilian history as bad as this."[7]

In the Philippines during this same period, the Marcos regime supported the forceable consolidation of peasant landholdings into large estates financed by foreign capital, managed by political cronies, and protected by private armies. By the mid-1970s, 45 percent of Philippine farming acreage was devoted to export crops—sugar, coconuts, bananas, rubber, pineapple, coffee, and cocoa—while the caloric intake of the average Filipino had declined almost to the anemic norm of Bangladesh.[8]

The United States Department of Agriculture has calculated that, whereas in 1950 world food supplies were slightly less than the amount requried to provide the minimum recommended caloric intake for every person on earth, by the late 1970s—despite population growth—the world was producing enough food to exceed minimum requirements by 8 percent. Nevertheless, the USDA concluded, "The number of malnourished people worldwide quite likely increased from 100 to 200 million in 1950 to more than 500 million at the end of the 1970's." Although agricultural yields had increased greatly during these three decades, the effective ability of humanity to feed itself had declined sharply. More people lacked the means to buy food or land to grow their own. The USDA also noted that American grain exports help to reduce the capacity of Third World countries to feed themselves.[9]

Although we imagine that North America helps to feed the poor in the Third World, most food exchanged on world markets is traded among developed countries that can pay for it. The truth is that poor countries send more food to us than we ship to them. Poor nations import more grain than they export, but they export far more protein than they import. Much of the meat raised in the Third World is raised for export, and much of the fish caught by fishermen in the Third World is sold to prosperous countries. Moroccans, for example, developed a cheap canned fish intended for Egypt and other Middle East markets, but they found that cat food merchants from the United States would pay more for it. American pet owners can easily outbid the poor people of Cairo. The huge Peruvian anchovy catch, one of the world's major protein resources, is sold principally to western Europe and the United States to be used for livestock feed. Soybeans grown in Indonesia do not contribute protein to the local diet but are shipped to Europe to fatten pigs and poultry. After Central American rain forests are cleared to graze cattle, the beef is sold to fast-food chains in the United States. Reviewing these facts, George Kent of the Environment and Policy Institute in Hawaii concluded, "Surely, one good way in which the United States could help poor countries to increase their food self-sufficiency would be to increase its own food self-sufficiency—that is, by reducing the amount of food it imports."[10]

Grains sold cheaply to poor countries, and free food sent in response to starvation crises, can disrupt local economies and further damage Third World agriculture. Regional farmers may be forced to abandon their land if they cannot compete with subsidized grain shipments from abroad. After urban populations in Third World countries develop a taste for wheat products, they may scorn traditional sorghum or millet that can be grown in their own regions. Indeed, U.S. government officials have promoted our "Food for Peace" program for this very reason: Third World recipients are expected to develop a taste for American products and to move "from aid to trade." Even in times of disaster, food aid has not been coupled with forgiveness of debts. British analyst Jon Bennett has noted that

> in 1985, an incredible 2,500 million [£ Sterling, about $4 billion] was raised by voluntary and government agencies for famine victims in Africa. Yet, in the same year the famine-striken countries paid back to Northern banks, governments and financial institutions *double* that amount in debt repayments.[11]

Our food donations may keep some starving people alive, but our policies do not help them to provide for themselves. We may show mercy at times of crisis, but we avoid the truth of why people starve. Susan George, the most clearheaded analyst of world hunger, puts it this way: "charity, however necessary it may be to alleviate distress, is not the relevant virtue for fighting hunger. That virtue is justice."[12]

* * *

Western observers often attribute the spread of hunger in Latin America, Africa, and southeast Asia to the high birth rates in these regions. The relationship between birth rate and malnutrition is, however, more truly the reverse of what we commonly suppose. A high birth rate is not the principal cause of hunger; rather, economic and social deprivation, which lead to malnutrition, are the principal causes of high birth rates. Modern methods of contraception, while an important factor, exert less influence upon population trends than does economic security. In countries where economic and social security for the poor are improving, the birth rate tends to decline. In countries where large populations are impoverished, the birth rate will remain high. Developing countries with extensive social welfare systems, such as China, or rising per capita income, such as South Korea, have been able to reduce the rate of population growth significantly; whereas nations with declining per capita incomes or deteriorating social structures, such as Nigeria, Philippines, and Brazil, retain high rates of population growth.[13]

Susan George explains why birth rates remain high among poor families in societies that lack economic opportunity and social welfare systems. In industrial countries where parents support their children through long years of education and do not expect their support in return, children are a financial liability. In underdeveloped countries, however, children may be the only asset that poor parents possess:

> Another baby for a poor family means an extra mouth to feed—a very marginal difference. But by the time that child is four of five years old, it will make important contributions to the whole family—fetching water from the distant well, taking meals to father and brothers in the field, feeding animals. Later the child will help with more complicated tasks which would all devolve upon the mother of the household if she could not count on her children. Women may have to suffer the biological servitude of pregnancies, but at least they can be spared—in poor, "overpopulous" families—the much longer and far more burdensome servitude of carrying out all the household and many of the farming tasks without even simple

conveniences like running water and without any help whatsoever. Most Third World mothers have only a 50/50 chance of seeing their children live beyond the age of five. Once we realize that children are an economic *necessity* for the poor, then we can understand that poor families will have to plan their births every bit as carefully as couples in Westchester or West Harrow—and allow for the predictable mortality rate.

Would you think quite the same way about children if you lived in a country which had never heard of old-age pensions, social security, health insurance and the like? . . . The poor age quickly. One of the family's sons may turn out to be bright and will get some education followed by a paid job in the city. He will help to support his parents, but they know they will be able to count on all their children, educated or not. How else are the poor to survive when they are too old or exhausted to work?

George concludes from population studies that if a nation wants to reduce its birth rate, "the best way to go about it is not to distribute condoms and IUDs and hope for the best, but to give people effective land reform and more income."[14]

After land reform and opportunities to earn income, two other factors have proved influential in lowering birth rates: one is a birth control program that achieves broad social support; the second is improvement of the social status of women. China's birth control program, the world's most effective, was built upon institutions of social security as well as modestly rising income expectations, and this rigorous program has apparently won social approval. India's extensive birth control effort has been ineffective because the poorest people have not been helped economically and because many perceive the program as an arbitrary imposition by authorities. Thailand achieved significant population control even prior to economic development, according to the Worldwatch Institute, through a well developed public health program that supported social and economic gains for women.[15]

Enough food is grown each year to provide every person on earth with an adequate diet. Despite continuing population growth, there is little doubt that food will be produced sufficient to meet human needs through the remaining decade of this century. That does not mean, however, that adequate nutrition is at hand, awaiting only improvements in the transportation and distribution of food. Nourishment for the masses will become increasingly difficult to achieve. Hunger and malnutrition are chronic conditions for half a billion people, or perhaps one billion people, depending upon whether one accepts the definition developed by the United Nations Food and Agriculture Organization or the one proposed by the World Bank. One person in ten on the planet today—or perhaps one in five—is hungry and malnourished most of the time. From available estimates Susan George has calculated that "the number of people who die as a direct result of malnutrition is equivalent to dropping a Hiroshima bomb *every three days*."[16] There are heavy concentrations of hungry people in Central and South America, in Africa, and throughout Southeast Asia, with smaller pockets elsewhere.

Overcoming world hunger will require these political actions, and perhaps others as well:

• Land reform throughout the world to give the rural poor, the largest body of the hungry, access to means of subsistence.

• Rebuilding cultures of food production based on families, small collectives, and communities—as appropriate to the needs and cultures of people in different regions—which combine traditional agricultural wisdom with modern ecological understanding and appropriate technologies.

• Curtailment of most Third World cash cropping for export markets so that croplands, rangelands, forests, rivers, and oceans can be utilized for the benefit of the hungry people nearby.

• The forgiveness of international debts by creditor nations, or their repudiation by debtor nations.

• Radical reduction of the use of fed-grains and protein products to fatten beef, pork, and poultry in developed countries, so that these commodities may be available to people, directly and inexpensively.

• New investment in social welfare on a scale equivalent to present military expenditures, so that employment, education, health care, and retirement assistance may be available to the poor throughout the world. This would, in time, reduce population growth.

These measures address the crisis of human hunger in the near term. To resolve the crises created by the human abuse of the natural environment, which weakens the capacity of the earth to sustain life over the long term, additional measures are required:

• In temperate regions, a significant portion of the land now used to grow crops must be returned to pasture and woodlands to protect soils from depletion; and the use of artificial fertilizers and pesticides must be greatly reduced in order to curtail the poisoning of lands and waters.

• In arid regions, livestock populations must be reduced and reforestation undertaken to protect lands and climate and therefore slow the spread of deserts.

• In tropical regions, the wholesale clearing of rain forests must cease. Rain forests should not be clearcut for timber, pasturage, or tillage, because they are essential to the earth's ecosystem. There are, however, ways to harvest sustenance from rain forests without cutting the trees.

• Developed countries must reduce their use of fossil fuels by at least half, substituting engineering efficiency and solar technologies, to slow the dangerous "greenhouse" warming of the earth's atmosphere. Then the reductions should proceed further.

• Developed countries must also cut their use of metals, minerals, and wood products in half through better design and more efficient productive processes, by making quality products that remain in service longer, and by recycling used materials.

• Developed countries must curtail the creation of wastes and their disposal in the air, in waters, or on land, through efficient design, operation, and recycling.

• The world community must stabilize human population; furthermore, depending upon the efficacy of other measures, we may need to reduce human population in order to retain healthy environments for ourselves and the other species who share this planet with us.

• The world must keep the peace. Nuclear war could reverse all other gains in a few hours.

Further, while we halt the destruction of fundamental environmental systems, we need to protect our long-range ability to meet human needs with the help of new forms of agriculture:

• More intensive cropping can support more life, including more human life, on the land. When of our best farmland is devoted to a single crop like corn or wheat, it is underutilized.

• Tree farming has enormous potential for reclaiming arid regions and marginal lands while producing livestock feed and human provisions.

• Perennial grain ecosystems, the subject of Wes Jackson's research, may increase the productivity of fragile grasslands.

• New grazing systems that remove fences and supplement cattle with a diversity of ungulate species can increase meat harvests in semi-arid regions while protecting grasslands.

• Aquaculture, the intensive cultivation of fish and other acquatic life in ponds, lakes, streams, and estuaries, as well as more sophisticated use of ocean resources, can produce enormous quantities of high-quality protein and other nutrients for human consumption.

• Rain forests have supported small populations of hunters and gatherers, but they are the richest of all terrestrial environments, where the life is most abundant above the ground rather than close to the soil. As we learn to understand these systems we can draw more resources from them without damaging their remarkable vitality.

Difficult as they appear, none of the twenty measures listed here is beyond human competency. Taken together, they would assure the wholesome continuance of human life in association with healthy ecosystems in all parts of the world.

* * *

The changes required of humanity exceed reform. Indeed, they reach further than the type of changes generally implied by the word "revolution." They involve alterations in human relationships with nature as profound as any since agriculture began. To resolve the crises of the modern world, humanity must modify agriculture to embrace not only the production of food and fiber but also the sustenance of natural systems. Agriculture must evolve from the culture of provisioning human society to become the culture of provisioning the whole of earthly life. Social justice must embrace ecological justice so that we recognize all species and systems of life as citizens of an interdependent commonwealth, entitled to live and to flower alongside us.

If we continue to oppress our human brothers and sisters and to exploit natural systems as we have been doing, we will surely bring the house of life—the natural economy—down upon our own heads. Given that alternative, the reforms listed in this chapter should not be considered sacrifices but adventures. The changes that we and our children need to accomplish are awesome, but each reform can be rewarding in itself and can support our enthusiasm for building a healthy world.

We are called to express the image of God and to realize the garden of Eden. Eden was not simply a place for hunting and gathering, for God charged the first family to till the ground and shepherd the livestock. Neither was Eden merely an agricultural environment for human consumption, for God commanded the first family to attend to the needs of all species—even those like the Tree of Life whose fruit they were forbidden to consume. Eden was an ideal image of the covenant community that the Hebrews were struggling to establish as an alternative to earthly oppression, a community where diverse species would nurture and respect one another even as they fed upon each other in the ecosystem of life.

For three thousand years the God who fashioned the earth and loves it has called men and women to repent of callous exploitation and to return to moral relationships with creation. Only in our generation, however, has it become an inescapable fact that the survival of the human species depends upon our incorporating all of life, and the systems that support life, within our moral regard. Fortunately, human society is acquiring knowledge of the natural forces upon this earth—the atmosphere, oceans and estuaries, soils and climates, biological life, and ecological interacions—sufficient to inspire hope that we might, with fresh determination, learn how to protect the earth.

God has placed us, it appears, at the most profound crisis of the earth's long history, and God asks us to make our choices with eyes open to the consequences. Fears of hardship tempt us to intensify our exploitation of nature in order to protect a privileged portion of humanity, who must then raise walls and alarms against the poor of the earth. The beauty of nature, on the other hand, calls us to embrace all of life and to risk the reforms necessary to nurture our earthly companions. Jesus' words are more apt today than ever before: "Those who would save their life will lose it, but those who lose their life for my sake will find it" (Matthew 16:25, ILL). We must take the risk.

Part III.

Civil Rights

Liberating changes can spring from simple ideas that make sense to people. New ideas take hold most effectively when they bridge creatively from traditional wisdom to address the contemporary realities that society finds disorienting. When people accept new ideas that clarify their social outlook and give fresh self-understanding, human energies once blocked by confusion or despair are released in creative expression. This series has considered how, in biblical history, God offered ten commandments to the bewildered refugees from Egyptian oppression. These clear standards made such good sense that they freed the popular imagination from subservience to capricious authorities. From these revolutionary insights a new people formed who liberated a land from oppression as well.

To help Americans choose revolution, Thomas Jefferson built new insights upon classic political theory:

> We hold these truths to be self-evident, that all men are created equal, that they are endowed by their Creator with certain unalienable Rights, that among these are Life, Liberty and the pursuit of Happiness. That to secure these rights, Governments are instituted among Men, deriving their just powers from the consent of the governed, That whenever any Form of Government becomes destructive of these ends, it is the Right of the People to alter or to abolish it, and to institute new Government, laying its foundation on such principles and organizing its powers in such form, as to them shall seem most likely to effect their Safety and Happiness.[1]

In this spirit I propose three concepts intended to win for nature both respect and protection within our culture, with the hope that they may inspire the release of creative energies to reclaim our landscape from its present degradation.

The first concept is a human right of access to nature. Behind Jefferson's affirmation of "Life, Liberty and the pursuit of Happiness" he held a conviction, as we have seen, that people share a right to the land needed for subsistence. However, access to nature in the broadest sense—frequent contact with plants and animals, as well as personal experience of sun, winds, and flowing waters—was so much a part of American experience in Jefferson's day that its infringement would have been unimaginable. Today human technologies and concentrated urban populations separate a growing portion of humanity from these realities. Alongside Jefferson's fundamental triad we need a fourth affirmation—the right of access to nature—in order to guard the integrity of human personality and the vitality of human culture.

The second concept is land reform. During the first century of our republic, the frontier served adequately to substitute for periodic redistribution of land, which justice would otherwise require. Now after a century without a frontier, most Americans are separated from their land while the landscape itself is dying. Much of our countryside is bereft of human life as well as of the vital ecosystems of plants and animals. Meanwhile a growing underclass of men, women, and children are held prisoner within urban social structures that deny them opportunities to live decently and work productively. We need land reform to reopen the frontier not upon some distant territory but within the familiar and beloved lands of our common heritage.

The third concept is a constitutional amendment to confer civil rights upon all the species, systems of life, and distinctive natural features that—along with humanity—comprise America. A mature republic should no longer be content to colonize the great majority of that which lives within its borders and rule them without voice. At the adoption of the Constitution, political participation was reserved to white male landowners, but over two hundred years the excluded have cried for justice and have won the extension of civil rights to most men and women. Now is the time to expand our republic to enfold our lands and waters—the life upon, above, and within them—and the natural forces that sustain life, within the institutions of society. It is time to confer upon each of these the rights that are appropriate to their sustenance.

10. *A Natural Right*

The genius of the human species is our ability to create culture. Other species may exhibit a specific sensory acuity that we lack, such as an eagle's sight or a deer's sense of smell. Some domesticated species are so alert to human emotions that they may sense our feelings before we become conscious of them: a horse grasps its rider's mood and may rely upon the rider's confidence. Bees and ants achieve social efficiency beyond the aspirations of bureaucrats or factory managers. If we think that only humans are conscious and intelligent, or imagine that human awareness and intelligence are always superior in every respect to those of other species, we reveal our ignorance and perhaps our anthropocentric arrogance.[1] Still, no other species exhibits the complexity, diversity, and adaptability of human culture.

In this series the word *culture* has carried the broadest sense my dictionary allows: "The totality of socially transmitted behavior patterns, arts, beliefs, institutions, and all other products of human work and thought."[2] We are animals that require cultural support to realize our humanity, for both the tools in our hands and the language in our minds have been shaped by a long cultural history. Like bees separated from the hive, we would be lost without the support of society. If the hermit, the castaway, or the lonely explorer survives, it is because they carry cultural wisdom within them or meet another society that embraces them. You or I can think about what is "good" because, with God's help, human culture has developed some capacity for moral reflection, however uncertainly that capacity is applied.

Human culture is a beautiful addition to life on this planet even though the products of human work threaten, in our age, to destroy the natural world. We may distinguish culture from other natural life for purposes of analysis, but nature in its broadest sense includes the human cultures that have evolved within it. Humanity has often contributed complexity, diversity, awareness, and reflective capability to the surrounding ecosystem. The relation of culture to nature can be harmonious and, when it is, culture should not be regarded as alien to nature but as part of the flowering of earthly life.

This series has highlighted the ways that the human perception of beauty, in particular, contributes to the quality of natural life. To see the beauty of a tiny flower or a Grand Canyon, to take them fully into our consciousness and to celebrate them, adds qualities to the particular plant and to the great landscape that enrich their ecological relationships. The Bible teaches that when we honor the beauty of natural lives and praise God for them, while they also praise the Lord with us, then God's enthusiastic creativity is completed among us all. This perspective provided the Hebrews with an antidote to religious anxiety over powerful, capricious natural forces, an anxiety so common in agricultural communities.

Now we must address the modern-day anxiety not over the strength of natural forces, but over the the vulnerability of nature to the destructive impact of human society. So acute is this concern that some environmental philosophers regard wild nature as good while considering human culture to be evil because it distorts natural life and now places it in jeopardy. Both nature and culture are profoundly good, however, even though they may exhibit unhealthy, corrupted development. Each needs the other to know itself fully. Human culture needs nature—of that there can be no argument— but nature also needs human culture to grasp its own beauty.

We are fortunate that John Muir, who set the tone for the modern environmental movement a century ago, appreciated this truth. His strategy for environmental protection was twofold: he drew people into wild areas so they might fall in love with the beauty there, and then he harnessed that affection to secure political consideration for these landscapes. Without the protection of those who love her, nature would remain vulnerable to the depredations of the greedy, the thoughtless, and the desperate.

Muir's strategy grew from his spiritual experience. When he was wounded by human society his life was revived by the ministry of wildflowers, mountains, and canyons; nature even restored the communion with God that had been inhibited by the severity of his religious upbringing. In response, he gave nature his keen perception and loving enthusiasm. These, in turn, led to his geological insights and advocacy of wilderness protection. He achieved such intimacy with Yosemite that he became part of its ecosystem and expanded its consciousness, as the first representative of Western culture to grace this landscape with such understanding and appreciation. When John Muir celebrated its beauty, Yosemite's very being, its experience of itself, was expanded.

Muir appreciated the contribution of wilderness to human welfare, and—at the dawn of America's industrial development—he fretted about the harried pace of factories and mechanized farms that separated people from this natural beauty. He believed that men and women, to remain healthy, need habits that keep them in touch with nature, and that society must institutionalize these habits just as it provides systems for sanitation and public education. While walking through the Sierra mountains in 1875 to observe the giant Sequoia trees, Muir wrote the following lines in his notebook:

> Pausing in my studies this peaceful afternoon, I chance to think of the thousands needing rest—the weary in soul and limb, toilers in town and plain, dying for want of what these grand old woods can give. And though I suppose it may be of no avail, I yet shout: 'Ho, come to the Sierra forests. The King is waiting for you—King Sequoia!' There is health and life in his very looks, in the air he breathes, in the birds he keeps, in the squirrels that gambol in his arms, and the flowers that blow and the streams that flow at his feet. . . .
>
> Our crude civilization engenders a multitude of wants, and lawgivers are ever at their wits' end devising. The hall and the theater and the church have been invented, and compulsory education. Why not add compulsory recreation? . . . Our forefathers forged chains of duty and habit, which bind us nothwithstanding our boasted freedom, and we ourselves in desperation add link to link, groaning and making medicinal laws for relief. Yet few think of pure rest or of the

healing power of Nature. How hard to pull or shake people out of town![3]

Freedom cannot be forced. Yet Muir wrestled with a problem that requires attention: how modern men and women may continue to experience nature.

Hidden behind the dense constructions of human culture, natural environments have disappeared from the daily lives of most people in western societies and from the lives of urban populations in developing countries as well. If we encounter natural materials in our work, they have probably been shaped to fit the requirements of machines. The fruits and vegetables we buy have been bred to accommodate the stresses of modern marketing and come to us packaged or prepared. The wood trim in our homes, the lawn outside, and the dog on the front porch are mere decorative remnants of natural life stretched upon a framework of human construction. Even when people take the vacation that John Muir recommended and visit one of the parks that he helped to establish, most do not walk far from their automobiles. They do not smell much; hear, taste, or touch much. They engage the landscape only with their eyes, and even this contact is so tentative that they cannot trust themselves to remember the experience unless they capture the scene on photographic film for subsquent verification. The experience of nature recedes as technology surrounds us.

Other experiences also fade as we are enveloped by the artifacts of human society. During the 1960s, at the height of modern enthusiasm for technological progress, certain liberal Christian theologians revived from Nietzsche's madman the cry "God is dead!" and proposed it as a motto to convey the position of modern sanity. David Edwards of Cambridge University, for example, wrote that as God recedes from human experience "millions have felt some of the excitement of the liberation; they have felt godlike." He ascribed the stubborn persistence of religion in the United States to "a failure of nerve amid the dramatically revolutionary early stages of the birth of a new technological civilization."[4] In America, *Time* magazine led the chorus reporting God's departure—with the secret hope, I suspect, that mass media and advertisers might take God's place to arbitrate and merchandise moral values. However, others who heard the cry "God is dead!" realized that people infected with this anthropocentric enthusiasm had lost their bearings. During this same decade some people, sobered by the warning issued in Rachel Carson's *Silent Spring,* discovered a related truth—that the "new technological civilization" was killing nature as well as God.

Although there has been little formal investigation of the psychological cost of physical separation from natural life, some of the consequences are obvious. Noise on the streets and in workplaces, crowds of people who must be ignored, and persistent visual and auditory assaults by commercial advertisers, all produce sensory overload. In order to survive we learn to hear less, to see less, to smell less, and—in consequence—to feel less. We experience tension, however, as we continually screen sensory stimuli simply to focus upon the few we must absorb. We may let off some of this tension on a vacation to the mountains or the beach, or revel in stolen moments of "peace and quiet." The remedy, however, does not rebuild our sensory acuity. An old Bushman in southern Africa who led me through tall grass where lions might lurk, had sight and hearing far more keen than mine because he had stretched them to encompass an environment that was often quiet and motionless. His liveli-hood—indeed, his life and mine—depended upon noticing each footprint in the dust, hearing any distant sound, and seeing every movement. By contrast, my efforts to learn farming skills have been slowed by my limited ability to observe subtle changes in the living community around me. I fear that as modern culture overloads our senses and dims our acuity, the primary skills of the human species deteriorate.

Withdrawal from nature also deprives us of an important emotional resource and makes us more vulnerable to the anonymity of modern society. Emotional health is supported by the variety of those from whom we draw sustenance and to whom we express our feelings; both the depth of these relationships and their diversity are important. These "significant others" have included, traditionally, family members from several generations, friends upon whom we learned to depend, the God we worshiped, and the familiar land-scapes, animals, and plants among which we lived and worked. We came to care deeply about all of these. Under the best circumstances the human personality flourishes in response to a variety of intimacies: sexual bonding and release; relations with parents, children, and friends; communion with God; and expressive contact with animals, plants, and landscapes. Each type of relationship expands the range of our emotional expression and adds to our sense of personal identity.

Modern society induces us to reduce the number of deep personal bonds and to replace them with functional contacts, to enjoy fewer stable relationships and more transitory ones, and to compensate for lost contact with nature through increased consumption of goods. Although functional contacts and short–term friendships are useful, these changing patterns reduce our opportunities for emotional interraction. Lonely, we may eat well and yet feel starved within.

The earlier books in this series emphasized the importance of sexual energy for human health and encouraged sexual release within intimate relationships formed with knowledge and respect, mutual desire and commitment. Here I would note that in urban culture, where it is more difficult to sustain the traditional range of satisfying associations, it is tempting to try to meet all of our emotional needs through sexual expression. Sex may appear to be the only "natural" thing left. Some people are even tempted to cultivate new relationships through genital contact, and so they become extremely vulnerable to disappointment, disease, and abuse. Experience with nature is not a substitute for human associations. Nevertheless, when we reach out to form a bond with a garden, a riding horse, a fishing lake, or a favorite park, we form relationships that support emotional health. Intimate contact with nature generates vitality while extending the range of our sensory awareness and our emotional expression.

Isolation from nature also threatens grave political consequences. The most important function of human culture has been to connect individuals to the realities beyond the human—principally the natural world and God—with which society must interract in order to survive. Cultures grow when people learn from their experience, deepen their understanding of the lives beyond human life, criticize accepted techniques for interracting with the world and develop new ones. However, now that people are losing touch with the life beyond human culture, they are losing experience that can ground them in reality and provide perspective on the social order.

Those who believe that humanity can manipulate the world without consequence have already lost touch with reality, while those who trust technology to solve all problems have equally abandoned realism. People can lose the capacity to imagine alternatives when human society overwhelms. In the absence of refreshing experiences, we may forget the justice that the Lord has taught us and also lose our sense of the beauty of natural life. We become vulnerable to such reassuring cultural fantasies as the exhibits at Walt Disney's Epcot Center, where the rides carry us into futures benignly controlled by corporate technologies, while we are soothed by surprisingly lifelike animal robots and human attendants programmed to mimic personal warmth. To protect our sanity and our society, people need real experiences of life beyond human culture.

Thomas Jefferson believed that democracy required a large class of yeomen whose political participation would be undergirded by ownership of land or the tools of their craft so they would not be intimidated by the powerful. Today, to protect us from similar manipulation, a democratic people must maintain contact with living realities beyond human culture. I do not imagine that humans can experience any reality without reference to their culture, for even our sense of God and our sense of nature are conditioned by the language, images, and expectations to which we have been educated. Nevertheless, since God and nature have life independent of human culture, our personal interractions with them can modify cultural training. Those who stay in touch with God and with nature acquire experiences that help them to evaluate their culture critically. People who do not maintain such relationships are vulnerable to manipulation by those who direct cultural institutions. In America, powerful voices flood the media with attractive inducements to consume more and demand less, and to trust experts with the welfare of the world. Freedom, however, requires that people stay in touch with reality for themselves and delegate that duty to no other authority.

The mallability of the human species that has undergirded our cultural development now gives cause for alarm. People gradually accommodate themselves to crowding, to polluted air and water, to adulterated food, to the loss of God, to the absence of nature, to oppression, and to poverty—particularly if they are deprived of awareness that there may be alternatives. Those who have bred tomatoes to fit in their boxes and who now breed pigs to fit in their pens may soon wish to breed people to fit in their factories and their slums. It can happen to our children's children unless we protect their understanding of justice and their feeling for life by assuring them opportunities to experience nature and to know the Lord.

* * *

We must defend our humanity by claiming rights to relationships that were once available to the vast majority of men, women, and children, but that can no longer be taken for granted. *Every person has a right of access to nature and must be assured opportunities to exercise that right.*

This right of access is inherent in the "unalienable Rights" of "Life, Liberty and the pursuit of Happiness" proclaimed by the Declaration of Independence. It derives from God's command that we "cultivate and take care of" the earth (Genesis 2:15, JB); from our social vulnerability to nature; and from our psychological character and needs. The implications of this right for the modern world—like those of any other fundamental insight—will become clearer as society acknowledges the principle and seeks to honor it. A right of access suggests these further rights: to breathe air and drink water that do no harm; to have untainted food available at affordable prices, or land on which to grow it; to tend a small garden and care for a pet, if one chooses, in any residential setting; to have parks or other beautiful landscapes accessible on one's day of rest from work; and to experience wild landscapes and seascapes during special vacations, with social support adequate to overcome fear of the unknown and to encourage recognition of nature.

City life does not have to frustrate these opportunities. Indeed, protecting both wild and cultivated landscapes for human enjoyment requires that most people cluster in towns and cities, and yet that these not overburden the surrounding countryside. Ever since Frederick Law Olmsted designed Central Park in New York and Golden Gate Park in San Francisco more than a century ago, the best city planning has attempted to provide interractions with nature. Olmstead sensed that "we grow more and more artificial day by day," and he thought that the willingness of civic leaders to support park development expressed a "self–preserving instinct of civilization." Parks, he believed, served as an antidote to "vital exhaustion," "nervous irritation," and "constitutional depression."[5] In *Design with Nature,* a brilliant modern study of the urban environmen, Ian McHarg explains: "It is not a choice of either the city or the countryside: both are essential, but today it is nature, beleaguered in the country, too scarce in the city which has become precious." Implementing the human right to experience nature will lead not to the abandonment of cities but to their humanization through better provision for trees and animals, plants and parks, sun and clean air. McHarg explains the importance of nature to humanity this way:

> Clearly the problem of man and nature is not one of providing a decorative background for the human play, or even ameliorating the grim city: it is the necessity of sustaining nature as source of life, milieu, teacher, sanctum, challenge and, most of all, of rediscovering nature's corollary of the unknown in the self, the source of meaning.[6]

Furthermore, urban men, women, and children need convenient access to the outlying countryside. This has implications for rural residents. Respect for the right of all people experience nature must temper landholders' sense of private ownership. Society, in turn, owes farmers and other landholders respect, not simply for their production of commodities, but equally for their conservation of the landscape to the benefit of all. In addition to a fair price for their crops, farmers need compensation for otherwise "uneconomic" efforts to protect and enhance the health and beauty of the land. Conservation and production must be placed upon an equal footing. "Set aside payments" for fragile lands removed from tillage, as well as other conservation subsidies, play a role in the farm economy now, but they remain a patchwork without a coherent design. Government payments should purchase sound environmental protection and distinct public benefits.

The public should have access to private lands in ways that do not damage productivity or destroy the privacy and tranquillity of rural life. In many parts of Europe, traditions of access accommodate both the public interest and the needs of private landholders. I enjoy walking across picturesque farms in southern England on historic public footpaths with their convenient gates to cross the fences and stiles to climb over the walls. The farms themselves are obviously maintained with aesthetic sensibility as well as practical intent. They are a tribute to the community's pride in natural beauty and its accommodation of visitors' interests. McHarg explains that these English landscapes, among the most beautiful pastoral scenes in the world, are the result of careful and deliberate reclamation from a previous age of rampant timbering, overgrazing, and environmental degradation:

> Starting with a denuded landscape, a backward agriculture and a medieval pattern of attenuated land holdings, this landscape tradition rehabilitated an entire countryside, allowing that fair image to persist today. [Eighteenth-century landscape architects] used native plant materials to create communities that so well reflected natural processes that their creations have endured and are self–perpetuating.
> The functional objective was a productive, working landscape. Hilltops and hillsides were planted to forest, great meadows occupied the valley bottoms in which lakes were constructed and streams meandered. The product of this new landscape was the extensive meadow supporting cattle, horses and sheep. The forests provided valuable timber and supported game, while free–standing copses in the meadows provided shade and shelter for grazing animals.... The ruling principle was "nature is the gardener's best designer"—an empirical ecology.[7]

English reclamation might inspire Americans who wish to reclaim our landscape from the devastation inflicted by industrial agriculture and the rampant clearcutting of forests.

Public lands would also benefit if human rights of access to nature were given greater recognition. Our National Forests are being depleted by excessive timber cutting, which drives timber prices so low that taxpayers must subsidize the sales. Most of our vast public grasslands are leased to support private herds of beef cattle so large that they degrade the ecosystems even though they produce less meat than would buffalo, antelope, deer, and other wild species were they given free range on the same lands. Proper recognition of human rights would give greater weight to hunting, fishing, and recreation—along with the the protection of aesthetic and healthy ecosystems—in the management of these lands.

Second only to protecting their vitality, the social purpose of public lands should be to provide experiences with nature that expand human awareness. Harvesting resources should be held to third priority. Public lands can provide not only relief from workday pressures but also opportunities to employ and attune senses dulled by the urban cacophony. A century ago Olmsted theorized that natural scenery opens the human spirit to contemplation by inter-rupting the anxious, practical, and self–absorbed thoughts which otherwise occupy our minds.

> In the interest which natural scenery inspires . . . the attention is aroused and the mind occupied without purpose, without a continu-ation of the common process of relating the present action, thought or perception to some future end. There is little else that has this quality so purely.[8]

In his book on the role of public lands, *Mountains Without Handrails,* Joseph Sax suggests that hunting and fishing become deeply satis-fying when they stretch one's senses beyond their accustomed limits. As he notes,

> neither the setting nor the activity *in itself* seems to be decisive; rather, it is the presence of something capable of engaging, rather than merely occupying, the individual—a stimulus for intensity of experience, for the full involvement of the senses and the mind.[9]

Aldo Leopold suggests that hunting challenges the individual's ethical capacities and provides an antidote to the group pressures common in urban life. The hunter is informed both by laws and by informal codes of sportsmanship, but he or she is often alone when decisions must be made:

> A peculiar virtue in wildlife ethics is that the hunter ordinarily has no gallery to applaud or disapprove of his conduct. Whatever his acts, they are dictated by his own conscience, rather than by a mob of onlookers. It is difficult to exaggerate the importance of this fact.
>
> Voluntary adherence to an ethical code elevates the self–respect of the sportsman, but it should not be forgotten that voluntary disregard of the code degenerates and depraves him.[10]

Joseph Sax urges the National Park Service to lead visitors away from familiar recreational patterns and nature–based amusements, inducing them to expand their experiences and risk more intimate encounters with nature. Americans must step from their automobiles, turn from those activities where sociability, competition, and technical equipment draw attention to themselves, and enter natural surroundings unencumbered enough to experience these environments on their own terms. "To promote perception," Aldo Leopold argues, "is the only truly creative part of recreational engineering. . . . Recreational development is a job not of building roads into lovely country, but of building receptivity into the still unlovely human mind."[11] Parks have a healing mission.

Rights of access to nature require compensatory provisions for the handicapped. Indeed, in this instance, most Americans are handicapped because we have been deprived of adequate experiences for so long. Society needs to develop remedial programs. In urban schools, learning to know nature can become an educational process that is as important as learning to read and just as necessary for healthy personal development. Young children need pets and plants, parks and field trips, while older children require biological and ecological studies in addition. Children living in unhealthy neighborhoods have a right to summers in the country. Any city family too poor or culturally deprived to broaden their own experience has a right to publicly subsidized travel to the beach or the mountains, to a farm or a forest.

To fulfill this right of access to nature, Americans must also claim our right to a new beginning with a share of the American landscape. The homeless and the hopeless who crowd our cities in growing numbers, and indeed all those who find themselves overwhelmed by urban life, have rights to a new start in a natural setting if they choose. We must reclaim the American landscape for the living.

11. *Reopening the Frontier*

The vast rural landscape of America stretching from sea to shining sea is again a frontier ripe for settlement. Beyond the suburban fringes and the interstate exits, human population is dwindling to the levels sustained by Native Americans before the first European adventurers disturbed them, while the populations of many animal and plant species not favored on commercial farms are declining toward extinction. The landscape, littered with machinery, is defined by the expanding boundaries of consolidated ownership and thinly garrisoned by those required to attend the machines. Except for these remnants, the land is available to a society that might wish to reclaim it in the interests of life.

It is time to reopen this frontier and to claim the land for humanity and other species essential to a healthy ecosystem. Personal freedom is not secure when the majority of Americans are denied access to the land that is our birthright; nor can there be social justice when land is withheld from the poor. The land erodes and life upon it declines because it is exploited, rather than tended by people who come to know it intimately and love it fervently.

"Land reform" is a political program to take land from the control of the few and place it in the hands of the majority—or, at least, all those who wish to occupy land and attend to it. Land reform must move beyond familiar efforts to "save the family farm," because in America most such farms were absorbed into large enterprises years ago. Our land, possessed by impersonal corporations and by families that have learned corporate ways, suffers under machinery too huge and chemicals too harsh. It needs to be liberated.

"Reopening the frontier" names a set of land reform proposals built upon American values and traditions. These do not reject "private property" as some land reform proposals have done; rather, they modify ownership with the recognition that land is more than property and requires respect as well as possession. Personal relationships with land are so important to human welfare that every person's right to this opportunity must be assured; such relationships are so important to living landscapes that none of them should be managed impersonally or exploited dispassionately. The frontier should be reopened not only to ease economic injustice but also to reduce environmental degradation. Land reform, nevertheless, is not a panacea for these ills but one of several fundamental reforms that are required.

Since land reform has deep roots in the biblical tradition it should recommend itself to Christians. In the previous books I have examined the land reforms that flowed from the biblical covenant. The Lord gathered the nation of Israel with a summons to redistribute the land among all the people, and the call for periodic redistribution animated the biblical vision of a just society. By summoning a people—"You shall be holy to me, because I the LORD am holy" (Leviticus 20: 26, NEB)—and joining them in covenant with a holy land—"for the land belongs to me" (25: 23, NJB)—the Lord liberated both people and landscape from social oppression.

The Ten Commandments, God's freedom charter for this covenant community, required that social and environmental relationships be governed by ethics rather than by power. The first, "You shall have no other gods to rival me" (Exodus 20:3, NJB), warns against the deification of natural forces and also cautions against blind faith in human technology. The fourth commandment, "Observe the Sabbath day and keep it holy" (Deuteronomy 5: 12, NJB), established cycles of rest, reflection, and access to the fruits of the earth that upheld rights for dependents, domestic animials, wildlife, and the land itself. Sabbatical justice required periodic forgiveness of debts and redistribution of land to restore equitable relationships among people and to protect human contact with the earth.

The Tenth Commandment required God's people to share the land equitably and without jealousy:

> ... you must not set your heart on your neighbor's house, or field, or servant—man or woman—or ox, or donkey or anything of your neighbor's possessions. (Deuteronomy 5: 21, NJB)

Calling this self-restraint "the practice of neighborliness," Wendell Berry points out that the Amish continue to exemplify the biblical standard by deliberately limiting the size of their farms in order to make room for many neighbors:

> I do not think that we can make sense of Amish farming until we see it . . . as belonging essentially to the Amish practice of Christianity, which instructs that one's neighbors are to be loved as oneself. To farmers who give priority to the maintenance of their community, the economy of scale (that is, the economy of *large* scale, of "growth") can make no sense, for it requires the ruination and displacement of neighbors. A farm cannot be increased except by the decrease of a neighborhood. What the interest of the community proposes is invariably an economy of *proper* scale. A whole set of agricultural proprieties must be observed: of farm size, of methods, of tools, of energy sources, of plant and animal species. Community interest also requires charity, neighborliness, the care and instruction of the young, respect for the old; thus it assures its integrity and survival. Above all, it requires good stewardship of the land, for the community, as the Amish have always understood, is no better than its land.[1]

In America, from the colonial settlements through the first century of the federal republic, society thrived upon the availability of land to all free people. As we have seen, the right of access to land was central to Thomas Jefferson's political vision, though not all those who influenced American institutions shared this conviction. Even when a majority of Americans lived on the land, however, many farmers chose the aggressive exploitation of cash crops in preference to self-reliance and the culture of neighborliness. After the frontier was exhausted, labor-saving technologies tempted the most enterprising farmers to covet their neighbors' fields, while periodic agricultural depressions led to foreclosures and consolidations that continued to depopulate the rural landscape. Now that most Americans have been removed from the land and absorbed within a technological culture, many of us enjoy more material comforts than our grandparents did. Yet we may have less real security because we lack independent means of sustenance and are more vulnerable to unpredictable changes in economic conditions we cannot control. Our separation from nature grows even as, beyond our sight, the landscapes of memory are degraded by modern exploitation. An idolatrous technology has taken both land and people captive.

Yet America, if we choose, can open the frontier again and make land available to all citizens who are willing to prepare for responsible landholding, to live upon the land, and to invest themselves in it. Profit-making corporations are not appropriate landholders, as I will explain, and their holdings should be appropriated with just compensation and distributed to human beings who desire them. Large private holdings can also be appropriated and subdivided if they are desired by the landless. Public lands, in addition, can be made more accessible to the people and can be managed in smaller units by those with immediate and personal knowledge of their character.

* * *

Land reform is most often proposed with reference to agricultural lands, but this proposal is more comprehensive. While it is important to redistribute American farmland so many more people may participate in agriculture, it is equally desirable to disperse concentrated ownership of forests, grazing lands, and mineral-bearing lands. Our society needs to provide open space for those seeking retirement, for artists, for naturalists, and for anyone else who wishes to engage with nature.

Land reform is commonly advocated on behalf of the poor, in the hope that they might sustain themselves upon the land even where education, employment opportunities, and social welfare systems are deficient. Though many impoverished Americans might benefit from land redistribution, this reform is proposed on behalf of all citizens who wish to overcome their separation from the earth. Particularly in a time of environmental crisis, land redistribution cannot substitute for welfare, employment, and educational reforms, for society must provide those who tend the land with the training they need to protect it and the social support required to fashion more wholesome and frugal communities. Sophisticated culture of the earth requries alert, informed, and responsible landholders who are supported by a network of social resources. Sound land reform must restore life and vitality to America's landscape while protecting it from further degradation at the hands of the greedy, the careless, or the ignorant.

In an underdeveloped country where the majority have been forcibly removed from the land yet continue without secure employment, redistributing the land may be essential to the survival of the poor even if the society does not possess wealth sufficient to compensate large landowners for their holdings. Under those circumstances the expropriation of land is just; indeed, it follows the precedents set by God's people in the Bible. Most of the wealth that Americans value, however, is not in land but in the creations of human society. Taxation of this wealth can provide ample resources to pay for appropriated lands.

Land reform can implement the *human right of access to nature* articulated in the preceding chapter, but it must also guard the *civil rights of natural life* (to be considered in the next chapter). The political energy for reform must spring from a dual awakening to human needs and to the claims of the earth. Some land reform proposals by radical environmentalists are utopian in that they imagine perpetual justice and security once social abuses are corrected and proper relationships with nature are reestablished.[2] The expectations here, influenced by biblical prophets, are more modest. The goal of reforms is not to achieve perfection but to honor the demands of justice and to secure some opportunities both for people and for our natural companions upon the earth. Any reform is subject to corruption and will need to be renewed from time to time. Like the biblical laws requiring the forgiveness of debts every seven years and the redistribution of land every fifty years, realistic reform strategies should anticipate a continuing need for social correction.

Under the American Constitution as the courts have interpreted it, land reform may be used to achieve public benefits but not to redistribute wealth. Governments may condemn and reassign land for roads and public works, for urban renewal, for parks and national forests, and for a multitude of other social purposes—so long as the takings are done under law and the owners receive just compensation.

Although the government may use taxation to redistribute wealth, it may not seize land in order to do so. The Fifth Amendment to the Constitution of the United States prescribes that

> no person shall . . . be deprived of life, liberty, or property, without due process of law; nor shall private property be taken for public use, without just compensation.[3]

Speaking for the Supreme Court in 1907, Justice Oliver Wendell Holmes eloquently portrayed the reach of governmental power:

> . . . the State has an interest independent of and behind the titles of its citizens, in all the earth and air within its domain. It has the last word as to whether the mountains shall be stripped of their forests and its inhabitants shall breathe pure air. It might have to pay individuals before it could utter that word, but with it remains the final power.[4]

Later, Holmes would express the Court's insistence upon compensation with equal clarity:

> . . . a strong public desire to improve the public condition is not enough to warrant achieving that desire by a shorter cut than the constitutional way of paying for the change.[5]

Even though there is moral and biblical justification for expropriating lands without payment in very poor and oppressive societies where land is held by a few, we Americans have the means to achieve reform while honoring the constitution that protects so many of our liberties.

* * *

The redistributions proposed here would affect corporations, persons who own large tracts of land, and public land administration—but each in a different way.

Corporations for profit should no longer be permitted to own land having biological value, or to own other living things. While it is appropriate for human society to cultivate and harvest natural life, all life has moral value, and no life exists simply for profit. Since corporations are dedicated to profit, they are not appropriate holders of land, plants, or livestock. However awesome their power in modern society, corporations are abstract creations of law that exercise only the privileges society chooses to assign them. Unlike people, animals, or land, corporations have no reality apart from their social definition. Profit-making corporations are useful devices for combining capital with labor, information, and equipment in order to accomplish complex tasks for the benefit of their owners. Corporations benefit society as well when they efficiently provide goods and services. However, as strictly economic organizations, corporations accommodate awkwardly at best to noneconomic social values.

Land, livestock, and other living things are important sources of social wealth, yet they are always more than economic entities. Their moral use must respect their inherent character and their natural relationships. The earth has been severely damaged by practices that reduce life to economic quantities.

Nine midwestern states already curtail the power of profit-making corporations to own agricultural lands and livestock.[6] As part of a land-reform strategy, federal legislation should redefine the legal character of for-profit corporations to prohibit further acquisitions of living creatures or of lands, unless those lands have been set apart by zoning from the biological community. Then, to open new frontiers for homesteading, the government should begin to acquire by condemnation corporate lands that retain the potential for biological life. Compensation should be based upon the fair value of these lands at the time the law restricting corporate ownership was passed. Corporations would be allowed to sell their lands to individuals prior to condemnation. They could also lease land from individuals for business purposes other than cultivation or speculation—to provide an office or factory site for example, but not to raise crops or grow timber.

These reforms would place upon the market, or make available for homesteading settlement, the vast corporate farms in California—now tended by migrant workers and alien wage labor—which irrigation financed by taxpayers made possible. These reforms would also free Appalachia from the grip of absentee corporations that own 80 per cent of the land in the coal-producing mountains where a working family often cannot find a house site, much less a farm or woodlot to make its own.[7] From coast to coast, huge tracts of farmland, forestland, grassland, mineral land, and land held for speculation would be available once again for purchase or for homesteading.

Large private landholdings—when the demand for homesteads warrants—should also be subject to condemnation by the government, for a fair price, in order to redistribute property to the landless. The object is not to discourage the private holding of land but to extend that opportunity to all Americans as part of our birthright.

Legislation authorizing the condemnation and redistribution of large landholdings would discourage holding of America's land, by wealthy citizens or foreigners, for purposes of investment. Some people consider land to be the most fundamental wealth of society. Yet its monetary value is only one of the characteristics important to society; vitality, environmental integrity, beauty, productivity, and democratic accessibility are others. In modern societies the economic value of land is overshadowed by the value of buildings and improvements, tools of production, consumer goods, and the stocks and bonds that convey ownership and financial participation. To the degree that society tolerates the accumulation of great wealth, it is more suitable to hold such wealth in those instruments that are human creations. Land and the life upon it need to be shared widely and held more intimately, so that personal communion with the landscape may curb the temptation to manage land for economic ends alone.

To further discourage holding land for investment purposes, states should tax land progressively, as Thomas Jefferson recommended, with a higher rate for larger holdings. They should also copy Vermont's *increment value tax* upon land. The Vermont statute derives from the theory that, while landowners at the time of resale should benefit from the value of improvements that they have made to their property, rising value in the land itself is nearly always the result of general social growth rather than the landowner's efforts. At the time of sale, therefore, Vermont taxes the increase in land value exclusive of improvements and—to discourage speculation in land—the state applies the highest tax rate to lands held the shortest period.[8]

Since many wealthy individuals and corporations would prefer selling their lands voluntarily over the uncertainties of condemnation, land reform legislation would place a great deal of land on the market. This would tend to depress the price of land, making purchase more attractive to those who prefer to select their own property instead of occupying a parcel assigned to them by the government agency responsible for homestead distribution. In addition, many large landholders would deed lands to their relatives so the family might continue operate a large farm or ranch together. It is likely that under threat of condemnation, more land would be redistributed by sales and other private transactions than by government taking. These distributions would also broaden land ownership and contribute to the social objectives of land reform.

To achieve land reform's environmental objectives, federal and state governments would need to regulate pollution more carefully and to assist with the costs of conservation practices that provide no direct economic return to the landowner. Society should reward landowners' social role as protectors of environmental integrity, just as we now compensate their efforts to produce food, fiber, timber, and minerals. This need not be an uneconomic "handout," for much of the cost of conservation practices can be recaptured by taxes on the land and commodities associated with it. Coal, oil, and lumber, for example, should be taxed heavily to encourage their conservation and to fund the restoration of lands previously degraded by rapacious mining and timbering. Agricultural chemicals and fertilizers should also be taxed heavily to discourage their use and to underwrite the costs of coping with the soil erosion and water pollution that these agents generate.

Dependable incentives for conservation practices would make lands, now economically marginal, more attractive to settlement. Since the Second World War, agricultural production has been concentrated on the flat, open, and irrigated lands suitable to large machinery, while both productivity and land values have declined in regions of small farms and rolling hills. Conservation payments would provide incentives to modify the most abusive aspects of farming, and they would also create new interest in lands that require restoration. Some people who did not wish to farm commercially might be eager to homestead more marginal lands if they could derive some income from their efforts to control erosion, improve water quality, revive life in the soil, reforest, or provide wildlife habitat. The devastated lands of Appalachia, with which I am familiar, call out for such people.

Public lands can play a vital role in land reform. Although the variety of parks, wilderness areas, forests, grasslands, waterways, roadways, and other public lands have functions distinctive to their characters, their managers should pursue two overriding purposes: to protect natural health and vitality with effective conservation management, and to provide public access to nature.

Our national forests, the largest category of public lands, illustrate the deficiencies of management when those who set policy are remote from the lands they administer. Fewer foresters work in the woods where they can observe natural life; more work at remote computers and drafting tables. Timber harvest plans dictated from Washington, D.C. commonly exceed the rate of regrowth possible on site. The Forest Service continually extends its network of forest roads at public expense, encourages the cheap, destructive practice of clearcutting rather than careful, selective cutting, and sells timber at a net loss to the taxpayer.[9] These practices also demoralize private woodlot owners, who cannot afford to tend their own forests wisely because the government holds the price of logs below the cost of good management.

Sound forest policy would place most foresters back in the woods, with responsibility for the welfare of particular tracts that they learn to know intimately and manage with personal affection as well as professional devotion. These positions of environmental trust are too important to relinquish to computer calculations and bureaucratic planning. Professional foresters in the field should be assisted by entry-level workers who learn responsible relationships with nature as they prune and thin trees, maintain watercourses, stock fish and game, maintain camping areas, build roads and trails, and give the forests the personal attention they deserve. There could be many more opportunities for people to live and work in our national forests.

On most public lands, reforms to improve environmental quality would also increase employment opportunities. Vast public grazing lands should be cleared of cattle and restocked with buffalo, antelope, and other species that utilize grass efficiently , along with predators to keep the herds moving and healthy. When the grasslands recover some of their ancient vitality, then herds of sheep and cattle—tended by watchful shepherds—may be reintroduced with care.

Parks and other public lands, both urban and rural, are important sites for the educational programs necessary to equip citizens to relate to nature. However, most of our public lands have not received adequate maintenance since the work programs of the Great Depression. They could benefit from new employment maintenance programs. Every American who needs a job should be offered the opportunity of two years of conservation work on public lands doing tasks that teach responsible relationships with nature.

* * *

Every American citizen should be entitled by law to homestead once in his or her lifetime, regardless of means, provided the citizen has not owned land for the previous five years. To secure title to the homestead, the citizen would need to undergo a year's training at public expense, occupy the land assigned for five years, and maintain it in a satisfactory manner during that time. The land would be secured without cost, but buildings and equipment that came with the land would usually need to be purchased over time.

People could homestead for a wide variety of reasons and

claim their right to a land allotment reasonably suited to their needs. If they wished to farm they could specify the type of farming for which they were qualified. Retirees and people planning to work off the land might seek small subsistence acreages to supplement their principal livelihood. Some might wish to manage a small forest, or to reclaim abused land in return for government conservation payments.

Many countrysides are dotted with houses abandoned during the long decline of rural population, while our cities and towns swell with homeless people. There are scores of houses standing empty in the county where I live that might be rehabilitated by someone needing shelter. People who wished to occupy and improve a rural residence during the five-year homesteading period could be excused from paying for a house worth less than the improvements necessary to meet basic standards.

Land condemnation efforts would be facilitated if laws required full disclosure of land ownership so that federal and state governments could inventory landholdings by owner, size, and type. Regional land courts would then appraise the homesteading demand and proceed to condemn appropriate lands, moving first upon corporate lands. If necessary, a court would employ a lottery system to condemn private lands above the size specified by law, although the owners should retain their residences and reasonable acreage of their choice. The court would subdivide lands into economic units depending upon climate, terrain, soil quality, and intended use, and apportion them to appropriate applicants. A corporate cattle ranch in west Texas might be divided into plots of several hundred acres, while a tract of land in New Jersey might be split into five-acre plots for intensive vegetable cultivation. Either division would create an economic unit for an enterprising homesteader. An old house with room for a garden could adequately meet the needs of some. Unreclaimed strip-mined land in Appalachia might be parceled into watersheds of a hundred acres or more, with the opportunity to earn significant reclamation payments for careful regrading, pollution control, and reforestation.

Modern homesteaders need education and training to respond to the environmental constraints and social opportunities of our time. This might typically require a full year of resident education at a college near the homesteading site prior to moving upon the land, to be followed by continuing education throughout the homesteading period. The educational program should support values and aspirations relevant to the homesteading challenge, help the homesteader become a participating member of a new community, introduce ecological understanding and conservation technologies, and teach work skills relevant to the homesteader's particular opportunity.

To succeed, most homesteaders would need to master the the companion virtues of *self-reliance* and *community support,* and learn to rely upon these more than the market. Their small parcels of land may not yield sufficient cash crops to finance all the equipment required for successful commercial production, much less automobiles and other "necessities" of modern life. Homesteading would require a frugal style of life in the midst of a wasteful society that has tolerated deterioration of the community infrastructure that once facilitated thrifty exchange. Most homesteading households would need to emphasize sustenance, not production. They would need to exchange work, goods, and services in their neighborhood, and therefore they would need to cultivate the relationships of trust and respect that undergird such community support.

Modern homesteading need not be a solitary experience. People could enter new communities together. Churches and other neighborhood organizations in urban areas where unemployment is high might sponsor group homesteading so that friends who share a common commitment could move to a rural community. Once the homesteaders were established on the land, their urban connections would serve as a bridge for continued migration.

Homesteaders would enter communities that—however depleted they may have become by comparison to previous decades—contain established institutions and resident families with traditions, convictions, and prejudices. This is one reason why training within the new community would be important before homesteaders occupy their land. People need time to understand and appreciate one other, to learn to cooperate as neighbors. Yet the urban skills that homesteaders bring could replenish rural communities bled by adversity. In many a country town, a family willing to reopen the dry-cleaning shop, the bakery, or the local restaurant—and to hang on while patronage builds slowly—may be just as valuable as the one that wants to farm.

* * *

"I am talking about the idea that as many as possible should share in the ownership of the land," said Wendell Berry, "and thus be bound to it by economic interest, by the investment of love and work, by family loyalty, by memory and tradition."[10] Wes Jackson, in turn, wondered how many this might be:

> If we tried to put every family of four on 40 acres, or one person on every ten acres, given our population of 225 million, we would need about 2.25 *billion* acres. We have roughly 400 million acres of agricultural land, an additional 100 million acres of marginal land and about 800 million acres of range land about equally divided between private and government ownership. . . . We would need to double our total acreage just to accommodate each family on 40 acres.[11]

The homesteading proposed here would not be for farming purposes alone, but would accommodate many personal desires and social needs, each with distinctive land requirements. It will be *agricultural* in the broadest sense—accommodating a broad range of vocations and aspirations upon the land. If some rural areas became crowded again, communities could adopt more labor-intensive and ecologically complex farming techniques. They could also devote more labor to the range of crafts, manufactures, and services that enrich a rural community.

Homesteading might benefit millions of people from urban areas who are unemployed or otherwise unsatisfied, but the land will not accommodate everybody. Homesteading is not a substitute for addressing the social and economic problems of our cities. Yet even those who did not exercise their right to homestead would benefit from having the right, just as bank depositors benefit from their right to withdraw their funds on demand even when they choose not to do so. Banks prosper only when depositors are so confident of their access to their funds that they don't all try to withdraw them at once. Just so, people with a right to a homestead would have more freedom and security even though only a small percentage might choose to exercise this right at one time. The land would benefit from this human right because Americans who know they have access to land will value the landscape more highly and guard its health and beauty more jealously, whether or not they choose to live upon it.

12. *Civil Rights for the Earth*

Aldo Leopold begins his famous discussion of land ethics by recalling the way that Homer's ancient hero reasserted his property rights after years away from home:

> When God-like Odysseus returned from the wars in Troy, he hanged all on one rope a dozen slave-girls of his household whom he suspected of misbehavior during his absence. . . . The girls were property. The disposal of property was then, as now, a matter of expediency, not of right and wrong.
>
> Concepts of right and wrong were not lacking from Odysseus' Greece: witness the fidelity of his wife through the long years before at last his black-prowed galleys clove the wine-dark seas for home. The ethical structure of that day covered wives, but had not yet been extended to human chattels.[1]

Homer's story is three thousand years old, but it has been only 125 years since chattel slavery was brought to an end in America by the Thirteenth Amendment to the Constitution, ratified in 1865. Indeed, following the Civil War, blacks and those in sympathy with their rights had to continue a difficult struggle for liberty, equality, and opportunity, over against prejudice and resurgent segregation. Some consequences of slaveholding still linger on despite striking progress in recent decades.

During these same 125 years, rights have been extended to other members of our living community who were once regarded as property. I remember as a child listening to my grandmother, a

Methodist evangelist, while she told of her role in a campaign that won women the right to vote in East Cleveland, Ohio, several years in advance of the Nineteenth Amendment which would secure women's suffrage throughout the land. The brutal exploitation of children in mines and factories during the late 1800s made their lack of civil rights vividly apparent also; this led to child labor laws, school attendance laws, and eventually to statutes protecting children from abuse within the home. When the factory system disrupted other social conventions and threatened to reduce all laborers to commodities, workers fought for laws to protect their rights to organize and bargain collectively, to provide social security, and to regulate workplace safety and health. However halting such progress must appear to those who continue to suffer injustice, from the long perspective of history the pace of change during the past century has been swift.

Being a naturalist, Aldo Leopold interpreted these extensions of social ethics by drawing an analogy to the ecological processes by which species that depend upon each other evolve techniques to accommodate one another:

> an ethic, ecologically, is a limitation on freedom of action in the struggle for existence. . . . The thing has its origin in the tendency of interdependent individuals or groups to evolve modes of cooperation.

This ethical evolution, Leopold continues, has not progressed far enough:

> There is as yet no ethic dealing with man's relation to land and to the animals and plants which grow upon it. Land, like Odysseus' slave-girls, is still property. The land-relation is still strictly economic, entailing privileges but not obligations.[2]

Leopold, writing in the 1940s, was not the first to imagine extending rights to land and natural life. The English legal philosopher Jeremy Bentham suggested in 1789, during the time that the American Constitution was being publicly debated, that "the date *may* come when the rest of the animal creation may acquire those rights which never could have been withholden from them but by the hand of tyranny."[3] That date is at hand, I believe, and now is the time to protect animals, other living species, and the land itself, from the human abuse and pollution that threaten the vitality of the biosphere.

From an environmental perspective, the fundamental flaw in America's constitutional order is its *anthropocentrism*. The system is designed to accommodate human welfare alone. This remains true despite the impressive array of legislation enacted to control pollution since the foundations of a new policy were set in the National Environmental Policy Act of 1970. The preamble to this important statute proclaims the goal of "restoring and maintaining environmental quality to the overall welfare and development of man," while it also promises, in more inclusive language, "conditions under which man and nature can exist in productive harmony." However, the law itself is directed narrowly to "federal actions significantly affecting the quality of the *human environment*."[4] The "Environmental Impact Statements" required under this act are not intended to protect the health of nature as such. Rather, they assess whether any environmental degradation resulting from a proposed federal action will so injure human welfare as to outweigh the human benefits anticipated from the proposed action. The influence of environmental quality upon human welfare is recognized, but the rights of nature and natural life—apart from society's interests in them—are not.

The Endangered Species Act of 1966 was exceptional in that it gave categorical protection to species found to be threatened with extinction. In due course the Supreme Court held that the Tennessee Valley Authority, which had spent $100 million on the Tellico Dam, would have to suspend construction because the snail darter, a small fish so endangered, would be placed at risk if TVA closed the floodgates and disrupted the species' only known habitat. Those who favored unrestricted development ridiculed Congress for enacting a law that protected an obscure species of tiny fish at the cost of a giant dam. Lawmakers eventually amended the statute to allow the dam to be completed after populations of darters were moved to another river nearby. Because the "right" which the law conferred upon this endangered fish was inflexible, because it lacked adequate constitutional context and legal precedent, and because the public was not committed to the rights of obscure creatures, the legal protection crumbled under determined pressure from the few who hoped to profit from the dam. Mercifully, the darters survive in their new habitat, though this outcome was not certain when the Tellico floodgates were closed. The dam, however, has proved to be an economic disappointment to its prospective beneficiaries.

The United States Constitution defines the system that governs 250 million people. The Constitution also provides the legal context for human relationships with 3.6 million square miles of land within our borders, as well as more than one million square miles of coastal and territorial waters over which our government claims jurisdiction. These lands and waters teem with life in complex ecosystems. At one time these ecosystems maintained their own vitality without human intervention, but now many of them have been modified for human use and have become dependent upon human management. Given the spread of human population and the growing impact of industrial processes upon the biosphere, even the most wild and remote regions are vulnerable to pollution if society does not protect their integrity and limit society's intrusions. Although our culture is dangerously ascendant over nature, human life comprises only a small percentage of the life within the borders and waters of these United States. Only this human portion has received rights under our Constitution. Only humanity, along with some of our social constructions such as corporations, has access to our courts and to our legislatures for protection. It is time to correct this disparity.

The trees and soil, the rivers, lakes, and estuaries, the populations of birds, fish, and mammals within this nation, along with the insects and microorganisms that complete the web of life, have God-given rights that must be considered in relation to human rights. The systemic interrelations of earth, air, and water with living organisms must also be represented in the decisions that affect them. A just constitutional order should protect civil rights for the land, waters, and air, and all the creatures within them, providing a framework that relates human rights to the rights of nature itself.

* * *

The first public figure to suggest how the American legal system might be adapted to this need was Supreme Court Justice William O. Douglas, who for thirty years was America's leading defender of civil rights and the most prominent conservationist to hold high public office. In 1972, Douglas wrote a dissenting opinion to support the Sierra Club's claim to represent the interests of a living environment within California's Mineral King Valley. The club had sought an injunction to prevent the U.S. Forest Service from leasing Mineral King to Walt Disney Enterprises for the construction of a sky resort designed to accommodate fourteen thousand visitors daily. In the lawsuit, however, the club deliberately refrained from claiming that its members who hiked and camped in the valley would suffer loss or injury as a consequence of the Forest Service's action, asserting only that the area's aesthetic quality and ecological balance would be degraded. By declining to claim personal loss they avoided the traditional legal grounds for "standing"—which means the right to bring a suit—and forced the court to rule upon their novel claim to represent a natural environment itself.

The District Court granted Sierra Club a preliminary injunction, but the Court of Appeals ruled that the club failed to justify the standing they sought. The Supreme Court upheld the Court of Appeals by a vote of four to three. Writing for the majority, Justice Potter Stewart reasoned that

> aesthetic and environmental well-being, like economic well-being, are important ingredients of the quality of life in our society, and the fact that particular environmental interests are shared by the many rather than the few does not make them less deserving of legal protection through the judicial process. But the "injury in fact" test requires . . . that the party seeking review be himself among the injured.[5]

The majority were not willing to recognize interests other than human interests.

Douglas, in his dissent from this opinion, proposed to expand the community of those who could seek protection under our legal system. He cited Aldo Leopold's observation that "the land ethic simply enlarges the boundaries of the community to include soils, waters, plants, and animals, or collectively: the land."[6] Douglas argued that

> the critical question of "standing" would be simplified and also put neatly into focus if we fashioned a federal rule that allowed environmental issues to be litigated before federal agencies or federal courts in the name of the inanimate object about to be dispoiled, defaced, or invaded by roads and bulldozers and where injury is the subject of public outrage. Contemporary public concern for protecting nature's ecological equilibrium should lead to the conferral of standing upon environmental objects to sue for their own preservation.[7]

Several inanimate human creations have already received such recognition within our legal tradition; most conspicuous among these are corporations, which are immaterial inventions of law and yet receive many of the constitutional protections that people enjoy. Furthermore, those who are alive but unable to speak for themselves—small children, the severely retarded, the comatose—are represented in court by persons recognized as competent to speak on their behalf. Douglas continued:

> So it should be as respects valleys, alpine meadows, rivers, lakes, estuaries, beaches, ridges, groves of trees, swampland, or even air that feels the destructive pressures of modern technology and modern life. The river, for example, . . . speaks for the ecological unit of life that is part of it. Those people who have a meaningful relation to that body of water—whether it be a fisherman, a canoeist, a zoologist, or a logger—must be able to speak for the values which the river represents and which are threatened with destruction. . . .
>
> Those who have that intimate relation with the inanimate object about to be injured, polluted, or otherwise despoiled are its legitimate spokesmen.[8]

Douglas' use of the phrase "inanimate object" to characterize an environmental system that includes inarticulate life, is awkward, for it was the living system, as well as its environmental support, that Douglas wishes to recognize with legal standing.

The real problem, Douglas insisted, was not the range of human interests in nature that should be permitted a voice in court, but rather the rights of the environment itself. Douglas was an avid hiker, explorer, and sometime nature-writer who understood environmental systems. He knew that the protection of the whole was more important than the rescue of certain species that might charm the popular imagination. He therefore directed his argument to the rights of these systems—as represented, for example, by a river—rather than to the rights of particular plants or animals within an ecosystem. "The problem" Douglas pointed out, "is to make certain that the inanimate objects, which are the very core of America's beauty, have spokesmen before they are destroyed." He went on:

> That is why these environmental issues should be tendered by the inanimate object itself. Then there will be assurances that all of the forms of life which it represents will stand before the court—the pileated woodpecker as well as the coyote and bear, the lemmings as well as the trout in the streams. Those inarticulate members of the ecological group cannot speak. But those people who have so frequented the place as to know its value and wonders will be able to speak for the entire ecological community.[9]

During the two decades since Justice Douglas offered his dissenting opinion, the federal courts have liberalized slightly the requirements for standing in environmental litigation, but they have not taken the major step Douglas recommended, to confer upon those possessing intimate experience of a threatened environmental system the right to represent the interests of that system in court. Public concern for the welfare of the natural environment has grown steadily throughout this period, while laws to control pollution have been expanded and improved. However, neither law nor popular understanding has expanded—beyond the human need for safe, productive, and pleasant natural environments—to affirm the rights of nature itself. Most leaders within America's environmental movement respect nature for itself, not simply for its social utility. Nevertheless they feel constrained by political expediency to promote, for example, rain forest conservation on the grounds that the species and genetic material that can be preserved thereby may someday be useful to humanity.

Unequivocal moral defense of environments and species on their own behalf, such as Justice Douglas recommended, has not yet become acceptable in American legal and political discourse. Yet it is unlikely that we can protect nature appropriately until we step across this barrier to speak clearly and candidly for the interests of the earth. We must draw nature within culture as a full partner to humanity.

* * *

Here is language for an amendment to the United States Constitution to recognize civil rights for the earth. Each clause is indented separately to help the reader visualize the relationships among the several rights and duties that the amendment recognizes:

> The earth and all its life shall be treated considerately
> > for they are vulnerable to human culture.
> > Although cultivating natural life,
> > harvesting from species and natural resources,
> > and physical expressions of culture
> > are appropriate for humanity,
> it shall be a constitutional responsibility to preserve
> > living species,
> > the natural systems that support life,
> > and natural features that are unique and beautiful.
> > Species, natural systems, and natural features
> shall have standing before the law to protect these their rights
> within the general welfare.

Like the Bill of Rights, which forms the first ten amendments to our Constitution, this amendment would confer rights upon particular communities and individuals—in this instance ecosystems, species, and natural features—to shield them from arbitrary abuse by the powerful and assure their access to governmental institutions in defense of their rights. Like other proposals (such as the Equal Rights Amendment which would require equitable opportunity for women), this one is designed to focus political dialogue in the hope that many changes can be achieved before the amendment itself is approved. Respect for nature's rights requires such a fundamental change in popular attitudes and such thorough reform of institutional conduct that a constitutional proposal is an apt way to claim public attention. Even after ratification, this new statement of rights would grow in meaning and significance as American society deepened its respect for natural life. All the affirmations of civil rights in our Constitution have developed in this way.

The amendment requires that society treat nature with consideration and preserve natural life and beauty. Conversely, the amendment recognizes nature's rights to preservation and considerate treatment and grants the legal standing necessary to protect these rights. The particular rights conferred here are limited by the "general welfare," a traditional legal conception that is broadened here to embrace the welfare of the ecosystem as well as the welfare of human society. The amendment affirms the appropriateness of human activities that deliberately alter nature—such as cultivation, harvesting, and mining—as well as the physical expressions of human culture that have an impact upon the natural environment secondarily—such as buildings and roads—so long as these expressions do not contravene these particular rights: the continuation of species, the vitality of natural systems that support life, and the preservation of those natural features that society values as unique and beautiful.

The amendment addresses the earth, natural forces, and living creatures from an ecological perspective. It recognizes their common interests as well their competing interests. Following the thought of John Muir and Justice Douglas, it does not make a sharp distinction between the living and the inanimate but affirms their interdependence and their mutual claims upon humanity.

For example, California condors have been so poisoned by their polluted habitat that the few remaining alive must be held in captivity to protect new chicks. Before condors can be released again, their natural setting must be cleansed of pesticide residues. Therefore the ecosystem to which they may return must be protected now from further toxic poisoning. Indeed, it needs protection for its own sake, and also for humanity's sake, as well as for the condor. This rugged Big Sur coastline also requires protection from aesthetic degradation in order to sustain the human spirit and to honor the rocks, the sea, and the birds that together form the area's special beauty. There is a complex interdependence among environmental interests, aesthetic interests, the geology, natural life, and human society. When society redirects its attention away from the techniques of dominion and toward the ethics of life-support, many distinctions made by our scientific culture to separate humanity from other creatures, or to separate the living from the inanimate, lose their relevance.

The amendment begins with *consideration*. While this notion may appear inoffensive, it implies conduct that expresses regard for the needs of natural life. The meaning of consideration may expand as social understanding of the needs of natural life deepens. Consideration is justified by nature's vulnerability to human culture. When humanity struggled to survive against overwhelming natural forces we prayed for mercy and compassion, but now the relationship has significantly reversed and we must show compassion toward the earth.

Nevertheless, the amendment affirms the value of human culture. If we are sensitive, considerate, and not fundamentally destructive, then the cultivation of plants and the tending of animals—including improvements to domesticated species—can enrich the fabric of earthly life while meeting human needs. The ores we mine and the timber we cut can be fashioned into beautiful and serviceable goods that honor their origins. The places occupied by cities and the other artifacts of civilization are removed appropriately from nature if the resulting communities are just, handsome, and healthy, and if they relate in a wholesome manner to the surrounding ecosystems.

The amendment recognizes the rights of three aspects of nature. The first, "living species," is the most specific and unambiguous. We know how to define a species: it is composed of organisms capable of producing fertile offspring. The United States has already made a legislative commitment to protect endangered species, and our efforts to do so are becoming more sophisticated. The amendment would strengthen this commitment. There will continue to be some species, such as the Mediterranean fruit fly, that society considers noxious and resolves to remove from agricultural environments in the interest of general welfare. The amendment, however, would require that viable populations of even these species be allowed to flourish in other areas.

The "natural systems that support life" are a less specific collection of interests. This critical environmental envelope that surrounds life includes: sunlight filtered by ozone in the upper atmosphere to screen ultraviolet radiation; air that contains suitable amounts of oxygen and is free from chemicals at toxic levels; a stable climate within which overall heat, rainfall, and acidity are not artificially distorted more rapidly than ecosystems can adapt; water that is healthful and not poisonous; soil that is not toxic and can support microorganisms; and other factors that we may not yet understand. Clean-air legislation, pure-water regulations, sewage-control requirements, toxic waste requirements, and other pollution control laws relate to these interests. Although it is difficult to ascertain the level of protection truly necessary to sustain life, it is vital that society achieve such protection. By granting natural systems standing to defend their interests, just as corporations and others who now pollute have standing, the amendment would give balance to disputes about pollution standards and their application. The amendment does not protect natural systems from all changes but only from those changes so radical as to undermine their capacity to support life. Nor does this proposal imply that life prefers static conditions; indeed, evolution and adaptation are characteristics of vital, healthy ecosystems. Modern pollution levels, however, can modify life-support systems so rapidly and radically that ecosystems cannot adapt. The amendment would give natural systems a defense against destructive change.

The third interest granted constitutional protection, "natural features that are unique and beautiful," is one that joins nature and culture. This interest relates to the aesthetic interaction between humanity and nature. "Unique and beautiful" are human criteria pointing to aspects of the landscape that we admire. This aesthetic interaction has led our society to determine, for example, that the Grand Canyon portion of the Colorado River gorge is more appropriate for a national park than for the hydroelectric reservoir once proposed at the site. Much of the environmental protection achieved during the past century—including national parks, wild and scenic rivers, and national monuments—expresses this desire to protect natural features that are unique and beautiful.

The amendment gives constitutional recognition to this cultural bonding with nature. It affirms nature as a part of culture so that one generation may protect for the next what we value. Not every natural feature that some person has loved will find protection, yet when the bulldozers of progress threaten something unique and beautiful, those who love it will have a tool to defend it. Legislatures will need to give further definition to this protection, and courts will need to develop precedents in its application. Most importantly, the unique and the beautiful will have standing for their defense. The cultural value of a place where humanity and nature have exchanged joy will be measured against the worth of a new development, in the light of a "general welfare" that embraces the earth as well as human society.

The amendment will not confer standing upon particular animals or trees, individuals within a species, or inanimate things unless they are adjudged to be "unique and beautiful" or their degradation threatens life support. This may reduce, though not eliminate, the fears that one wag expressed in the *Journal of the American Bar Association*:

> If Justice Douglas has his way—
>   O come not that dreadful day—
> We'll be sued by lakes and hills
>   Seeking a redress of ills.
> Great mountain peaks of name prestigious
>   Will suddenly become litigious.
> Our brooks will babble in the courts,
>   Seeking damages for torts.
> How can I rest beneath a tree
>   If it may soon be suing me?
> Or enjoy the playful porpoise
>   While it's seeking habeas corpus?
> Every beast within his paws
>   Will clutch an order to show cause.
> The courts, besieged on every hand,
>   Will crowd with suits by chunks of land.

> Ah! But vengeance will be sweet
>   Since this must be a two-way street.
> I'll promptly sue my neighbor's tree
>   for shedding all its leaves on me.[10]

The amendment will not treat animals and plants like people, to confer rights upon them as individuals. However, because it specifies that all life be treated considerately, it will give constitutional assistance to the animal welfare movement in its important struggle to curb abuse of these fellow creatures. As our cultural understanding of consideration toward life grows, the amendment may come to imply more responsible treatment of plants and other forms of life as well. It will not, however, give particular animals or trees standing in court to defend themselves, but only species, ecosystems, and distinctive natural features.

The amendment will confer civil rights upon aspects of nature—both directly and indirectly. It states directly, "Species, natural systems, and natural features shall have standing before the law to protect these their rights." Indirectly, it would create "a constitutional responsibility to preserve" these aspects. This reponsibility to preserve lays a duty upon governments to enact laws designed to achieve the protections specified by the amendment and to administer the laws effectively. It also lays a duty upon persons to protect these rights. In doing so, it opens the way for those in a position to speak for endangered species and natural systems, or for unique and beautiful natural features, to represent them in court. Our society has always recognized that people have responsibilities as well as rights, but to specify citizens' responsibilities within our Constitution is a novelty. In this instance to do so will be appropriate because the natural interests that the amendment protects are inarticulate and depend upon human initiatives to secure their civil rights. Individuals and organizations that become aware of threats to natural life can claim the authority of the amendment when they stand in court on behalf of natural interests that require protection.

Adding this amendment to our Constitution will expand the "general welfare" to include the lands and waters under the jurisdiction of the Constitution along with all creatures within these boundaries and the natural systems that support life here. The amendment will bond culture and nature together by recognizing the rights of nature within civil society. No right is absolute, however. In the classic example, the right to free speech does not include the right to cry "Fire!" in a crowded theater. When more rights are recognized, the interractions among them become complex and the task of resolving competing claims becomes more difficult. As Aldo Leopold observed, a culture is like a natural environment in that it tends to develop an ever more complex ecology. If human civilization is to flourish and not to choke upon its own pollution, we must embrace the earth with all its life and join nature to culture within a framework of justice.

* * *

A constitutional amendment is not a panacea. It will not substitute for political efforts to clean the air, to protect the range of the grizzly bear, or to set aside natural features of special beauty. It will not remove the natural environment to some realm of safety beyond politics. Rather, it will empower nature that has already been drawn into politics by the pervasiveness of human culture. If it is adopted without adequate public understanding and support, as the prohibition amendment was, this amendment will accomplish little. Consideration for nature will test our social resolve more thoroughly than abstinence from alcohol ever could. If discussion of a "Civil Rights for Nature" amendment strengthens other environmental efforts, then it will be valuable.

On Chestnut Ridge Farm I wish the rights of the earth were recognized under law, for the responsiblity I bear is oppressive. Whatever my good intentions, I am still "Massa" on Chestnut Ridge and the land is still slave. I am a kind master, but that is not the same as sharing rights and responsibilities with another. Our cultural definition of property assigns me more power than is good for me or for the earth. The future of Chestnut Ridge is clouded because the landscape is not truly recognized by the culture that surrounds it.

America is not yet the "land of the free" when the earth itself remains enslaved. We are not the "home of the brave" if we fear to share our freedom with all who live among us.

Part IV.

Open Communion

Praise God, from whom all blessings flow;
Praise Him, all creatures here below;
Praise Him above, ye heavenly host:
Praise Father, Son, and Holy Ghost.

Readers who have tuned their ears to inclusive language about God and the people of God—a practice that prevails throughout this series—may be disconcerted by the sexist tone of this doxology, sung every Sunday in many churches. It seems to exalt the masculine in heaven and, by reflection, upon earth as well. Yet another dimension of the doxology challenges Christians to make our fellowship more inclusive than it is at present. In words worn smooth by familiarity, the doxology extends the communion of faith to "all creatures here below." Like the Psalms that inspired it, the doxology opens the community of the faithful to enfold all the creatures that God created, whether sharing the same soil, the seas around us, or the sky above us. If we are to help redeem the world from destruction, Christians must confess this inclusive communion, bring it alive in our liturgies, and embody it in our actions.

This series *Environmental Theology* has examined the Bible and reconsidered fundamental tenets of Christian faith, laying a foundation for Christian experience of nature and moral behavior toward the earth. This final part provides a conclusion to the series as a whole by suggesting how environmental theology and ethics may be institutionalized in the worship and work of Christian churches. Churches must change to accommodate nature, but these reforms can revive biblical faith and need not lead us away from it. We can embrace nature without becoming pantheists. We can exhibit the beauty of the Lord when we protect the beauty of the earth. The traditional concept of a "parish" with a geographic character, for example, can be used as a vehicle for the inclusion of nonhuman life within the conscious Christian community. To carry the image of God to distressed environments and, indeed, to redeem the land, Christians need to develop new forms of community as well. Here I suggest one such experiment as appropriate to the plight of agriculture.

When Christians resist the extinction of species, the oppression of peoples, the disruption of both cultures and ecosystems, and all that pollutes human and natural life, we will suffer with the afflicted and have occasion to lament the many unnecessary deaths around us. In this we share the sufferings of Christ for the world. Yet the gospel gives hope to the earth and can inspire our strivings for both social justice and natural abundance. Although the spread of pollution may create anxiety and sow confusion within the human community, Christian hope points toward a wholesome future for life on earth.

13. *Going Natural, Staying Faithful*

Two threads of anxiety run through the long weaving of biblical history and Christian tradition. One is that nature will entice God's people to depart from faithfulness to the Lord. Intertwined with this thread is a companion anxiety about human nature, that our sexual desire will offend the Lord and must therefore be curbed. Book 3 of this series, *Hope for the Land,* showed how these anxieties took hold in the early Hebrew communities in Canaan, which had to defend their distinctive allegiance to a God of moral integrity against the entrenched but decadent pantheism of the Baals—the fertility gods of the regional culture. Although the Lord challenged the Hebrews to bring their agriculture within the framework of covenant ethics and promised them that justice would lead to fruitfulness, the culture of the Baals tempted them to use sympathetic sexual magic, along with human sacrifice and other religious cruelties, to entice crops to grow and herds to multiply. Protracted struggle with the Baal cult fanned fears of the power of sexual desire to lead people to apostasy and the power of nature itself to corrupt human relations with God. Similar fears resurfaced in the early churches as they tried to develop communities of justice and compassion amid the moral and religious decadence of the declining Roman Empire.

These anxieties do not emerge from the creative heart of biblical and Christian faith but are scars from long, uncertain struggles with oppressive cultures. God's covenant of salvation, as announced by Moses and again by Jesus, offers freedom from these anxieties and all our fears so that we may learn to express ourselves morally and fully in our relations with other people and the natural world. Moses brought ten commandments from the Lord which, while rigorous, were clear enough to provide a moral understanding that freed people from dependency upon hierarchies or arbitrary power. Jesus challenged his hearers to listen with their own ears and see with their own eyes; to abandon moral compromises, hypocrisy, and self-condemnation; to live as though the new kingdom were present and thereby bring it nearer; and to be born again so their deepest desires might emerge and find answer in experience with the Lord and within the new community. This is the Christian psychological perspective of Book 2 in this series, *Beauty of the Lord.*

Three reforms to the institutional life of Christian churches follow from the environmental theology developed in this series. First, we can help our churches to lay aside their repressive tendencies so that they may become, instead, *communities of redemptive expression.* Then churches can offer clear alternatives to the patterns of oppression that afflict both human society and the natural world. Second, we can encourage our churches to step beyond anthropocentrism to become *communities embracing both God and nature.* Churches will then provide a more visible witness to the importance of moral relationships with all of earthly life. Third, we can deepen our expectations for the future, our "eschatology," so that churches may become *communities of earthly hope.*

* * *

When the exciting energies that initiate religious communities wane in the passage of time, churches often become repressive, tightening their discipline and cultivating fears of punishment in order to sustain the moral qualities remembered from earlier generations. The unfortunate psychological and spiritual consequences of this pattern of development were examined in Book 2. Concerns about environmental pollution might easily reinforce this pattern, because obvious responses to the fearful threats posed by human abuses of nature include asceticism, self-discipline, and stronger social controls of polluting behavior. If churches respond to the ecological crisis only with such patterns of discipline, however, and fail to cultivate communion with nature itself, they will not convey a biblical hope or provide a redemptive witness. Indeed, they may inadvertently reinforce characteristics of modern culture that stimulate overconsumption and foster pollution.

When we are conscious of our desires we may seek to satisfy them deliberately and appropriately, but if we repress emotions below the level of consciousness we are more likely to act in ways that damage our health and disrupt the social order. Hidden fears and yearnings can push us in directions we do not understand. When society encourages patterns of repression that induce people to bury feelings, they become vulnerable to leaders with the skills to manipulate these hidden fears and desires. Jonathan Edwards—as we saw in Book 2—developed a religious revival rhetoric that did just this, though he himself was unaware that his novel techniques were manipulative. In the modern world many leaders understand how to subvert the feelings of their followers. Advertisers have applied psychological understanding of the unconscious to induce customers to buy products not simply for their usefulness, but in response to urges of which the customer may not be aware. They subvert sexual desires, in particular, to sell products that cannot bring sexual satisfaction. Advertisers use the media to sow confusion about what we want, diverting us from direct efforts to meet our needs, as we consume more products of industry and commerce instead. These same advertising techniques are used by politicians who prefer to cultivate good feelings and deflect popular anger toward scapegoats rather than address pressing social problems. The commercial exploitation of repressed emotions and unfulfilled desires leads to an enormous waste of natural resources, while the political exploitation of these desires and fears subverts freedom and confuses efforts to deal with the problems of social justice and environmental integrity.

Love for the natural world that is active and expressive can motivate changes in human behavior and sustain new relations through difficult times in a way that fearful, anxious motives cannot serve. It is human expression, not our repression, that is truly responsive to the creative beauty of the Lord and the moral demands of Jesus. Happy expressions of our love—whether they be creative *eros* or self-giving *agape*—will meet human needs effectively and are likely to protect nature as well. We need, therefore, to question whether our religious fellowships encourage people to discover their freedom in Christ, to express their deepest loving character, and to fashion their lives in responsive, responsible interraction with the living world around them.

Within the moral universe of God's love and purpose, human expressiveness is not an enemy to be feared. We who believe that the Lord created the world have reason to expect that our desires can be satisfied within a moral ecology of mutual benefit. The promise of the covenant is that God will help us form a society where we may be whole while also honoring other lives. The self-discipline and group discipline required to build this society need not be arbitrary and oppressive. Both Jesus and Paul condemned the abuse of God's commandments by religious authorities who would make them instruments of fear rather than hope, repression rather than liberation. The commandments, indeed, guide us toward self-expressions that culture can sustain and nature can support.

Christian *communities of redemptive expression* can have great appeal to people in this confused, frightened society, for many people despair that life can be whole. Christians trust a God of moral beauty who responds to our deepest yearnings; who eases our fears, forgives our sins, and quiets our self-condemnation; who welcomes our creativity and self-expression; who challenges us to build a society of justice and love where people experience freedom and give each other security. We believe that the needs of each can complement the needs of others if they are expressed within a culture of sustenance, justice, and peace. Within their fellowship churches can develop many of the personal ideals and social skills that are needed to reform society and redeem nature from destruction, and they can become creative centers for the infusion of the kingdom of God into the world.

Our Lord's goal is a community of satisfaction that embraces the whole earth. Because we know the God who is revealed in the Bible, we have reason to recommend to the world that trust in the Lord, hard work, loving engagement with persons and nature, and personal creativity tempered by a careful regard for just relationships together can assure a natural fruitfulness and cultural responsiveness that meet human needs and those of our natural companions. All the earth may yet join together in a sabbath of praise.

* * *

To respond to the gospel expressively in this age of environmental crisis, Christian churches need to open their liturgies to include nature as a welcome participant in praising the Lord, and they need to expand church life to incorporate surrounding species and ecosystems within the fellowship of moral concern. This can be a constructive supplement to efforts, already under way in many denominations, to make Christian fellowship more inclusive by reforming sexist language and dismantling patterns of racial and sexual discrimination.

A previous chapter concluded that as people are hemmed in by the complex structure of technological, urban society, human culture fails to discharge what has traditionally been its most significant function: helping people relate to the realities beyond the human. The radical anthropocentrism of modern society makes it difficult to recognize a God who is not simply the product of human imagination, while it also makes it difficult to imagine that other creatures have meaning and integrity apart from our need for them. Churches concerned about perpetuating knowledge of God should, therefore, have a keen interest in reviving contact with nature. Each of these relationships can reinforce the other and provide an antidote to the anthropocentrism that threatens to turn the magnificent edifice of human culture into a windowless prison.

Christians need to regard nature *directly,* not just *instrumentally.* In times of repose we may find that the beauty and vitality of natural settings arouse strong feelings within us that include religious emotions. The Christian tradition has encouraged us to consider these evocative natural characteristics as metaphors for divine qualities. Jonathan Edwards drew elaborate metaphors and similes from nature in order to direct toward God, in an orthodox fashion, those feelings of love and awe that are stimulated in natural settings. It is even more important, however, that we accept our feelings toward natural beauty and power as important in themselves, and not only as symbols of our feelings toward God. Emotions bonding us to nature are necessary to a life that is fully human, just as are emotions that bond us to the Lord. We honor neither God nor nature when we confuse one set of feelings with the other.

John Muir frequently described nature as a manifestation of God, yet he rarely allowed religious emotion to obscure his direct appreciation of the natural object before him. He developed a remarkable sense of the distinctive vitality and moral integrity of each species and every natural force. He came to respect both mountain sheep and mountain glaciers for themselves, and he treated them with the brotherly regard to which all life, he was convinced, was entitled. Muir's delight in nature and natural forces, his enthusiasm for wilderness where nature might be experienced apart from its instrumental value to human society, and his determination that human society must protect the range of life provide an example of the finest human communion with nature.

As we come to appreciate that human sustenance depends upon protecting the earth's vitality, we may ponder our obligations to "stewardship." Stewardship ethics express our sense of responsibility for the resources that God has placed in our hands and under our administration. However, "stewardship" is too constricted an idea to express the full moral relationship with nature that is conveyed by the biblical images of covenant, sabbath, and redemption. Stewardship objectifies nature as things, whereas the Bible emphasizes the vitality and moral responsiveness of natural life. Nature is our partner, not our possession. Land, livestock, and resources do not "belong" to us. Rather, both "holy land" and "holy people" belong to God. In this mutual relationship to the God who frees each from oppression, we are challenged to know, enjoy, and care for each other with love and respect. Therefore it is not enough for churches to teach stewardship. We must provide, in the presence of God, experiences of companionship with nature and solidarity with the earth. Then we will be *communities embracing both God and nature.*

* * *

There are surprising contrasts between the biblical visions of hope that were detailed in Book 3 of this series and the expectations that commonly prevail in modern Christian communities. When we attend funerals we comfort one another with words that express our hope for the continuation of life. Where congregations participate actively in modern culture and regard its values positively, churchly comfort often takes the spiritual, abstract form of a hope that the immortal soul survives the body to join God in a heaven whose location and attributes are unclear to those who otherwise accept a scientific view of the cosmos. A century ago such liberal, acculturated Christians might also have affirmed that the kingdom of God would eventually come upon earth thanks to the spread of moral enlightenment and modern technology. Today's liberal Christians, on the other hand, are aware of intractable social problems and are less likely to speculate upon the future of society.

Where congregations feel isolated from modern society or even abused by it, Christian hope assumes the more concrete form of a vivid community of redeemed men and women beyond the grave, a community where God rewards the faithful for their suffering. This heavenly hope bears no relation to the cosmos that science describes, but that matters little to those who are eager to reject "the wisdom of this world" (1 Corinthians 1:20 KJV) that has served them poorly. Their hope for earthly society is usually negative. That is, they anticipate that the earth will be destroyed, as it deserves, in a conflagration that may be society's own doing but that expresses the judgment of God.

There are many variations on these two themes, but the point is that neither form of hope acknowledges a place for natural life in God's saving intention. Neither form of hope relates creatively to modern cosmological, ecological, biological, or even psychological understanding. Neither form of hope includes a vision of the earthly future for culture and for nature.

Biblical hope has characteristics quite different from these modern religious expectations. Each biblical vision of the future, from Jesus' words of comfort to the most elaborate apocalyptic, was sharply tuned to the crisis of the believers to whom it was addressed so they might receive strength and guidance to face the problems of their time. Each vision of the future built upon the worldview—including cosmology and psychology—of the society from which it emerged. Priests of the Lord took the story of a great flood that was known by all peoples and filled it with fresh moral promise. Similarly, Jeremiah accepted the popular psychology that the heart was the organ where human feelings were located, and then he promised its renovation. Furthermore, the overwhelming majority of biblical visions expressed a hope for natural life as well as human life. There are variations among biblical visions, but they do not diverge sharply on the inclusion of nature within God's redeeming purpose.

Biblical visions do diverge on the question of whether the promised hope rescues a small community—Israel, or God's elect, along with their promised land—or embraces the whole earth. They also diverge concerning the transition from the present to the future. No biblical vision anticipates a smooth evolution to the new community of redemption. Some imply a sequence of judgment, catastrophe, repentance, and rebuilding within a recognizable framework of earthly history. The more pessimistic visions suggest that "heaven and earth" as we know them must be destroyed and replaced by quite a new creation.

Christian hope for the future, our "eschatology," must be a moral vision and not simply a reasonable forecast. Christian hope may depart from the modern worldview and, indeed, must so depart when the sciences that shape popular understanding lack moral insight. Yet when Christian hope fails to speak to modern concerns it loses its prophetic character. Despair for the world is understandable and may prove justified, but escape from concern for this earth and indifference to the future of others do not honor the God who loved the world so much as to send Jesus. The truth of an eschatology is not found in its predictive accuracy—exactly when to expect a great change and what things will look like afterward—so much as in its moral responsiveness to the crisis of the age.

When Christians, faithful to the Lord, read the signs of our times in light of the Bible's rich promises, we may come to appreciate that hope has these dimensions:

• Hope unites us with the full community of those that God

created and loves. We will find our future in solidarity with our brothers and sisters who are now afflicted, and with the creatures, species, and ecosystems that are now abused.

• Hope springs from repentance. God does not offer us a way around the crisis of our age that avoids taking personal responsibility for our participation in the oppression and pollution now pervading the earth. Only as we repent does God show us how we, and the world, may change.

• Hope prepares us for tribulation. The crises of human justice and environmental integrity have become so acute that profound human suffering and environmental degradation must follow. Those without hope will try to isolate themselves from their needy neighbors and their polluted environment, and as they do so their futile efforts will compound the agony of others. Those with hope, however, will learn ways to care for the earth and their companions. They will ease the pain of others by sharing it. They will build those communities and tend those ecosystems that eventually emerge from the crisis.

• Hope is ecological, embracing the beauty and diversity of God's creation. We will accept death as a gift that makes room for life. Christians will hope for a living community, not a static one. We will desire the flowering of life.

• Hope is in the Lord. The presence of God gives us courage. We can respond to the environmental crisis with personal hope and creativity because God has responded to us:

> Rain righteousness, you heavens,
> let the skies above pour down;
>   let the earth open to receive it,
>   that it may bear the fruit of salvation
> with righteousness in blossom at its side.
> All this I, the Lord, have created.
>   (Isaiah 45:8, NEB)

As Christian hope becomes more biblical it will also be increasingly relevant, until churches become *communities of earthly hope* that make a difference.

14. *The Parish*

Despite all that has been said about our cultural isolation from natural life, the most promising efforts to integrate nature into the local church will begin with communicants' existing relationships with the natural world. Pastors and teachers in the church can encourage members to deepen their experiences with nature, to reflect upon them, and to share these experiences in the church fellowship so that, in due course, the congregation may be able to discuss conduct toward the natural world in the light of biblical teachings and environmental constraints.

John Muir discovered a century ago that we are more responsive to nature when we are at rest and at play than when we are employed. At work our attitudes are so conditioned by economic needs that, if we engage with nature at all, we are likely to see it merely as a commodity to be exploited and to protect ourselves from more sensitive interactions. Thus, while there may be farmers, miners, florists, or biologists in the congregation, it is more useful to begin efforts toward environmental awareness by building upon people's recreational roles as hunters, hikers, fishers, gardeners, pet owners, golfers, skiers, sailors, or vacationers.

These folks have experiences with natural life to share, and if the church invites them to do so—in Sunday School classes or at family night suppers—then the experiences are given added value. Since the best stories will be those that exhibit keen sensory observation, members will be encouraged to pay closer attention to already familiar environments. Churches can also plan picnics and retreats that gather members in natural settings, and then make the experience with nature, and reflection upon it, featured parts of the event rather than merely decorative background to other activities. We can encourage each other to relate to nature more directly, to simplify the rituals of recreation, and to reduce the amount of equipment standing between us and other life, so that opportunities for sensual and emotional intimacy are enhanced.

Recreational activities, of course, raise ethical questions. Is hunting a moral activity? Do our vacation homes scar the very environments we seek to enjoy, while our motor boats shatter the tranquillity of lakes? Do even our hiking boots erode the hillsides? Each of these questions becomes relevant when those who participate in the activity are able to consider it, but when the congregation is just beginning to pay attention to nature it is not kind for some Christians to disparage the activities of others. I don't hunt, and as a farmer and a hiker I have found hunters annoying and even dangerous. However, some hunters I know love the environments they walk through and the prey they seek with an intensity that inspires me. Others are less distinctive, but their times in the woods provide the growing edge of their sensual and moral relationships with nature, so these times deserve to be affirmed by the church rather than rejected. In churches that develop communion with nature, the day will come when Christians sensitive to animal rights can talk with Christian hunters and together ponder ethical behavior toward creatures that they both love.

As a pastor I have found it difficult to guide people to ponder the impact of their work upon nature. My own work with nature, however, has been influenced by the congregations I served. In Book 2 I told how Pennsylvania farmers introduced me to love for the land, while coal miners in West Virginia convinced me that grief for a ravaged land can be as intense as anger for an abused daughter might be. On the other hand, I have known strip miners who took pride in their work and were careful for the land according to the standards they recognized—even though the results of their labor were catastrophic in my opinion. I could not persuade them to change their practice, and they were not pleased when I advocated laws that would force them to do so.

Pastors should be alert for the sorrow that may live beneath the defensiveness of those who abuse the earth in their work. Some farmers, loggers, miners, and real estate developers who bristle at any hint of criticism nevertheless mourn inwardly the decline of natural environments that they have known intimately. They may feel coerced by cultural pressure and economic neccessity, so they bury their emotions and their memories in order to press on. If they can be encouraged to tell stories about the land they have known and loved, and if their expressions of affection are heard, this may release some of their grief and ease some of their defensiveness. When such people do change their practices, their conversions may be sudden and emotionally compelling, like farmer Dick Thompson's account of how God led him to "quit using chemicals cold turkey." At such times people need pastoral encouragement and congregational support.

When a congregation is ready to discuss the environmental consequences of particular human endeavors, such as agriculture or electric-power generation, it might begin by asking thoughtful farmers or utility employees in the membership to ponder the question and make a presentation. Their capacity for self-criticism may be limited, but if the church gives their views recognition they may be more receptive when the church solicits other viewpoints. In the Middle Ages the Catholic Church tried to enforce specific standards for the conduct of trades and professions, but churches in modern society have little influence upon professional ethics because the issues have become so complex—and, indeed, there are too many issues. Nevertheless, churches can raise moral questions and repeatedly call attention to abused persons and environments. It is difficult to help the abused while retaining love for the abuser, but this is the unique Christian calling, and we will be supported by the Holy Spirit when we make this effort. What is most important, when some people take a stand at work because they honor social justice and respect environmental integrity, their congregation can rejoice to give them recognition, moral support, and practical assistance.

* * *

The heart of the Christian community is worship where we celebrate our faith and form the religious affections that influence our behavior. Praise to God creates the fellowship of believers.

Nothing is more important, therefore, than to open Christian worship to embrace the praise of all creation that is party to God's covenant of redemption.

Many resources to help us are readily at hand. *Hope for the Land* cited hundreds of Bible passages that embrace nature within the praise, promises, and purposes of the faith. Although more hymns need to be written on these themes, most hymnals include a few. None are finer than "All Creatures of Our God and King," setting the prayer of Francis of Assisi to magnificent music by Ralph Vaughan Williams:

> Thou flowing water, pure and clear,
> Make music for thy Lord to hear,
> Aleluia! Aleluia! . . . [1]

The problem is not lack of resources but the need for a *shift of consciousness* so the congregation experiences itself as an ecosystem—as a people joined to the living environment that is, by God's grace, our partner in redemption. New patterns of worship can make this shift possible. For example, many services include a time when participants suggest persons and needs to be remembered in prayer, and this can be extended to embrace the needs of the natural environment. Better yet, we can draw nature into the church's communion at the opening of the service when prayers of praise are offered. Members might be asked to observe some aspect of natural life and add it to the congregation's praise:

> "Last night from my porch I heard the tree frogs offer a chorus of praise, and later the fireflies performed their dance of light. Let us join with them as we worship God."

> "The stream behind my house sings over the rocks, thankful for the recent rain. I offer its praise, with ours, to the Lord."

If the opening of worship regularly included images such as these, a feeling for the breadth of the covenant community would grow.

Other symbols can also be employed. Many churches decorate the altar with flowers every Sunday. Rather than buying from the florist, we might choose plant materials from the parish and place a note in the bulletin identifying them, celebrating their characteristics, and telling where they may be observed. This would incorporate representative plants from the neighborhood within the visible community of worship. The offering ceremony might also be modified to convey a sense of environmental responsibility. When money is the only acceptable gift, the offering becomes abstract and sterile, and it gives unwitting endorsement to the ascendancy of money over all other values in modern culture. During the earliest centuries of Christian history when the church was an alternative to the predominant culture, the offering included bread and wine for the Eucharist, along with produce and other items that Christians used in their life together. Modern Christians could also give tangible witness through the offering that we value personal relationships over abstract transactions and that we support thrift, creativity, and environmental responsibility. It would take thought to rehabilitate the offering so that personal creations and pledges of service could be received and put to good use (God protect us from old rummage items and stray cans of soup!), but such reform might bring the offering down to earth, express the real character of Christian community, and help to make stewardship a more vital part of Christian life.

Nature would be honored if the eucharistic elements at the very heart of Christian worship were made more sensual. The bland wafers and tiny squares of white bread that are now commonplace were designed to be inconspicuous so the communicant might think only of God and not be distracted by a taste. It is poor psychology, however, to expect a bland experience to convey the mystery of the sacrament, and this may be one reason that God remains indistinct and without personality for many communicants. A symbol without engaging characteristics is also poor theology because it understates Christ's saving incarnation in the tangible, sensual, and expressive flesh of this world. Environmental theology suggests that the bread and wine provided for the sacrament be the finest that the people of God can make from the grain and fruit of the earth. The elements should be tasty and distinctive, prepared with skill and attention, so they testify to the church's care with the fruits of the earth, convey the excitement of Jesus' presence, and give witness that Christ's incarnation will make all of life more excellent. "O taste and see that the LORD is good" (Psalm 34:8, KJV).

Many thoughtful congregations take prayer and the sacraments of the church to those who are ill and those who are dying. Christian communities that embrace the natural life around them will also find occasions to take their prayers outside to places that need recognition or comfort. A proposed shopping center, for example, may eliminate a stately grove of trees. Quite apart from the question whether the congregation wishes to protest this development, the church may wish to meet with this grove to offer comfort and prayer or, if the bulldozers have already done their work, to memorialize the beauty that has departed; for no death is more tragic than one that is lonely and unnoticed. Sad to say, churches that embrace the life around them will have many opportunities to perform such service.

* * *

Energy conservation, of all the environmental strategies available to us, can make the largest contribution to reducing pollution and conserving the earth's natural resources. Many churches are in a position to demonstate the value of energy conservation and to promote other environmentally responsible patterns of living as well. Most church buildings constructed before the 1970s are inefficient in their use of energy, while many congregations are hard pressed to pay their heating bills. Remodeling for energy conservation can save money while slowing the depletion of natural resources. Congregations that plan such improvements carefully will learn conservation techniques that members can apply at home.

Agencies in several cities help churches and other nonprofit institutions with conservation planning. In Ohio, for example, the Cleveland Non-Profit Energy Conservation Fund conducts energy audits and recommends those improvements that nonprofit institutions can fund from fuel and utility savings. The fund can assist with financing and oversee the work. A church might benefit from insulation in ceilings and around the hot-water heater; from storm windows; from boiler repairs; and from heat zoning monitored by clock thermostats that direct heat to those parts of the building actually in use. Most homeowners could benefit from one or more of these practices as well. If church members are involved in the analysis and planning, help with the work, learn to operate the improved systems, and see the savings in the church budget, they are more likely to carry these ideas home and to their places of work.

When a congregation considers a new building or expanded facilities, it must decide whether such an investment is a better use of its resources than other forms of ministry might be. If building is indicated, the congregation faces an additional challenge to make the structure a witness to resource conservation. Many churches are tempted to construct as cheaply as possible so as not to divert funds from their ministry, but often the result is an ugly, inefficient building that burdens a congregation with high operating costs. Jesus' words apply: "Would any of you think of building a tower without first sitting down and calculating the cost . . . ?" (Luke 14:28, NEB). A passive solar building, carefully planned for the needs of the congregation and designed with architectural distinction, can be both efficient and inspiring. Good design can reduce the fuel energy required for heating, lighting, and air-conditioning by 50 or even 75 percent. Beauty also has conservation value, for a handsome structure will give more enjoyment to its users; it is likely to be maintained with greater care and used for generations longer. Such a church can capture the attention of the surrounding community and witness to qualities of design that help us live more responsibly on a planet that is threatened with depletion.

Various aspects of church life may be designed to inspire environmental ethics and to promote a sense of "elegant frugality" among church members. This study has expounded a fundamental psychological principle that can be applied within the local congregation. *Church life should provide a responsible setting for expanding sensuous enjoyment, emotional expression, and personal creativity, for only as we learn to satisfy our needs more directly with families and friends, with God and with nature, can we reduce our consumption of those products and services that tax the natural environment.* If we fear our feelings and desires, and distrust our ability to find pleasure within a community of moral responsibility, we are vulnerable to those who pander products and services that deplete the earth and yet fail to satisfy. God's covenant of redemption promises that as we are attentive to the Lord, we may build a new culture where joys can be found and desires expressed in ways that build a healthy community of life. We need not fear our deepest longings, but—in God's presence and with care for one another—they can be answered.

The church supper may serve as an example. As a rural pastor, I have shared memorable feasts. "Cemetery Clean-up Day" each Memorial Day weekend at the Fruit Hill Presbyterian Church in Pennsylvania was a culinary event renowned in the region. Men eagerly clipped, mowed, planted, pruned, and mulched so they might carry their plates down the long tables laden with delights that women had thought about for weeks and labored over for hours. What joy, what fellowship, beside the rivers of cholesterol and the mountains of sugar! In my city pastorate, and more recently as a guest speaker at urban church suppers, I have seen the other side: bland institutional meals, often prepared by a hired cook, eaten hurredly to make way for something else that will, one hopes, prove more inspiring. Sometimes an environmentally aware member will tell me that the church has recently stopped using styrofoam cups and paper plates—or that a campaign is under way to make this change.

Please aim higher! The church supper will waste resources until it is fun again. An urban church might sponsor small, intimate suppers where one or two cooks from the congregation share their best dishes in a relaxed atmosphere. The dinners could promote regional produce and sound nutrition, but they should also feature exciting tastes and good conversation so participants rediscover the joy of eating. Afterward, those who did not help with preparation can sing songs as they wash dishes. For people who worship the God of Abraham and Sarah, archetypal hosts of the ancient world, a real meal does not need a supplementary program to make it a holy event. Our church should help liberate us from fast food, bland food, and solitary food. Some creatures—plants and animals—gave their lives for our dinner, and if we do not enjoy the offering, then they died in vain. A good meal can provide physical, sensuous, and social nourishment. When we appreciate this and learn how to achieve it regularly, we will be able to live more lightly upon the earth.

* * *

God's covenant of salvation embraced not only a people chosen to be holy to the Lord but also a holy land and all the life, whether wild or domesticated, upon that landscape. In the Bible, redemption is an ecology that involves both social justice and responsible relationships with nature. Within this ecology of redemption, nature itself will become more fruitful in response to God's love and human nurture, so that even those who were once homeless or poor can find what they require.

Christian churches have traditionally understood ourselves to be expressions of God's new, or renewed, covenant. We have responded to God's call that we form communities of redemption expressing a new order. As we come to understand that nature is also party to the covenant of renewal, this conviction will change our sense of congregational identity. We must move beyond our image of the congregation as *faithful people* gathered in the presence of the Lord and embrace a new image of *faithful life*—human, animal, plant—gathered before the Lord who is the hope of redemption for us all. This is the worshiping community heard by John of Patmos in the Book of Revelation:

> Then I heard all the living things in creation—everything that lives in the air, and on the ground, and under the ground, and in the sea, crying, "To the One who is sitting on the throne and to the Lamb, be all praise, honor, glory and power, for ever and ever." (Revelation 5:13, JB)

The particular congregation that shares this doxology will see itself composed not only of those people who have professed their faith in the Lord and joined this church, but also the animals, plants, trees, insects, fish, reptiles, microorganisms, and systems of life that share the neighborhood with these people of God. Seen ecologically, the local church is a *parish:* God's neighborhood community that bears responsibility for the renewal of all the life of that place.

Christian denominations have historic disagreements about the signs of redemption that reveal who God's people are, and this proposal to extend membership in the church to all forms of life will raise new theological issues. The community of the new covenant does not appear to embrace all people, for some have rejected it while others do not know the Lord well enough to choose the faith. Are all nonhuman creatures automatically members of the covenant community, or if not, what criteria distinguish the redeemed from the lost? We do not usually think that nature shares moral culpability with humanity for the fall into sin, though nature certainly shares the consequences. Therefore nature need not "repent" to choose God, and indeed, God's curse upon the ground delivered at humanity's expulsion from Eden was explicitly revoked when God covenanted with Noah and all the creatures that emerged from the ark following the great flood.[2] The review of biblical promises in Book 3 of this series suggests that nature is redeemed when it is healthy. Vitality, abundance, complexity, and a peaceful relationship among the species are biblical signs of nature's participation in the covenant of redemption. This biblical vision of peace does not necessarily imply that predation and other cycles of consumption within the earthly ecosystem will come to an end; rather, it implies a healthy, balanced ecosystem within which all forms of life may flourish while each species serves needs for others as well.

Therefore the *evangelical* call of the church toward nature is to bring it to health so it may exhibit the signs of redemption, while the responsibility of Christian *communion* with nature is to protect the vitality already present. Healthy wilderness does not need to be redeemed for it is already in full communion with the Lord. This, surely, is part of its religious attraction, and Christians will benefit from alert communion with the wild. On the other hand, eroded lands and polluted ecosystems do plead for redemption, and reaching out to them is part of the church's mission responsibility. A sick landscape or foul stream within our parish lays a moral claim upon us that is just as real as the claim brought by a neighbor lost in sin. It is our evangelical calling to bring hope and help.

In addition to the wild and the polluted, however, a third category of nature has a particular moral claim upon us. This is the natural life that we have domesticated and brought within human culture: our pets, plants, lawns, and farms. The Bible makes clear that when these are part of a believer's household they have rights that are just as specific as the rights of children, servants, and other dependent persons. The ancient Hebrews spelled out these rights in their sabbath laws. As modern Christians learn to take our obligations toward other life seriously, we will want to articulate the rights of domesticated creatures and dependent landscapes with special clarity. Otherwise we remain slave-lords over a household of creatures who should, instead, become members of our family within the covenant community of the redeemed.

Within the local parish, therefore, the communion of faith is privileged to become a moral ecology. Mature believers assume obligations toward domesticated creatures and dependent landscapes that are morally similar to our obligations toward our children or the vulnerable members of our congregation. We want to guard them all from cruelty, and help them to flower so they may taste the redemption that our Lord offers us all. An ecological parish establishes overt communion with wildlife, the birds and small animals, the dense woods and the deep bog. These already praise the Lord as beautifully as we do. If we join them in an ecumenical chorus, our faith will be enriched while their future will become more secure. Furthermore, we need a new "home mission evangelism" that reaches out to the abused creatures, the denuded earth, and the polluted air and water in our neighborhood. The residents of animal shelters need our ministry along with the residents of hospitals and prisons. Those who dump toxic wastes need as stern restraint as those who beat wives and children. We need to sow new seeds on barren ground, mulch them, and water them faithfully. When we perform these ministries literally, biblical metaphors that give them spiritual meaning may also come alive.

As a practical matter, most American congregations are not "parish churches" since they share a neighborhood with several churches of other Christian denominations, while few congregations are strong enough to shape their neighborhoods decisively. Nevertheless, each awakened congregation can do something, for if you cannot take full responsibility for a neighborhood ecosystem you may still take some responsibility for parts of it. Let your commitments be as specific as possible. In theory the governing board of a local church can recognize its communion with all life in the neighborhood, but far better would it be for the board specifically to "affirm our Christian communion with the splendid grove at the top of Andover Street," to devote next year's Vacation Bible School to humane treatment of pets and their place in God's family, and to "clean up Cherry Creek and replant its banks as part of our local evangelism." When more complex projects call to the congregation's conscience, it may undertake them on an ecumenical basis with other congregations and civic groups in the neighborhood.

A congregation's participation in larger environmental issues can be interpreted by extending traditional ideas of "national missions" and "foreign missions." The church that affirms its Christian communion with "the grove at the top of Andover Street" may discover that, along with other threats, the trees are vulnerable to acid rain. The air itself must be redeemed lest it corrupt those forests that remain healthy. This might lead the congregation to undertake an acid rain education and action project in association with regional and national organizations, whether religious or secular, that are working for clean air. Churches that contribute to particular mission projects overseas could profitably study the environmental problems that impinge upon those efforts. The demands of survival in Third World countries may make it difficult for people there to restrain environmental abuse. Despoiling nature may be encouraged by the lure of trade with the United States and other affluent nations. In consultation with mission leaders, a church might support a project to fabricate simple stoves that burn wood more efficiently and thereby slow deforestation, or it might protest the purchase by fast-food chains of beef raised on land cleared from rain forests. In all such situations, whether domestic or foreign, it is better to do a few things well than many things haphazardly.

When a church comes to know itself as an ecosystem, a parish that attempts to embrace all life with God's redeeming love, this can make a world of difference.

15. *Redeeming the Land*

When ancient Jerusalem was besieged by the armies of Babylon and all hope for her was lost, Jeremiah made a final prophetic gesture before the city fell. He redeemed from the money lenders a tract of family farmland that had been foreclosed—and which now lay, inaccessible, beyond Nebuchadnezzar's siege works. "For these are the words of the LORD of Hosts," he announced, "The time will come when houses, fields, and vineyards will again be bought and sold in this land" (Jeremiah 32:15, NEB).

* * *

The following story is not yet true.

It is now fifteen years since 1989, when the Rev. Anne Stem, pastor of two small Luthern churches in rural Redemption County, fashioned the plan during winter evening conversations with Wally Boggs, who taught agronomy at Central College, and Father John McKay, who chaired the Economics Department at Mercy College, to buy the whole county, or as much as was for sale, and redistribute lands, homes, and workplaces to people willing to covenant together for a just society that respected the earth. They would show to America an alternative to the harsh exploitation and rapid depopulation of landscapes that prevailed elsewhere. They hoped this example would arouse demand for land reform across America before our free institutions were eroded by further consolidation of property and power. They believed the plan could double the county's population in twenty-five years and create a vital, self-sufficient community with a diverse culture that would inspire people elsewhere to work for similar changes.

Although many Lutheran farmers had resisted the temptations to expand during the 1970s and were more secure than others in the county, Reverend Stem could see that the Lutheran community had been in steady decline for thirty years. Her two congregations were both aging, and although a lot of land was on the market, only a few young men and women considered buying a farm or taking up another trade in the community. Dr. Boggs saw his agronomy classes dwindle year by year while Central College, a Presbyterian liberal arts school that had once made an important contribution to regional culture, turned to students from the East who had been refused by colleges of their first choice. Father John was disappointed that Mercy College, principally a technical school, had so little impact upon the community other than providing the training that helped young men and women to move away. The Catholic population had dwindled to less than half of what it had been when he was ordained in this diocese; indeed, the future of the college was now under official review.

Because Redemption County was somewhat hilly and thus less well suited to farm consolidation than other counties in the region, the credit crisis had not struck here as swiftly. Nevertheless, for several years farm credit banks and insurance companies had been foreclosing larger farms. Then, in the waning days of the Reagan presidency, the county office of the Farmers' Home Administration began a broad foreclosure campaign against smaller farmers who had dropped behind on mortgage payments. Soon the Bush administration made clear that its farm policy would focus upon the repeal of agricultural trade restrictions and farm protections in other countries so America's largest producers might penetrate more world markets. Redemption County would probably compete poorly, but even if farms here were consolidated further and devoted to export commodities, the result would be continued declines in population, economic vitality, and local culture, coupled with intensified abuse of the land.

The new plan required a great deal of money, for at the

beginning the Covenant Community Trust, as it was called, needed to raise the capital for land reform without access to governmental tax receipts. The three leaders enlisted the participation of several Christian denominations, and then two large philanthropic foundations that supported agricultural policy research agreed to provide major funding if large tracts of land and other properties could be assembled. Another breakthrough came when the president of an insurance company took personal interest in the project. He arranged a land swap among several banks and insurers who together held about a fifth of the county's property in foreclosures, so substantial acreage could be optioned to the trust.

Meanwhile, the organizers led intense and often heated discussions across Redemption County. The plan offered immediate relief to farmers who were overwhelmed by debt and promised economic growth for which the county had longed, but the proposal was uncoventional and unfamiliar, and it would encourage an influx of people of uncertain race and background. After many local church congregations voted to support the plan and welcome new people, and the trustees of both colleges agreed to direct their educational programs to the effort, the county Board of Supervisors also resolved to cooperate.

These were the goals of the Covenant Community, as it came to be called:

• To make land and shelter available to those who need them at a price they can afford

• To modify traditional property rights on these lands in the interest of environmental integrity

• To provide training in new farming techniques and other necessary trades

• To establish networks of neighborhood support and economic discipline based upon voluntary commitment rather than collective ownership or the pressure of debt

- To give preferential incentives for trade and exchange within the community in order to build a county economy with some self-sufficiency and a culture with some resiliency

- To inspire the spread of such values in American society

The pages that follow will explain how these goals were pursued.

* * *

The Covenant Community Trust serves not only as the instrument to redistribute lands and free them from debt, it also retains a legal interest on behalf of the land itself and the the biotic community upon it. When the trust deeds lands to individuals or families, it retains 50 percent ownership of the land—although not of buildings or other improvements—as trustee for the nonhuman community upon the tract. Each participating landholder prepares an annual conservation and production plan for review by the trust, and trust representatives periodically inspect landholdings. In cooperation with the colleges, the trust provides training for prospective landholders as well as continuing education and field support in ecology, conservation, forestry, animal health, and other disciplines. Where reclamation and restoration of a healthy ecosystem are particularly difficult, the trust may provide financial assistance to the landholder. Under agreement with each participating landholder, the trust receives 10 percent of all agricultural sales, though not of barter and other exchanges. After five years' residence, landholders may sell their homes, lands, and other facilities, or portions of them, and may purchase additional lands, but the trust's legal interest in the natural vitality of these lands continues. Experience has shown that farms encumbered with such co-ownership by the Covenant Community Trust sell for 15 to 25 percent less than comparable farms held "free and clear," depending upon the proportion of value in house, barns, and equipment—in which the trust does not share ownership. The trust's encumberance also tends to keep these farms within the community of those who share common values.

That first parcel of lands offered to the trust by the insurance company included farmland of varying quality scattered throughout the county, plus several town and village properties: homes, old stores, service stations, and other places of business. The trust decided to purchase those lands and other properties, regardless of their quality, that could form the basis for rural neighborhoods, plus properties in Central City near one college or the other. Four potential rural neighborhoods, three of them surrounding small villages and one near Central City, emerged in the planning process. Land was evaluated for its reclamation requirements and productive potential, and then it was subdivided into small farms that families might tend with simple machinery. Many of these included an existing house either on the land or in a nearby village, some of which would require substantial repair. Other homes and buildings acquired by the trust were designated for mechanics, tradespeople, and professionals who might contribute to the neighborhood culture and economy. When established county residents who were in financial difficulties asked for assistance, the trust attempted to purchase their farms for a fair price regardless of the location, assuring the owners that after retraining they might return to their former homestead. In the case of a few large farms, however, the trust insisted before purchase that it be allowed to subdivide portions for other homesteaders. When local people who had previously lost their farms asked to join the Covenant Community, they were given preference, and a few were even reestablished on the land they had once tilled.

The trust advertised, both locally and in national Christian journals, that rural homesteads were available to those who were ready to commit themselves to an experimental community. All participants were required to spend a year in residence at Central College for orientation and training, and then work a five-year apprenticeship on the land before they received title to their property. Those having means paid for their training, land, and home as they were able, while others received training and homestead without cost. When the popular media picked up the news, applications flooded in. This enabled the Covenant Community, from the beginning, to select diverse and promising participants.

Even local residents who wished to participate were required to let their farms grow fallow for a year and to move with their families into the college housing. This requirement was resented at first, but it quickly proved a saving grace for the program. Men and women, many of them middle-aged, halted patterns of work that had become inflexible and began to think more seriously about their lives and their environment, while the opportunity for locals and newcomers to get acquainted on campus was indispensable preparation for the cooperation they would need to exhibit in the neighorhood communities to be developed. Participants shared a core curriculum on homesteading techniques, environmental science, community relations, practical economics, and biblical covenant ethics. They also chose among specialized courses, many of which are taught at Mercy College, in such practical fields as carpentry, ironwork, engine repair, forestry, plant genetics, animal husbandry, and intensive gardening, as well as liberal studies in religion, literature, the arts, and political science. Some participants arrived with specialized training and experience, while a few were able to study longer than a year before taking up their homestead. All learned that regular, continuing education would be important to their covenant commitment. By the end of each year a few had dropped out and a few more had to be screened out, but usually three-quarters or more were ready to affirm the covenant and take up their homesteads.

* * *

Affirming the covenant requires commitments in three areas: ecological responsibility, economic discipline, and sabbath observance. Members must promise to respect the integrity of the land and the living community upon it including both wild and domesticated animals, and the natural systems that support life. They affirm that the well-being of the Covenant Community depends upon a healthy environment, and they pledge efforts to improve the quality of their land. The commitment to the land is institutionalized in ongoing dialogue with the Covenant Community Trust, which acts as a trustee for natural life.

Economic discipline takes three specific forms. First, members pledge to use the technologies approved by their neighborhood covenant council in return for neighborly assistance. This is the heart of the matter. Homesteading and subsistence living require a great deal of neighborly cooperation, yet neighbors can help each other efficiently only if their productive endeavors complement each other and, more particularly, if their technologies are compatable. The amazing efficiency of Amish neighborly assistance, for example, depends upon rigorous technological discipline so that one farmer may substitute his equipment for another and practice common skills with confidence. Forty men can erect a barn in a day because the design and building techniques do not vary from one barn to another or one year to the next. In these covenant neighborhoods, however, the intention is not to build a traditionalist society like the Amish but rather innovative communities, so the efficiency of neighborly assistance is somewhat less. Nevertheless, neighbors must harmonize their technologies if they are to be useful to each other.

Of the four original neighborhood communities, one decided to farm with horses rather than tractors although, unlike the Amish, they use electric power for many chores rather than diesel engines, and some farmers own a car or pickup truck. Farmers can support each other with compatible equipment, while the community includes a mechanic, an electrician, and a blacksmith. Over the years another neighborhood group has collectively acquired a fine tractor and a full range of tillage and harvesting equipment that are housed in an old garage in their village. One member works full time to maintain this equipment, while another operates it on the community farms. A third community is conducting field research on intensive agricultural techniques that utilize specialized knowledge and equipment, and this requires the members to work closely together. In one community, nearly half the families needed new homes and agreed upon a standard design so that materials could be prepared or purchased at lower cost and cooperative work could proceed more efficiently.

Neighborhood covenant groups meet every Sunday evening to plan cooperative activities for the week. While members are free to undertake novel projects on their own, the covenant standard is that where neighbors expect help from one another they shall agree on common technologies and procedures so that the assistance may be given efficiently, even in emergency situations.

The second element of economic discipline is a common wage-scale. Barter and neighborly helpfulness are encouraged to reduce the need for cash income to pay wages, and this contributes to the stability of each homestead. Nevertheless there are occasions when wages must be paid, and there are services for which salaries are required. The Covenant Community recognizes that a variety of vocations are needed in a healthy society—whether farming, medicine, teaching, carpentry, art, or preaching—and that those who practice any useful vocation are entitled to comparable dignity. Therefore it determined to make all professional wages the same. When one covenant member provides a skilled service to another in return for a wage, that wage is $10 an hour. Unskilled and apprentice labor is paid at the rate of $4 an hour. People are free to work outside the community without wage restrictions. However, now that Mercy and Central colleges are fully within the covenant community, professors, secretaries, and maintenance personnel all receive $10 an hour. Doctors and nurses at the new Covenant Clinic are paid the same. There has been no shortage of applicants for these positions up to now, for many people feel that the quality of life here provides an added reward.

The third aspect of economic discipline is *scrip,* a nominal paper currency that circulates among community members. A member must accept this paper currency, printed by the community, for one-fourth of the value of financial transactions with another member, and may accept it for more. This discipline is designed to stimulate trade within the community and reduce the temptation to purchase bargains from outside suppliers. If a quarter of my college teaching salary comes in scrip, I am sure to spend that portion within the community. If my neighbor who farms with horses and takes care of his land can sell me corn for $4 a bushel, $3 in cash and $1 in scrip, I will not be tempted to buy agribusiness corn at $3.50, in cash. As the community grows, the scrip system provides an incentive for the development of new crops, services, products, and businesses in the area.

Established merchants in Redemption County were irate when the covenant community introduced the scrip system, for they were sure it would deprive them of a share in the promised growth of local trade. When a few tried accepting the scrip, however, they found they could use it in partial payment for products and services from covenant members who were willing to take scrip even though not obligated to do so in this instance. Merchants became more resourceful in buying from the local community as well as marketing to it. As the Covenant Community has expanded, most county merchants have come to accept scrip for some portion of payment because it brings them trade. Business is growing.

The third covenant commitment, sabbath observance, is not designed to compel religious worship but rather to limit power and greed. Most participants in the covenant are religious, but it is not a specifically Christian community and there are no religious requirements for membership. Unlike the Amish practice, these neighborhood groups are not primary worshiping communities even though they usually begin their business meeting on Sunday evenings with prayer. Most homesteaders apply for a particular neighborhood because they prefer one style of farming or see a demand for their trade. On Sunday mornings covenant families travel in different directions to churches of personal choice where they worship alongside neighbors who are not part of this covenant. Few want the Covenant Community to become a sect, for most people appreciate its mission to strengthen the surrounding culture. While there have sometimes been problems assimilating newcomers into churches that were set in their ways, many local Christians have appreciated the influx of new people with fresh spirit.

The sabbath pledge is, instead, a promise to rest and allow others rest, to refrain from long-term debt, and to forgive one's debtors. Homesteaders pledge not to turn their difficult work into perpetual drudgery nor to impose drudgery upon family members, draft animals, or the land itself. They will rest every seventh day and allow others that rest. This pledge builds community, for neighbors need confidence that on one day each week they will not be needed for production assistance, and societies need collective rhythms of relaxation so that cultural and recreational events may be scheduled. Since the Covenant Community defines its sabbath from sundown on Saturday to sundown on Sunday, hardly a Saturday evening passes without a community supper, dance, musicale, play, or some other social activity, while sandlot baseball thrives on Sunday afternoons. Even if you are poor and tired—indeed, especially then!—you need recreation.

This pledge embraces "sabbatical" disciplines as well, including the biblical ethics that inhibit long-term debt. Indeed, the most important part of the whole scheme may be placing people on the land without debt and then giving them incentives not to borrow. Debt ties families to the money economy and forces farmers to specialize in those crops that will satisfy their creditors rather than meet their own needs and the needs of their neighbors. Debt erodes personal freedom and damages the social fabric of a face-to-face community. Therefore Covenant Community members must promise not to mortgage their land or otherwise borrow money—even from institutions outside the community—for terms longer than six years, and that every seventh year they will remain debt free. The community acknowledges that brief borrowings may be necessary, but long-term debt forces people into drudgery and threatens the homestead. Likewise, all covenanters must forgive debts to other members that run to the seventh year, for a community cannot flourish where some people hold others to perpetual debt.

The biblical injunction to let the land lie fallow every seventh year is given a more imaginative, less literal application. The Covenant Community Trust tries to insure that the biotic life and fertility of agricultural land are sustained and, if possible, improved. In addition the trust insists that one seventh of every farm be permanently maintained in a predominantly wild condition with good habitat for birds and other wildlife. This acreage can include forests from which wood is harvested occasionally, stream banks and bogs where native plants are allowed to flourish, and even wild fencerows.

Sabbatical also embraces the covenant members themselves. While nobody is forced to leave their farm or their job every seventh year, and no funds are available for subsidized sabbaticals, the community nevertheless encourages people to take a break from vocational routines every seventh year. If some have the means to travel, their neighbors will watch the homestead, care for their livestock, or temporarily rent their fields. Other people trade jobs on sabbatical, so farmers and craftspeople may help teach at one of the colleges while faculty get practical exprience in the field. Some spend the year working outside the community, while a growing number spend part of their sabbatical on tour interpeting the Redemption County experience to people in other parts of the country. The Covenant Community encourages sabbatical because those who work hard need both rest and new experiences if they are to continue growing as healthy and productive persons. Sabbatical leave, even when unpaid, challenges people to find their fulfillment in life rather than in wealth. It has ecological validity.

* * *

Life was hard for many homesteaders during the first years. The work was unfamiliar, housing was often inadequate, money was scarce, and even food was occasionally in short supply. Many people could not afford a car or a truck, and although the covenant community, anticipating this problem, provided a van network from the very beginning, some people found it galling to be so dependent. A few desperately searched for jobs that would provide quick cash. Most people, however, learned through experience what they had been told during their orientation year: neighborly support during hard times was more valuable than a marginal, uncertain job.

At the beginning, the challenge to each covenant neighborhood was compounded by problems of deciding upon technologies and economic disciplines, and by the unfamiliarity of cooperative work to get big jobs done. To remodel a house or build a barn, one could not ask a banker for a mortgage but instead had to ask neighbors for their time and talents. Each covenant neighborhood included a variety of people, and not all were poor. Fortunately some had resources that were helpful to others, but this also created tensions. Those who felt desperate resented having to turn to those who seemed more secure, while families with resources resented the nagging feeling that they should give more help to neighbors in difficulty with whom they worked nearly every day. It took time to learn the great variety of services and skills, including friendship and insight, that could be exchanged among neighbors, and to discover that a family who required a lot of help at first was indeed likely to return help at a later time.

Some of the most valuable assistance came from neighbors who were not members of the Covenant Community. They knew the land and the region, and while covenant farmers might wish to improve upon local practices, some of them had to learn the rudiments of farming, so a neighbor who could give advice was appreciated. Most local people were flattered to be asked, and many were generous with their time and assistance. Indeed, as the community of newcomers became more sophisticated, they learned how to tap the knowledge of the oldest residents who remembered how the land lay before too many trees were cut and too much sod had been plowed. These folks could recall what game and wildlife had thrived here, and this was helpful for reclamation planning. They remembered simpler farming techniques, some of which might again be useful. Some old-timers had rusty, horse-drawn equipment behind their barns that could be rehabilitated and put to work. Others sang the old songs and played the tunes that soon became popular at the Saturday night musicales.

Many new families on the land, however, differ from those that old-timers remember. Some homes are filled with children, but many families have just one or two, and some households include no children at all. Some are friends and companions rather than families in the traditional sense. Quite a few retired couples among the newcomers appreciate the community life and, supported by pensions, work at reclamation more than production. Black families have taken up farming here despite the harrowing tales of hardship they heard from their grandparents. Other families that had been migrant workers appear resilient to hard work, but some of them need special help to broaden their education and resolve traumas from the past. Some of the Vietnamese and Latin American immigrants bring distinctive cultural knowledge and skills to the community.

The traditional pattern of father in the fields and mother in the kitchen is no longer prevalent. Many women who do not choose to work on the farm find jobs elsewhere, so each covenant village includes a day-care center. The village restaurant has become a popular social center, for many families do not eat all three daily meals at home. Several restaurant managers have become sophisticated in obtaining neighborhood produce and other services in return for discount meals, so cash-short families can be accommodated. You need a reservation to eat at one village restaurant on a Friday night, for that is when the best cooks in the area take turns preparing a special menu.

In many families one or more people work outside the Covenant Community. Some teach in the public schools or work in the county hospital. Others provide sophisticated services to corporations or universities from their home computer terminals. The Covenant Community encourages interraction with the larger society, for it is not a goal to become isolated. Indeed, now that the community is being noticed, accommodating visitors and tourists has become a significant business. Frequent conferences are housed at Central College, and every summer visiting young people live on farms to participate in work and study that provide the farm family with assistance while expanding appreciation for the covenant experiment.

Nevertheless the community tries to provide for its own needs so that expensive "imports" from conventional suppliers may be reduced. Small canneries have opened in two villages to help homesteaders prepare food for themselves and items they may sell. One village set up a sawmill, added a planing mill, and is now building furniture that is popular locally. Mercy College has developed a sophisticated shop for the reconditioning of old farm equipment, and plans are under way to manufacture certain items for the small farmer that are hard to obtain. Last year the Covenant Community opened a sewing factory in Central City that is making work clothes under the "Back to Earth" label; these are popular in the community and it is hoped that visitors will like them as well. Another covenant member owns a car rental garage to supply those who have only occasional need for a vehicle.

As the Covenant Community matures, relations with the

surrounding society become more complex. A waiting list of applicants for homesteads in the county is maintained, but now that the Covenant Community Trust has interest in nearly a third of the farmland, additional land is more difficult to obtain and also more expensive. Some people who have the means purchase land for themselves and then deed an interest to the trust so that they may join the covenant. However, the community is becoming concerned that since it lacks political power, including the right to tax and the right to condemn land, opportunities for the poor are shrinking as land prices rise.

Other problems are also stimulating interest in political activity. At first the additional children from new families were a boon to local schools, filling underutilized classrooms and attracting more state aid. Now new classrooms are needed, and many covenant parents are dissatisfied with the quality of instruction. Two covenant members have already been elected to the school board, but finding acceptable sources of new revenue will not be easy. Since most covenant members live on modest cash incomes, they share the general distaste for property taxes. One member has announced her candidacy for the state legislature in hope of securing a law that would allow the county to add to the state income tax or sales tax as a more acceptable means to raise revenue for local use. She also advocates a statewide land reform program that would use tax funds to condemn land to make new homesteads available. Covenant Community members are learning that they must develop their political influence and encourage others to undertake reforms as well.

Every year a few resign from the Covenant Community. Some of these move away, but others remain on their farms and even continue some of the habits that they learned in the covenant. A few members have been expelled for blatant violation of covenant standards, and one neighborhood was nearly destroyed by controversy. The Community Land Trust, by policy, will not repurchase property that it has already encumbered, for it prefers to extend environmental protection to new tracts, but the market for this land remains strong. Indeed, as this culture develops and exhibits attractive characteristics, some people move to Redemption County who accept the

environmental constraints of covenanted land even though they
may not be interested in personal covenant membership. The revival
of old-time music has attracted two such musicians, while a fine
cabinet-maker works with the furniture shop but has not yet joined
the covenant.

The rapid development of culture in Redemption County
rests upon three pillars. The first is the religious commitment that
undergirds social and environmental efforts. People need deep resolve to persevere when the way is hard, and they need extra
strength to remain helpful when neighborhood relationships are
taxing. Since they did not organize as a religious sect, but institutionalized their efforts at the environmental and social levels instead, religious commitment can help the covenant people to remain
flexible in these areas. "When our faith is involved, but not at stake,"
Anne Stem observes, "We are more likely to criticize our social and
environmental behavior." The second pillar is education. Every
adult in the Covenant Community participates in at least one class
each week except during the harvest months. Education helps
people to reflect upon their experience. Through classes the discov-
eries of one can be shared with others and appraised by the group.
Continuing education also provides an opportunity to explore interests that have no apparent connection to daily work. In this community a poor farmer may become a philosopher and may even have
opportunity to teach. The third pillar is rest and recreation, enjoyment and expression, through arts, worship, music, sports, food, and
sensuous alertness to natural beauty. This is not a dour community
but a lively one, and the time taken for rest and recreation is used to
the full. This is the flowering of a culture.

* * *

The landscapes of Redemption County are becoming more
beautiful. Many of the larger fields are now divided with fencerows.
There are hedges, trees, ponds, and bogs that enrich the view. More
birds and frogs are heard, and more rabbits and squirrels are seen.
Many older, smaller fields that had been weedy and eroded are now
lush and neat. New timber stands are growing. Tired old farmhouses

have been remodeled, and gardens thrive beside them. The landscape is dotted with new homesteads where people can be seen at work. There are horses, cattle, hogs, and sheep, as well as chickens, geese, and turkeys. The countryside smells good and looks alive.

Even those who had been most fearful of the Covenant Community now enjoy Sunday drives on the country roads more than they once did. When they need to grouch they say "Well, some things look better, but . . . "

"Many of us have fallen in love again with the land we are tending and the place where we live," Anne Stem concludes. "We want to care for the life here because it is so beautiful."

16. *Earth to Earth*

Christian hope can no longer be anchored in another world to the exclusion of this earth, for the moral crisis of humanity and the environmental crisis of nature are interdependent. At the beginning of our faith history, the people who believed and the lands that they tended were oppressed. When *Yahweh* gathered a holy people, this God commissioned them to liberate a holy land as well. The Lord instructed them in compassionate attitudes and just behavior toward their human companions whether strong or weak, toward domesticated lands and livestock, and toward the wild species. The covenant community was a morally responsive ecosystem.

When oppression took root again within this distinctive society, God's prophets warned against injustice and pollution, calling the people to repent before the rains failed, the earth withered, and the land was overrun by those who did not know the Lord. God's people were eventually driven into exile but, while the blighted landscape rested, prophets imagined a return that would secure social righteousness and revive natural fruitfulness. Centuries later Jesus proclaimed, "The time has come; the kingdom of God is upon you; repent, and believe the Gospel" (Mark 1:15, NEB), and those who folowed him in Galilee witnessed stirrings of rebirth among the common people and signs of awakening from the natural environment as well. Although the Christian Church lost its connection with the traditional holy land, its apostles preserved the affirmation that all created life looks forward to "the same glorious freedom as the children of God" (Romans 8:21, NJB).

Viewing the frightening environmental crisis of our time through the lens of Christian hope, I see three admonitions pointing toward the future that God intends:

- Commune with the earth
- Prepare for its devastation
- Labor in hope for its regeneration

* * *

We commune with the earth as we cultivate sensuous, under-standing, and respectful relationships with living creatures that surround us, with natural forces such as sunlight and wind, and with the hills and fields, streams and lakes, that comprise the landscape where we live. Conscious communion with nature must become a part of daily Christian life if nature is to be recognized within the eucharistic praise of the church.

Since communion with nature has often been ignored in the Christian tradition, we have much to learn. Some eastern religions and some Native American practices have been more expressive in this regard, and we may profit from them. Recalling that Native American hunters honored prey and apologized to them for taking lives necessary to sustain human families, we might address our thanks before meals directly to the species of animals and plants that nourish us as well as to the God who watches over the fruitfulness of the earth.

The important thing is that we do, in fact, commune. Time spent in the woods is not wasted time, for unless we take time we will not learn. Attention focused upon a domestic animal or a free-flying bird is not idleness, for without attention we will not feel. The care required to construct a compost pile that will fertilize a garden is not extravagant, for life responds to our care. Our communion with nature provides the motivation we need to deal with the environ-mental crisis that threatens the earth, and no service to the God who loves the world is more urgent than this.

Our communion is not innocent, for our sustenance depends, in part, upon a culture that abuses the earth. The nature we meet is increasingly polluted: it still reflects the beauty of its Creator, but it also reveals the consequences of human sin. Therefore Christian meditation upon nature, while it may inspire our spirits, should also bring us to repentance. It is less likely to suggest passive acceptance of things as they are than to inspire efforts to reform culture and rescue nature from destruction.

Modern relationships with nature cannot issue from the sense of moral security that the Native American hunter once knew when, in a rich land with few people, he followed the traditons of his ancestors. There are no ancient rituals available to us that will assure harmonious relations with the natural world. We cannot simply retreat to the farming practices of our grandparents or even to the sabbatical ethics of the biblical Hebrews, however relevant these may prove to be in some respects. We must devise our own relationship with nature as we develop sensitivity to the species and ecosystems around us. Both ancient wisdom and modern science can help us if we are alert to feedback from those we affect and if we are humble enough to abandon techniques that work poorly. True communion with nature, Wendell Berry suggests, leads to discretion:

> That is not to suggest that we can live harmlessly, or strictly at our own expense; we depend upon other creatures and survive by their deaths. To live, we must daily break the body and shed the blood of Creation. When we do this knowingly, lovingly, skillfully, reverently, it is a sacrament. When we do it ignorantly, greedily, clumsily, destructively, it is a desecration. In such desecration we condemn ourselves to spiritual and moral loneliness, and others to want.[1]

Environmental relations now require the full communion, the respect from an "I" to a "Thou," that Martin Buber recommended for moral relationships among persons.[2] The lives around us can no longer be regarded as things to be exploited with impunity. We must recognize nature within the covenant of life.

* * *

The hardest part of loving the earth is preparing for the devastation that is coming. Those who exploit nature may remain indifferent to its fate, but those who love the earth are forced to notice the consequences of human abuse that are already apparent and to contemplate further, inescapable degredations. At high elevations trees wither from the toxic gases that spew from automobiles and smokestacks, while lakes lose their capacity to sustain life as acid rain descends upon them. Tropical rain forests, the richest assemblages of life on this planet, are ravaged for timber and deliberately burned to provide grazing land for cattle; whole species are exterminated before humanity has even identified them.

The smoke from these vast, deliberate fires adds to huge emissions from the world's use of coal, oil, and natural gas that raise levels of carbon dioxide in the air; this, in turn, slows the escape of solar radiation from the atmosphere so the earth warms. This "greenhouse" warming trend dries temperate forests so they also burn more readily; it may also bring drought to agricultural regions and reduce our ability to grow food; while the warming atmosphere can melt polar ice caps, raise the level of the oceans, and flood coastal regions. Other industrial gases have already opened holes in the stratospheric ozone layer that shields the earth from ultraviolet radiation, which can cause cancer in humans and genetic mutations in simpler forms of life. Solid and liquid wastes spread poisons through soils, streams, and groundwater.

Even as the planet becomes less hospitable, human population multiplies. Hundreds of millions of people are now so poor that they must pillage their biotic communities, cutting the timber, overgrazing the grasslands, and cropping marginal farmlands until deserts advance toward once productive regions. Yet millions of others who benefit from the exploitation of natural resources are rich enough to isolate themselves, for the time being, from the fate of the earth.

It is by no means certain that all life will perish from the earth, or even that humanity will propel itself to extinction. Ecosystems and natural forces may exhibit more resilience than we have reason to expect. People may repent of pollution, and human society may innovate in ways that cannot now be predicted. God may intervene to change the course of history. It does appear, however, that much of the natural beauty and vitality that we love will be damaged by the pollution already released, the technologies already in place, and the needs of people already born. Whatever hope our grandchildren may find in their time, they will live amid environmental degradation more intense than we now experience, and they will confront a human community in great distress as well. The future that we can see is bleak.

It is natural to reject such a somber forecast and insist that somehow, in some way, the worst consequences of human abuse of the earth can be avoided. It is also common for Christians to imagine that God will rescue us from the fate that others may have to endure. If we love nature and understand its place in God's moral covenant, however, then we can no longer imagine that our Lord will snatch us from the burning earth to hide us in a remote heaven while other species—more innocent than we—suffer the consequence of our sins.

When we recognize that God's community of renewal is a moral ecosystem, then we cannot seek redemption at the expense of those we have abused. Biblical prophets insisted that even God's chosen people must accept responsibility for their sins and endure the consequences of the injustice and the pollution which they tolerated. Amos gave a sharp reminder that God's judgment upon sin does not mitigate the natural calamities one might expect but rather augments them:

> Fools who long for the day of the LORD,
> what will the day of the LORD mean to you?
> It will be darkness, not light.
> It will be as when a man runs from a lion,
>   and a bear meets him,
> or turns into a house and leans his hand on the wall,
>   and a snake bites him.
> The day of the LORD is indeed darkness, not light,
>   a day of gloom with no dawn.
>
> (Amos 5:18—20, NEB)

Therefore Christians who love the earth must ask God for the grace to accept such judgment and the courage to announce it to others. *Devastation is at hand!* It is no kindness to mute these words. However swift our repentance, however broad its reach, however faithfully we tend the earth, however we redirect human desires, however innovatively we meet human needs, great suffering lies ahead. Many species will be extinguished; many ecosystems will be impoverished beyond recognition; many people will starve; many others will be sickened by polluted environments they cannot escape.

We must make these truths plain because those who would profit from the sufferings of others, and those who find it politic to be inoffensive, may propose remedies that actually compound the environmental crisis: if only we produce more, if only we expand mining and drilling, if only we add more chemicals to the fields, if only we subsidize nuclear power, if only we compete more aggressively for foreign markets; if only poor countries would pay their debts, manufacture the dangerous chemicals we need, store wastes for us, and grow crops we wish to buy; if only we keep those hungry people out, then the United States will have enough. In response to such evasions, Christians who love the earth must boldly proclaim the truth that Americans cannot avoid unpleasant consequences from our exploitation of the earth. Only after we repent and relent can we begin to build a happier culture in partnership with nature.

We must make these truths plain, as well, so that Christians and other concerned people may prepare ministries of compassion. The foremost of these is to be present with the suffering. Those who love the earth will renew their natural contacts with special urgency. Beautiful, vulnerable landscapes need human visitors who care: people with the scientific knowledge to understand them, people with artistic gifts to memorialize them, people with religious feelings to commune with them and pray for them, as well as people with the political skills to speak for these places to the larger society. The more desperate we imagine the fate of the earth to be, the more urgent it is that we meet, love, and understand those species and places that may be lost to the future. Although the preservation of memories does not substitute adequately for the preservation of life, and being present for dying species or decaying landscapes may be painful, it would be a greater tradegy for members of the family of life to slip away unknown and unrecognized.

This series has persistently maintained that a life of environ-

mental responsibility does not require painful sacrifice but rather
leads to more natural rewards and more wholesome satisfactions
than the exploitative life-style so prevalent today. Indeed, pollution
is now so widespread that all people will experience its unpleasant
consequences regardless of their life-style. Beyond a more healthful
life of "elegant frugality," however, some people will choose to
identify themselves with the needs of nature in ways that are indeed
costly and sacrificial. These, I believe, will play a special role in
redeeming the earth. Jesus our Lord identified with all forms of
earthly life and died for all of them:

> "Through him God chose to reconcile the whole universe to [God's]
> self, making peace through the shedding of his blood upon the
> cross—to reconcile all things, whether on earth or in heaven,
> through him alone" (Colossians 1:20, NEB, alt.), "that the universe,
> all in heaven and on earth, might be brought into a unity in Christ"
> (Ephesians 1:10, NEB).

Those who give of themselves for the sake of nature may participate
in Christ's sufferings, and since this sacrifice is a special calling, it
brings special rewards. "For just as the sufferings of Christ overflow
into our lives," the apostle Paul writes, "so too does the encouragement we receive through Christ" (2 Corinthians 1:5, NJB). Part of this
encouragement is knowing that one is among the children of God for
whom "the created universe waits with eager expectation" (Romans
8:19, NEB).

                                    * * *

Let us labor in hope for the regeneration of the earth—the
third admonition. Our God has called all forms of life into the
covenant of redemption, and if we trust the Lord with our own lives
we can trust God with the destiny of natural life as well. The toxic
burden of pollution may grow throughout our lifetimes, ecosystems
may weaken while species perish, and humanity may crowd more
densely upon the earth. Yet whatever land we protect, whatever
waters we cherish, and whatever seeds we plant may eventually
spread new life to the world. Like Jeremiah, we must reach beyond

the siegeworks of oppression to redeem some living things.

Biblical prophets, particularly those whose warnings of God's judgment were most uncompromising, held forth lush visions of a future when God and the people of God would redeem the earth. As oppression and pollution spread, these biblical visions become more important, for they were spoken to hard times so hope might not be lost. Like modern environmentalists, biblical prophets could write with nostalgia for earlier days when moral corruption and environmental pollution were less prevalent. Unlike many environmentalists, however, the prophets looked forward to times of renewal that would bring more fertility, productivity, environmental complexity, and peace among the species than in the golden past. Book 3 of this series, *Hope for the Land,* considered Ezekiel's vision of a redeemed ecosystem, fed by waters from the temple mountain, and overflowing with fruits and fish. These images infuse John's vision, on the final pages of the New Testament, of a new heaven and a new earth. According to Gospel reports, this anticipated abundance actually broke forth during Jesus' ministry in Galillee.[3]

Prophets believed in a future because they trusted the Lord. Their ecology was moral rather than scientific: without technical understanding of environmental relationships, they insisted that each species had a place in a moral community. They did not presume that the health which the earth had exhibited heretofore limited its potential for the future. Instead they proposed that, as social justice and relationships among species improved, the capacity of the ecosystem to sustain both human and natural life would grow apace:

> A time is coming, says the LORD,
>> when the ploughman shall follow hard on the reaper,
>> and he who treads the grapes after him who sows the seed.
> The mountains shall run with fresh wine,
>> and every hill shall wave with corn.
>> (Amos 9:13, NEB)

This promise still gives those who trust the Lord a reason for hope and a strong motive for environmental reclamation.

Christian hope that both justice and abundance are possible

may give a distinctive thrust to our political analysis and our social action. The population problem provides an example. Like most environmentalists, I believe that healthy relationships between humanity and nature will not be achieved until human population is stabilized and, indeed, reduced. This conclusion, however, troubles many Christians who believe that it encourages social tolerance of fetal abortions, and it is particularly upsetting to Roman Catholic leaders, who insist that all artificial technologies for birth control are morally unacceptable.

In fact nobody knows what human population the earth might support without environmental degradation. Those who lack ecological understanding imagine that humanity is in competition with other forms of life for space and sustenance and, therefore, a growing human population requires the decline of other species and ecosystems. The truth is quite different. A large human population can only be supported on this planet if natural life remains dense and complex, for the quality of air and water, the quantity of rainfall, the productivity of soil, and the ability of the earth to retain a habitable temperature, all depend upon a rich biotic community. The alarming rise in pollution and environmental degradation during the twentieth century is due to the character of modern technology and the consumption habits of the affluent, more than to the human numbers. If we cut human population in half but continue to maintain our present technologies, life-styles, and patterns of social oppression, environmental degradation will proceed.

On the other hand, if we changed our basic philosophy of farming from simplifying ecosystems in order to optimize human control, as we now do, to enriching farm ecosystems with as much diversity as possible, as Booker T. Whatley recommended, there is no reason why temperate farming might not achieve, in time, a density of life similar to that of tropical rain forests. More people could be fed from each acre of ground, more people could be employed, the quality of plant and animal life could be improved, and even the climate might benefit from the greater exchange of moisture and nutrients in such complex environments. While I continue to believe that birth control is a moral necessity, population policy can make a major contribution to ecological health only within the context of energy conservation by the affluent, accompanied by land reform and biologically sensitive renewal of agricultural practices.

Those who hope in the Lord must announce to the world that natural abundance, beyond all previous experience, is possible if we commit ourselves to moral relationships with all humankind, the other species, and the natural forces that share this earth with us. This is God's promise throughout the Bible. Those who love the Lord also have a special obligation to demonstrate this truth by fashioning righteous and compassionate communities that embrace the life around them, and by experimenting with techniques that give promise of sustaining and enriching the natural environment while improving human sustenance.

* * *

Biblical ecology helps me to anticipate death with more contentment. Throughout the years, the "me" of which I am conscious has been formed from the substance of countless plants and animals whose tissue became, for a time, my flesh. What I am depends upon what they were, although they had to surrender their own lives and consciousness to sustain me and others like me.

When we die, and our bodies are buried or ashes scattered to await the general resurrection, we won't just "sleep." We too will percolate through the lives of other creatures, beginning with bacteria and microorganisms, spreading to insects and plants, and eventually, perhaps, joining fish or animals. Our consciousness will have been surrendered, but we will sustain the senses of other species, returning their favor through physical communion.[4]

The more I love the earth, the more satisfactory this fate appears. There is a splendid sugar maple on my farm from which I have drawn sweet sap through the years. I hope to be buried nearby in a simple wooden box so I may quickly enter a community of life that I have enjoyed.

The general resurrection that we are promised in the New Testament is not a natural circumstance but a special work of God, so we may leave to the Lord the physical details of how this will be accomplished. However, Christians can join John of Patmos in the

moral conviction that "everything that lives in the air, and on the
ground, and under the ground, and in the sea" will join with God's
people to give praise to Christ, their Redeemer (Revelation 5:13, JB).
Wendell Berry writes of this inclusive sabbath:

> What stood will stand, though all be fallen,
> The good return that time has stolen.
> Though creatures groan in misery,
> Their flesh prefigures liberty
> To end travail and bring to birth
> Their new perfection in new earth.
> At word of that enlivening
> Let the trees of the woods all sing
> And every field rejoice, let praise
> Rise up out of the ground like grass.
> What stood, whole in every piecemeal
> Thing that stood, will stand though all
> Fall—field and woods and all in them
> Rejoin the primal Sabbath's hymn.[5]

Since by the mercy of God we depend upon one another, we share a
common hope.

Suggestions for Reading

Thomas Jefferson, *Writings,* selected by Merrill Peterson at the University of Virginia (New York: Library of America, 1984), reveals the range of this brilliant mind and engaging personality. Richard Matthews' brief study of *The Radical Politics of Thomas Jefferson* (Lawrence, Kansas: University Press of Kansas, 1984) clarifies Jefferson's social vision while challenging the traditional emphasis upon Jefferson's individualism.

Despite all that has been written since, Lewis Mumford's study, *The Pentagon of Power* (New York: Harcourt Brace Jovanovich, 1970) remains the most stimulating critique of the modern technological system. Just so, Amory Lovens' essay "Energy Strategy: The Road Not Taken,"included in *Soft Energy Paths* (San Francisco: Friends of the Earth, 1977), is the essential analysis for modern energy policy. The endnotes to my chapter 4 recommend additional books on the energy crisis.

Wendell Berry's magnificent indictment of modern agriculture, *The Unsettling of America* (San Francisco: Sierra Club, 1977), has become a classic among his many essays, novels, and poems that convey a vision of rural culture. Christian readers may find Berry's recent book of poetry, *Sabbaths* (San Francisco: North Point Press, 1987), particularly appealing. Wes Jackson's seminal study, *New Roots for Agriculture* (University of Nebraska Press, 1985) develops this biologist's vision of "perennial polycultures" within a philosophical and religious context. Together, Jackson and Berry have gathered exciting essays from several hands in *Meeting the Expectations of the Land* (San Francisco: North Point Press, 1984). Susan George shows that American food policies promote world hunger in

How the Other Half Dies (Totowa, New Jersey: Rowman & Allanheld, 1977). Marty Strange adds clear policy recommendations to his penetrating social analysis in *Family Farming: A New Economic Vision* (Lincoln, Nebraska: University of Nebraska Press, 1988). Francis Moore Lappé combines clear policy analysis with nourishing recipes in *Diet for a Small Planet* (New York: Ballentine Books, 1982).

In *Animal Thinking* (Cambridge, Massachusetts: Harvard University Press, 1984), ethologist Donald Griffin shows that many species have remarkable sensory and cognitive capacities, some of which exceed the human. Vicki Hearne, who trains horses and dogs, explores the emotional and cognitive interplay between humans and domesticated animals in *Adam's Task: Calling Animals by Name* (New York: Knopf, 1986). Ian McHarg's magnificent *Design with Nature* (Graden City, N.Y.: Doubleday, 1971) develops a philosophy of landscape management. Joseph Sax clarifies the cultural role of national parks in *Mountains Without Handrails* (University of Michigan Press, 1984). In *Ecotopoia* (Berkeley, California: Banyan Tree Books, 1975), Ernest Callenbach imagines a society in harmony with nature.

Christopher Stone wrote the law journal essay that helped to shape Justice William O. Douglas' landmark dissent in *Sierra vs. Morton;* it may be found, along with the court opinions in this case, in Stone's work, *Should Trees Have Standing?* (Los Altos, California: William Kaufmann, 1974). Stone continues to explore the philosophy of environmental law in *Earth and Other Ethics: The Case for Moral Pluralism* (New York: Harper & Row, 1987).

Appreciation

Marty Strange of the Center for Rural Affairs, Walthill, Nebraska, gave me my first training in agricultural policy, and he thoughtfully reviewed the chapters on agriculture. David and Elsie Kline graciously shared their hospitality, their words, and their deep Amish tradition. Christopher Stone of the Law Center, University of Southern California, inspired me fifteen years ago to begin thinking about civil rights for nature, so I was honored when he read the chapters on civil rights and gave me encouragement. Russell Stroup, to whom I dedicated Book 3, taught me forty years ago that Jefferson's democratic vision complemented Jesus' moral vision in the Gospels. None of these can be held responsible for what is written here, but each one has helped me to think.

On an emergency basis while I was changing publishers, Karen Ready edited the copy with grace and competence. Lori Ward Hamm, my editorial associate throughout this series, supervised the publication of this book with dedication and skill.

Notes

Part 1. America the Beautiful

1. Katherine Lee Bates, 1893.

Chapter 1. Jefferson's Vision

1. Thomas Jefferson, *Writings,* 17 (New York: Library of America, 1984), 706.
2. Jefferson, *Writings,* 1399.
3. Dumas Malone, *Jefferson the Virginian* (Boston: Little, Brown & Co., 1948), 238.
4. Jefferson attacked slavery in his draft of the Declaration of Independence, but his language was deleted by the Continental Congress before adoption of the Declaration. In the model constitutions he drafted for the state of Virginia, slavery was expressly prohibited, but his drafts were not adopted. Jefferson kept slaves, but deplored the practice throughout his lifetime. See Richard K. Matthews, *The Radical Politics of Thomas Jefferson, A Revisionist View* (Lawrence, KS: University Press of Kansas, 1986), 66–67. On Jefferson's personal relations with blacks and women, see Fawn M. Brodie, *Thomas Jefferson, An Intimate History* (New York: W. W. Norton, 1974).
5. Jefferson, *Writings,* 185–186.
6. Jefferson to James Madison, 28 October, 1785, *Writings,* 841–842.
7. Jefferson, *Writings,* 1309.
8. Jefferson, *Writings,* 290–291.
9. Jefferson, *Writings,* 293.
10. Jefferson, *Writings,* 894–895.
11. Jefferson, *Writings,* 1249.
12. Jefferson, *Writings,* 859.
13. Jefferson, *Writings,* 1181.
14. Jefferson, *Writings,* 290.
15. Jefferson, *Writings,* 818. Jefferson's preference for farming was so strong that he initially wished to discourage manufacturing on this side of the Atlantic so that the oppressive conditions in European cities would not spread to these shores. As president he came to realize, however, that lack of manufacturing ability made the new nation more vulnerable to the viscissitudes of trade. He supported "manufactures to the extent of our own consumption at least, in all articles of which we raise the raw materials," but he continued to oppose aggressive partici-

pation in world commerce, which he called "this protuberant navigation which has kept us in hot water from the commencement of our government, and is now engaging us in war." See *The Life and Selected Writings of Thomas Jefferson*, Adrienne Koch & William Peden, eds. (New York: Modern Library, 1944), 593–594.

16. See "Declaration and Resolves of the First Continental Congress, October 14, 1774," in *Documents of American History*, Henry Steele Commager, ed. (New York: Appleton-Century-Crofts, 1949), 83. The expressions derive from John Locke's triad "life, liberty, and estate."
17. *Documents*, 103.
18. *Documents*, 100.
19. Jefferson, *Writings*, 841–842.
20. See Aaron M. Sakolski, *Land Tenure and Land Taxation in America* (New York: Robert Schalkenback Foundation, 1957), 84.
21. Jefferson, *Writings*, 1386–1387.
22. Jefferson, *Writings*, 561–562. See *Radical Politics*, 53–75, 124.
23. Jefferson, *Writings*, 959.
24. Jefferson, letter of 25 January 1786, quoted in *Radical Politics*, 138, note 14.
25. Jefferson, *Writings*, 1400.

Chapter 2. The Pursuit of Happiness

1. Wilhelm Reich, *The Function of the Orgasm* (New York: Simon and Schuster, 1973), 201.
2. Paul Goodman, *Nature Heals* (New York: Free Life Editions, 1977), 68.
3. Reich, *Function of the Orgasm*, 156.
4. The exploitation of sexual repression by Facism was explored by Wilhelm Reich, *The Mass Psychology of Facism* (New York: Farrar, Straus and Giroux, 1970), and by Erik Erikson in *Identity: Youth and Crisis* (New York: W. W. Norton & Co., 1968). See also Book 2, Chapter 17.
5. Edmund Spenser, quoted in Geoffry Hill, *The Lords of Limit* (Oxford).
6. Jefferson, *Writings*, 859.
7. Jefferson, *Writings*, 859.
8. Jefferson, *Writings*, 1343.

Chapter 3. Good Work

1. Karl Marx, *Capital, A Critical Analysis of Capitalist Production*, ed. Frederick Engels, trans. Moore and Aveling (London, 1886), 163–164, 166.
2. Lewis Mumford, *The Myth of the Machine, The Pentagon of Power* (New York: Harcourt Brace Jovanovich, 1970), 358–359.

3. Mumford, *Pentagon of Power,* 127–128.
4. Mumford, *Pentagon of Power,* 154–155.
5. Sebastian de Grazia, *Of Time, Work, and Leisure* (Garden City, NY: Doubleday Anchor, 1964), 13.
6. Mumford, *Pentagon of Power,* 138.
7. Mumford, *Pentagon of Power,* 128.

Chapter 4. Elegant Frugality

1. Amory B. Lovins, *Soft Energy Paths: Toward a Durable Peace* (Cambridge, MA: Ballinger Publishing Co., 1977), 57.
2. Lovins, *Soft Energy Paths,* 8.
3. Lovins notes that "fluidized beds are simple, versatile devices that add the fuel a little at a time to a much larger mass of small, inert, red–hot particles—sand or ceramic pellets—kept suspended as an agitated fluid by a stream of air continuously blown up through it from below. The efficiency . . . is remarkably high." *Soft Energy Paths,* 46–47. American Electric Power Company, mentioned below, has built the first commercial plant of this type on the Ohio River near Steubenville, Ohio.
4. For details of this struggle see "The Battle for Brumley Gap," *Sierra* magazine, January 1984. The consultants were Energy Systems Research Group, of Boston.
5. Lovins, *Soft Energy Paths,* 102
6. Lovins, *Soft Energy Paths,* 150–151
7. There are several good evaluations of these opportunities. The lay reader will appreciate Barry Commoner, *The Closing Circle: Nature, Man & Technology* (New York: Alfred A. Knopf, 1971), and E. F. Schumacher, *Small is Beautiful: Economics as if People Mattered* (New York: Harper & Row, 1973). Students will benefit from Mihajlo Mesarovic and Eduard Pestel, *Mankind and the Turning Point, The Second Report to the Club of Rome* (New York: E. P. Dutton, 1974); *A time to Choose: America's Energy Future,* by the Ford Foundation, Energy Policy Project (Cambridge, MA: Ballinger Publishing Co., 1974); *Jobs and Energy: The Employment and Economic Impacts of Nuclear Power, Conservation, and Other Energy Options,* (New York: Council on Economic Priorities, 1979); and the continuing series of annual reports on the "State of the World" by the Worldwatch Institute (New York: W. W. Norton & Co.).
8. See Priscilla J. Brewer, *Shaker Communities, Shaker Lives* (Hanover, NH: University Press of New England, 1986).

Part II. Agriculture

1. Wendell Berry, *Home Economics* (San Francisco: North Point Press, 1987), 54.

Chapter 5. Failure

1. United States Department of Agriculture, *A Time to Choose: Summary Report on the Structure of Agriculture* (Washington D.C.: 1981), 73; Sakolski, *Land Tenure,* 219. In 1880 national census statistics were first gathered on this question. In the South, freeholding may have peaked a decade earlier; the reimposition of tenancy had already begun by 1880.
2. Alexis de Tocqueville, *Democracy in America,* ed. J. P. Mayer (Garden City, NY: 1969) 554.
3. See Sonya Salamon, "Ethnic Communities and the Structure of Agriculture," *Rural Sociology* 50, no. 3 (Fall 1985).
4. Quoted in Brewer, *Shaker Communities,* 85–86.
5. *Documents,* 415
6. See "Jefferson, Morrill, and the Upper Crust" in Wendell Berry, *The Unsettling of America: Culture & Agriculture* (San Francisco: Sierra Club Books, 1977).
7. Justin Morrill, quoted in Berry, *Unsettling of America,* 145
8. USDA, *A Time To Choose,* 73.
9. Sakolski, *Land Tenure,* 225–225; Sidney Baldwin in *The People's Land: A Reader on Land Reform in the United States,* ed. Peter Barnes (Emmaus PA: Rodale Press, 1975), 17–19. See also Sidney Baldwin, *Poverty and Politics: The Rise and Decline of the Farm Security Administration* (University of North Carolina Press, 1968).
10. Berry, *Unsettling of America,* 11. See Lester R. Brown, "Conserving Soils," in *State of the World: 1984,* Worldwatch Institute (New York: W. W. Norton & Co., 1984).
11. Wilson Clark, *Energy for Suvival: The Alternative to Extinction* (Garden City, NY: Doubleday Anchor, 1974), 168–174; Barry Commoner, *The Poverty of Power: Energy and the Economic Crisis* (New York: Alfred A. Knopf, 1976), 163.
12. Berry, *Unsettling of America,* 33.
13. USDA, *A Time to Choose,* 34–35, 133.
14. 1982 figures adaped from U. S. Congress, Office of Technology Assessment, 1985 report on "The Changing Structure of Agriculture," as reported in Shantilal P. Bhagat, *The Farm Family: Can It Be Saved?* (Elgin, IL: Brethren Press, 1985), 30. Other figures from USDA, *A Time to Choose,* 44, 47. Most tobacco is grown on farms with less than $40,000 income.
15. USDA, *A Time to Choose,* 73.
16. Berry, *Unsettling of America,* 41.
17. USDA, *A Time to Choose,* 62.
18. *The New York Times,* Sunday, 3 August, 1986, 3:1.
19. *The New York Times,* Sunday, 12 July, 1987, 3:1.

Chapter 6. Roots

1. Masanobu Fukuoka, *The One-Straw Revolution* (Emmaus PA: Rodale Press, 1978), 19, 15.
2. Berry, *Unsettling of America,* 86.
3. John A. Hostetler, *Amish Society,* 3d ed. (Baltimore: Johns Hopkins University Press, 1980).
4. Menno Simons, quoted in Hostetler, *Amish Society,* 118.
   This quote, and those that follow from David Kline, were transcribed from the recording of an address to the the the North American Conference on Christianity and Ecology, North Webster, Indiana, 20 August 1987, and are used with the speaker's permission.

Chapter 7. New Growth

1. Dick Thompson, quoted by Charles Isenhart in "Two Iowa Farmers Sow the Seeds of Change," *Sierra* (November/December 1987), 82.
2. Booker T. Whatley, "The Men Behind 'The Ultimate Small Farm'," *The New Farm* (September/October 1987), 24, 25–26.
3. Craig Cramer, "May The Best Produce Win, Too," *The New Farm* (July/August 1987), 27.
4. "Food Aid Program in Massachusetts Ties Farms to the Slums," *The New York Times,* 28 June 1987, 35.
5. J. Sholto Douglas & Robert A. de J. Hart, *Forest Farming: Towards a Solution to Problems of World Hunger and Conservation* (Emmaus, PA: Rodale Press, 1978), 4–6.
6. Wes Jackson, *New Roots for Agriculture* (Lincoln: University of Nebraska Press, 1985), 10, 94.
7. Wes Jackson, "The Unifying Concept for Sustainable Agriculture," in Wes Jackson, Wendell Berry, Bruce Colman, eds., *Meeting the Expectations of the Land: Essays in Sustainable Agriculture and Stewardship* (San Francisco: North Point Press, 1984), 224, 226.
8. Jackson, *New Roots,* vii.
9. Jackson, *New Roots,* 148, 145.
10. Jackson, *Meeting the Expectations of the Land,* 183.
11. Wes Jackson, *Altars of Unhewn Stone: Science and the Earth* (San Francisco: North Point Press, 1987), 27.
12. Quoted in Jack Doyle, *Altered Harvest: Agriculture, Genetics, and the Fate of the World's Food Supply* (New York: Viking, 1985), 15.
13. Jackson, *Altars of Unhewn Stone,* 23.
14. Doyle, *Altered Harvest,* 177.
15. "Diamond vs. Chakrabarty," quoted in Doyle, *Altered Harvest,* 71.
16. Jackson, *Altars of Unhewn Stone,* 152, 90.

Chapter 8. Cattle Culture

1. Exodus 23: 4–12, 24: 4; Deuteronomy 22: 6-10; Ezekiel 34; Luke 15: 3–7.
2. Vicki Hearne, "Language and Animals," *The New Yorker,* 18 August 1986, 37, 56.
3. John Muir, *To Yosemite and Beyond: Writings from the Years 1863 to 1875,* ed. Robert Engberg and Donald Wesling (Madison: University of Wisconsin Press, 1980), 121.
4. John Muir, *The Mountains of California* (New York: Viking Penguin, 1985), 220, 210–211.
5. Thomas Jukes, quoted in Orville Schell, *Modern Meat: Antibiotics, Hormones, and the Pharmaceutical Farm* (New York: Random House, 1984), 21. My information on antibiotics and sex hormones is drawn from this book.
6. Schell, *Modern Meat,* 23–24.
7. Schell, *Modern Meat,* 278–294.
8. Carol Tucker Foreman, quoted in Schell, *Modern Meat,* 317.
9. Schell, *Modern Meat,* 168.
10. Frances Moore Lappé, *Diet for a Small Planet* (New York: Ballantine Books, 1982), 67, 69, 70, 75.
11. William Glaberson, "Misery on the Meatpacking Line," *The New York Times,* 14 June, 1987, 3: 1, 8.
12. Glenn Oakley, "Allan Savory's Range Revolution," *Sierra* (November/December 1986), 31; see also K. L. Tinley, *An Ecological Reconnaissance of the Moremi Wildlife Reserve, Botswana* (Okovango [sic] Wildlife Society, 1973), 108.
13. For a list of farmers who raise drug-free beef, lamb, pork and other meat products, send $1.00 to Lean and Clean, *The New Farm,* 222 Main Street, Emmaus, PA 18098.
14. Information provided by Humane Farming Association, San Francisco.

Chapter 9. Harvesting Justice

1. See William Cronon, *Changes in the Land: Indians, Colonists, and the Ecology of New England* (New York: Hill and Wang, 1983), a brilliant study in historical ecology.
2. Jess Ennis, "The Failure of Successful Agriculture in Mexico," *The Land Report* (Salina, KS: The Land Institute), Spring 1987, 20–24; Angus Wright, "Innocents Abroad: American Agricultural Research in Mexico," in Jackson, *Meeting the Expectations of the Land,* 135–151.
3. Edward C. Wolf, "Beyond the Green Revolution: New Approaches for Third World Agriculture," *Worldwatch Paper* 73 (October 1986), 18.
4. Doyle, *Altered Harvest,* 262.
5. Sumanta Banerjee and Smitu Kothari, "Food and Hunger in India," *The Ecologist* 15, 5/6 (London, 1985), 260.

6. Jon Bennett, *The Hunger Machine: The Politics of Food* (Cambridge, England: Polity Press, 1987), 157.

7. Bennett, *Hunger Machine,* 143.

8. According to United Nations figures, 1,940 calories per day versus 1,840; see Susan George, *How the Other Half Dies: The Real Reasons for World Hunger* (Totowa, NJ: Rowman & Allahneld, 1977), 146.

9. USDA, *A Time to Choose,* 23.

10. George Kent, "Food Trade: The Poor Feed the Rich," *The Ecologist,* 238.

11. Bennett, *Hunger Machine,* 87.

12. Susan George, in Bennett, *Hunger Machine,* 1.

13. Lester R. Brown and Jodi L. Jacobson, "Our Demographically Divided World," *Worldwatch Paper* 74 (December 1986), 21. Significant exceptions include India, where the birth rate remains high despite a rise in average per capita income (perhaps because the rise is poorly distributed); and Argentina, a developed, middle-class society experiencing hard times, where the birth rate remains low despite sharp declines in per capita income.

14. George, *How the Other Half Dies,* 37–38, 41.

15. Brown and Jacobson, "Our Demographically Divided World," 37–39.

16. George, in Bennett, *The Hunger Machine,* 12.

Part III. Civil Rights

1. "The Declaration of Independence," in Commager, *Documents of American History,* 100.

Chapter 10. A Natural Right

1. See Donald R. Griffin, *Animal Thinking* (Cambridge MA: Harvard University Press, 1984), and Vicki Hearne, *Adam's Task: Calling Animals by Name* (New York: Alfred A. Knopf, 1986). Griffin argues that "under natural conditions animals make so many sensible decisions concerning their activities, and coordinate their behavior so well with that of their companions, that it has become reasonable to infer some degree of conscious thinking, anticipating, and choosing" (3–4). He goes on to point out that "if we can learn what nonhuman animals think and feel, we could base our relationships with them on factual knowledge in addition to our own emotional feelings, and at the same time we could begin to define what is unique to our own mental life" (12).

2. *The American Heritage Dictonary of the English Language* (Boston: Houghton Mifflin Co., 1969, 1970), definition of "culture."

3. John Muir, *John of the Mountains* (Madison: University of Wisconsin Press, 1979), 234.

4. David L. Edwards, *Religion and Change* (New York: Harper & Row, 1969), 30, 129.

5. Frederick Law Olmstead, from "A Consideration of the Justifying Value of a Public Park" (1881), quoted in Roderick Nash, *Wilderness and the American Mind, Third Edition* (New Haven: Yale University Press, 1982), 155.
6. Ian L. McHarg, *Design with Nature* (Garden City, NY: Doubleday/ Natural History Press, 1971), 5, 19.
7. McHarg, *Design with Nature,* 72–73.
8. Olmstead, quoted by Joseph L. Sax in *Mountains Without Handrails: Reflections on the National Parks* (Ann Arbor: University of Michigan Press, 1984), 20.
9. Sax, *Mountains Without Handrails,* 29.
10. Aldo Leopold, *A Sand County Almanac* (New York: Ballantine Books, 1970), 212.
11. Leopold, *A Sand County Almanac,* 290, 295.

Chapter 11. Reopening the Frontier

1. Wendell Berry, *The Gift of Good Land* (San Francisco: North Point Press, 1981), 261.
2. See, for example, Ernest Callenbach, *Ecotopia* (Berkeley, CA: Banyan Tree Books, 1975).
3. Commanger, *Documents of American History,* 146.
4. *Georgia v. Tennessee Copper Co.,* 206 U.S. 230 (1907), quoted in Ann L. Strong, *Land Banking: European Reality, American Prospect* (Baltimore: Johns Hopkins University Press, 1979), 35.
5. *Pennsylvania Coal Co. v. Mahon,* 260 U.S., at 416, 43 S.Ct., at 160.
6. Iowa, Kansas, Minnesota, Missouri, Nebraska, Oklahoma, South Dakota, North Dakota, and Wisconsin all have laws or constitutional provisions designed to prevent for-profit corporations, other than family farm corporations, from engaging in agriculture.
7. See, The Appalachian Land Ownership Task Force, *Who Owns Appalachia? Landownership and Its Impact* (Lexington, KY: University Press of Kentucky, 1983).
8. See John McClaughry, "Taxes for Land Acquisition," in Peter Barnes, *The People's Land: A Reader on Land Reform in the United States* (Emmaus, PA: Rodale Press, 1975) 154–159; and Sakolski, *Land Tenure and Land Taxation in America,* 257–261.
9. These aberrations are due, in part, to the political influence upon the Reagan administration of the lumber and homebuilding industries, in part to professional overconfidence within the Forest Service that "scientific management" can improve upon natural growth.
10. Berry, *Unsettling of America,* 13.
11. Jackson, *New Roots for Agriculture,* 88–89.

Chapter 12. Civil Rights for the Earth

1. Leopold, *Sand County Almanac,* 237.
2. Leopold, *Sand County Almanac,* 238.
3. Jeremy Bentham, *Introduction to the Principles of Morals and Legislation* (1789), quoted in Christopher D. Stone, *Earth and Other Ethics: The Case for Moral Pluralism* (New York: Harper & Row, 1987), 34.
4. National Environmental Policy Act, 42 U.S.C. §§ 4321–47 (1970), quoted in Christopher D. Stone, *Should Trees Have Standing? Toward Legal Rights for Natural Objects* (Los Altos, CA: William Kaufmann, 1974), 42, 36, emphasis added.
5. The opinions in *Sierra Club vs. Morton* are reprinted in Stone, *Should Trees Have Standing?,* 65. Two justices, newly appointed to the Court, did not participate in this case. Stone's original essay, bearing this title and included in this book, was rushed to print in the *Southern California Law Review* while the Supreme Court considered the case. In his dissent, Justice Douglas acknowledges his debt to Christopher Stone, Professor of Law at the University of Southern California.
6. Leopold, *Sand County Almanac,* 239.
7. Stone, *Should Trees Have Standing?,* 73.
8. Stone, *Should Trees Have Standing?,* 75–76.
9. Stone, *Should Trees Have Standing?,* 76, 83.
10. John Naff, *Journal of the American Bar Assocation,* 58 (1972): 820, quoted in Stone, *Earth and Other Ethics,* 5.

Chapter 14. The Parish

1. Francis of Assisi, c. 1225, paraphrase by William H. Draper (1855–1933), copyright by J. Curwen & Sons, Ltd.
2. See Genesis 3:17–18 and 8:21–22. As considered in Book 3, the role of the "serpent" in the story of humanity's first disobedience, Genesis 3, does imply some rebellion by nature against God.

Chapter 16. Earth to Earth

1. Berry, *Gift of a Good Land,* 281.
2. Martin Buber, *I and Thou* (New York: Charles Scribner's Sons, 1937)
3. Ezekiel 47, Revelation 22, and Mark 6 were compared in *Hope for the Land,* 209–217.
4. This discussion is primarily symbolic. The biotic value of a pile of ashes, or even a decaying corpse, is tiny by comparison to the bodily wastes from a human lifetime, which are usually flushed into a sewer system where they are treated as pollutants rather than nutrients. Improving this system would make a more substantial environmental contribution than the burials I describe.
5. Wendell Berry, *Sabbaths* (San Francisco: North Point Press, 1987), 14.

Acknowledgments

Index to Book 4

BIBLICAL CITATIONS

Index to Series Themes

This index locates themes common to several books in the *Environmental Theology* series: see also "Series Relationships" in *Hope for the Land*, 237–239. For additional themes, see the table of contents in each book; for additional detail, see the index in each book. A book is identified below by the first word in the title.